INDUSTRY VITALIZATION

Pergamon Titles of Related Interest

Fusfeld/Haklisch Industrial Productivity and International
Technical Cooperation
Fusfeld/Langlois Understanding R&D Productivity
Hill/Utterback Technical Innovation for a Dynamic Economy
Lundstedt/Colglazier Managing Innovation: The Social
Dimensions of Creativity
Nelson Government and Technical Progress:
A Cross-Industry Analysis

Related Journals*

Bulletin of Science, Technology & Society
Computers & Industrial Engineering
Economic Bulletin for Europe
Government Publications Review
Long Range Planning
Work in America Institute Studies in Productivity

*Free specimen copies available upon request.

INDUSTRY VITALIZATION

TOWARD A NATIONAL INDUSTRIAL POLICY

Edited by **Margaret E. Dewar**
Foreword by **Harian Cleveland**

PERGAMON PRESS
New York Oxford Toronto Sydney Paris Frankfurt

Pergamon Press Offices:

U.S.A.   Pergamon Press Inc., Maxwell House, Fairview Park,
Elmsford, New York 10523, U.S.A.

U.K.   Pergamon Press Ltd., Headington Hill Hall,
Oxford OX3 OBW, England

CANADA   Pergamon Press Canada Ltd., Suite 104, 150 Consumers Road,
Willowdale, Ontario M2J 1P9, Canada

AUSTRALIA   Pergamon Press (Aust.) Pty. Ltd., P.O. Box 544,
Potts Point, NSW 2011, Australia

FRANCE   Pergamon Press SARL, 24 rue des Ecoles,
75240 Paris, Cedex 05, France

FEDERAL REPUBLIC Pergamon Press GmbH, Hammerweg 6
OF GERMANY 6242 Kronberg/Taunus, Federal Republic of Germany

Copyright © 1982 Pergamon Press Inc.

Library of Congress Cataloging in Publication Data
Main entry under title:

Industry vitalization.

  Papers presented at a conference held at the Hubert H.
Humphrey Institute of Public Affairs, April 1981.
  Includes bibliographical references and index.
  1. Industrial promotion--United States--Congresses.
2. Industry and state--United States--Congresses.
3. United States--Industries--Congresses. I. Dewar,
Margaret, 1948-
HC110.I53I52 1982 338.973   81-23529
ISBN 0-08-028829-4   AACR2

Printed in the United States of America

Contents

Contents

Foreword:
Vitalization without the "Re"

Harlan Cleveland

The University of Minnesota's Hubert H. Humphrey Institute of Public Affairs is in business to educate future leaders and to clarify the issues of leadership in our time. Industrial policy is obviously one such issue, current enough and choice enough to qualify as the topic for the 1981 Humphrey Conference. The Conference, on "Industry Vitalization: Toward a National Industrial Policy," was held in Minneapolis from April 26 to 28, 1981. It was the first stage of a continuing inquiry on industrial policy, part of a policy project directed by Dr. Margaret E. Dewar of the Humphrey Institute's planning faculty. Through such projects as hers, groups of graduate students and University of Minnesota faculty work together on issues that jump ahead of current politics to future policy. The Conference was funded by earnings from a major gift by the AFL-CIO to the Humphrey Institute endowment.

The papers collected in this volume by Professor Dewar were commissioned for delivery at the Industry Vitalization Conference, and revised thereafter in the light of the conference discussion. They cover a broad range of issues related to industrial policy, but in the nature of things they do not encompass all sides of any issue. But taken together they frame the policy issues, and offer some provocative ideas about what the government might do—or stop doing.

*   *   *

We do not now have a national industrial policy. Ad hoc tactics by the federal government—rescuing Chrysler, suing IBM and A.T. & T., embargoing selective foods and feeds, and jawboning the Japanese—serve both as evidence that we don't yet have, and that we badly need, a "strategic" sense as a nation of where we are trying to go, what we are trying to do.

The purpose of the 1981 Humphrey Conference was to help us all focus on where we are, and on what we—government officials, business leaders, labor leaders, and those of us in the business of policy research and analysis—might be doing to help.

The common objectives of most Americans are clear enough, if we keep the discussion at a high enough level of abstraction. We want economic growth with social fairness. We want assured access to needed resources and energy; we want a steady growth in productivity as we use these resources to serve human purposes and meet human needs; we want a strong competitive position in the world markets by which, increasingly, are measured the success or failure of corporations, industries, and national governments in coping with interdependence.

The "re" in "reindustrialization" and "revitalization" has led us to focus on rushing rescue teams to the most beleaguered industrial sectors. Until recently "industrial policy" has meant mostly steel and automobile manufacturing, and heavy industry still predominates in the reports, the editorials, and the politics of "industrial policy." But most American jobs are not in heavy industry. Overwhelmingly, *new* jobs are not in manufacturing at all. "Today," says the Council of State Planning Agencies in a report published in March 1981, " 'industrial policy' should mean rebuilding the economy so that it is not the same economy." Even that proposition might be common ground among many who think about industrial policy.

From that point on, we are as a nation far from moving toward consensus. A national administration turned out of office a year ago thought government should act as facilitator, that government needs to correct market imperfections, protect disadvantaged social groups, and dislodge bottlenecks to higher productivity. A new administration says the economy will work best and industry will be healthiest if government gets out of the way. Yet another school of thought, which in an earlier era might have called itself "liberal," believes that government should more actively decide how investment should be channeled and into which industries.

The rhetoric often seems more clearly differentiated than the actions it leads to: in the most popularized case, nearly everybody backed the Chrysler rescue mission, though it is hard to find anyone, in Wodehouse's phrase, who is "gruntled" with the outcome so far. But the ideological battle, centered on the proper role of government in the scheme of things, has so far inhibited a search for consensus on the key questions at issue.

We thought the management of such an enterprise as our Conference owed its participants, at the outset, a couple of provocative questions as a basis for discussion. So I suggested that two key questions about industry vitalization are these:

1. The industries that become our "leading economic sectors" for the 1980s and 1990s will become obvious, one way or another. Should this happen by "planning," by "consensus," or by "accident?" In other words, do we the people care what sectors shrink or expand? And if we do care, what are our criteria for caring?

2. How should public policy operate to channel investment into the leading sectors, and away from the shrinking sectors? ("Public policy" can mean either doing something or doing nothing; both have pervasive effects and

constitute decisions about who wins and who loses.) In other words: How do we the people make sure that we do not, by design or by neglect, feed our problems and starve our opportunities?

This book addresses these questions, helps to clarify them, and even suggests some answers. The debate continues—and so does the policy research at the Hubert Humphrey Institute on industry vitalization.

Introduction: Toward a U.S. National Industrial Policy

Margaret E. Dewar

Financial difficulties in the auto and steel industries, declining industrial productivity, and the U.S. industry's shrinking share of domestic and world markets are causing great concern that the United States may be entering an era of industrial decline. Some voices emphasize that hundreds of thousands of workers have lost their jobs and that communities have been disrupted as autos, steel, and their supplying industries have closed plants and contracted operations in others. Others worry that the worst problems are in basic industries critical to national defense. In the view of others, the United States ought to maintain preeminence in the world as a manufacturing nation. Slow growth in productivity, some warn, means slow improvement in the standard of living. The concerns have stimulated a lively debate and have pressured the federal government to act.

The resulting policy discussions have had several recurring themes. First, most of the attention has focused on "*re*industrialization" and on *re*vitalizing industry. The emphasis has been on restoring the troubled sectors to strength rather than on capitalizing on new growth potential in other industries. Second, the attention concentrates on older manufacturing, most frequently the auto and steel industries, and neglects the sources of most new jobs in manufacturing and in other major sectors of the economy. Third, most of those who worry about industrial problems gaze with envy at Japan's success, seek to identify why Japan has done better than the United States, and look for ways that this country might learn from Japan.

While most discussions about industrial policy share these themes, the specifics of the debate over what should be done reveal sharply different philosophies. The Carter administration proposed an economic program in which government served as "facilitator." The proposals implied that the smooth functioning of markets produces the best outcome, but some markets do not work correctly without help. Government, therefore, should correct market imperfections and loosen bottlenecks to increase economic efficiency. Government should ease the hardships of workers who lose their jobs and of communities hit hard by declining industries; workers and communities adjust especially slowly to new market conditions. Government efforts should be targeted to assure that the right kinds of reactions to public programs are elicited in the private sector, responses that lead to growth and greater productivity. Administrators can determine, the Carter approach assumed, what kinds of private sector activities ought to be encouraged and what programs stimulate business to behave in those desirable ways.[1]

The Reagan administration has a very different philosophy. The economy will work best and industry will be healthiest if government interference is kept to a minimum, they believe. To unshackle the private sector, government should cut taxes and eliminate or ease regulations. The uneven effects of such measures on different sectors are not of particular concern. Efforts to stimulate industrial growth and productivity should not be targeted at specific industries or aimed at encouraging certain kinds of economic responses rather than others; instead, a favorable climate for economic growth should be created.[2]

Interest groups and individuals outside government have suggested a range of other approaches. The point of view most distinct from the Reagan and Carter administration positions argues that government must take a far more active role in influencing investment and disinvestment in sectors of the economy if growth and productivity are to increase. Felix Rohatyn and others, for example, argue that the government must intervene to revitalize troubled manufacturing industries that play an important role in defense. Those industries are too important to be allowed to die. Government is, they assume, capable of "turning losers into winners," to use Rohatyn's phrase. A somewhat more radical view, espoused by Lester Thurow of the Massachusetts Institute of Technology, Michael Barker of the Council of State Planning Agencies, and others, holds that government should and can identify the future "winners" and "losers" and direct investment to the winners. Japan's industrial success, this group says, has been due in large part to just that sort of government planning and intervention. They believe that markets work too slowly and respond to the wrong signals in channeling resources to future growth ("sunrise") sectors and withdrawing resources from dying ("sunset") industries. Growth slows when "sunrise" sectors are starved for resources. Dying industries deprive healthier ones of capital and labor.[3]

An administration's specific responses to industrial problems do not necessarily reflect the stands taken in general policy statements. Notably, the Reagan administration has outlined aid for the auto industry, endorsed some assistance to the troubled savings and loan associations, plans to extend trade restrictions to help the textile industry, and will probably do something for the integrated steel manufacturers despite the administration's avowals that government is not in the business of helping industry that cannot help itself.[4]

The Reagan administration's performance is not surprising. Sectoral policy—encouraging investment in some industries or "sectors," groups of industries linked through markets, and discouraging investment in others—remains at the heart of the industrial policy debate largely because political pressures from labor and management force government to respond to the pleas of its declining industries. The Carter administration backed aid for Chrysler and drew up a program to assist the steel industry. Within the Carter administration, capacity was growing to examine the problems of some industries and to identify the impediments to the growth of others. Policymakers in the Department of Commerce and in Congress were beginning to consider where investment should occur and how investment might be encouraged in some sectors and discouraged in others, with the hope that the government would not respond to crises in distressed industries on an ad hoc basis.[5]

As this brief examination suggests, industrial policy issues are especially pressing now and are likely to remain so. In an effort to offer ideas about what government should do, the chapters in this volume look at industrial policy questions in general, but especially at questions related to sectoral policy. What are the problems of our troubled industries? What are the solutions to these problems? How successful were past efforts to help troubled industries? How have U.S. policies affected other industrial sectors? What have been the effects of implicit sectoral policies such as tax policy, antitrust measures, trade policy, and government procurement? What are the industrial policies of other countries? What are the results of other governments' sectoral policies? What are the implications for sectoral policy in the United States? Should government try to influence which sectors shrink and expand or leave this to market forces? The discussion generated by these questions adds to understanding about how business and government interact. The chapters support some and challenge other assumptions behind the Carter, Reagan, and alternative approaches to industrial policy. Therefore, the discussion provides a stronger basis for evaluating and reformulating sectoral policy.

INDUSTRIES IN TROUBLE

The first session of the conference dealt with industries in trouble. The current troubles of major industries are largely responsible for bringing industrial policy questions to public attention. Autos and steel, which directly employ millions of workers and are responsible for the jobs of millions of others in supplying firms, have been considered central to the health of the economy, although that does not seem true any longer. President Reagan termed autos "the one industry in this country that can cause a depression all by itself."[6] Both industries are viewed as vital to national defense. These giants are not the only industries with which Congress and the administration must deal. Among the others, parts of the textile, shoe, and apparel industries have suffered intermittent decline for decades.

The chapters by Friedman, Hirschhorn, and Miller on the auto, steel, and men's clothing industries, respectively, suggest several conclusions about the dilemmas confronting policymakers.[7] First, of great significance to the Reagan administration's direction, even if government efforts succeed in slowing inflation, they cannot solve the problems of troubled industries except perhaps in a special case like the savings and loan associations. Slowing inflation is certainly important; inflation causes problems for all industries, including troubled ones. However, the root of difficulties lies outside inflation: in changes in demand for men's tailored clothing, for example; in the failure of steel management to invest in research and development and to adopt new technology; and in changes in auto demand because of rising oil prices. Correspondingly, potential solutions have little to do with easing inflation. Successful inflation policies will not reduce the pressures on government to do something for the distressed sectors.

Second, few troubled industries are homogeneous, although lobbying and policy discussion frequently present them as such. Within most troubled industries, some firms are healthy. For example, as Hirschhorn states, the nonintegrated steelmakers, often called minimills, and the alloy/specialty steelmakers have steadily increased their share of the domestic market and show consistent profits, while the integrated steelmakers are beset with difficulties. Some textile firms are consistently profitable, while others struggle to keep going. The characteristics of the healthy companies provide important clues about why the rest of the industry is in difficulty and about the ways that the troubles might be solved. But these lessons on the nature of the industry's problems and on how they might be handled generally differ considerably from the suggestions offered by lobbyists for the troubled companies. Indeed, some of the proposals to help the troubled firms would handicap the healthy ones even while the programs promise no long-term solutions to others' difficulties.

Third, the overwhelming thrust of the lobbying of troubled industries is to get government protection from change, usually through import restrictions. The industries' adjustment to new market conditions tends to come late and very slowly. Even if policymakers decided that the economy would be healthier if government encouraged disinvestment and eased the pain of adjustment, such a policy direction would only increase the pressures from the troubled companies. No industry advocates its own contraction.

Fourth, the distress of workers and communities affected by industrial decline requires that aid go beyond either restructuring an industry to put it back on a profitable footing or speeding up the departure of capital. What is good for the companies' profits or good for directing investment toward "winners" is not necessarily good for the workers. Workers and communities cannot adjust to rapid economic change quickly enough to prevent great hardship. In major industries now in trouble, workers may be powerful enough to get programs to preserve jobs. The United Auto Workers, as

Friedman's chapter shows, push for restraints on imports, as do the manufacturers, but also ask for "local content requirements" which would require manufacturers who sell in the United States to use U.S.–made components. Even if such a proposal does not find support and even if the spokesmen for workers ignore the difficulties of former constituents who have lost their jobs, policies have to reach beyond narrow notions of efficiency and market adjustment to consideration of the economic costs of unproductive labor and the social costs of joblessness and community decline. Indeed, politicians and administrators probably cannot ignore the pressure to address these problems for long.

Fifth, government policies may be able to transform the troubled segments of industries into healthy ones, to make industries competitive in international markets; but those results may come only at great cost. A critical question is: What is it worth to us to revitalize the distressed parts of an industry? Although that question probably cannot be answered adequately without a better sense of goals for an industrial policy, the public probably should not bear the cost of trying to make our losers into our winners with little regard for the nature of markets.

GOVERNMENT INTERVENTION ON BEHALF OF TROUBLED INDUSTRY

The United States government has a substantial history of assisting industries in trouble. The second session of the Conference examined that experience. Jantscher's chapter on the merchant marine and shipbuilding industries, and the discussions of fisheries and agriculture at the Humphrey conference,[8] suggest a number of conclusions. Perhaps most important, efforts to help these industries have not accomplished their stated goals. Programs failed to make the merchant marine, shipbuilding, and fisheries into prosperous industries. Programs aimed at preserving the family farm failed to stem the exodus from agriculture. However, they may have had the unintended result of reducing the risk enough and providing high enough profits to stimulate the investment that led to today's prosperous large farms and agribusinesses.

Government aid programs failed to turn around the fortunes of the fisheries, the merchant marine, and shipbuilding for a number of reasons. Generally, efforts to help have been ad hoc and piecemeal. The direction of efforts has changed often. Government rarely made a full commitment to solve problems; programs principally served to relieve political pressure for a time. Further, the causes of industry problems proved remarkably hard to understand. When programs were based on wrong definitions of problems, they failed to help. Even when industry representatives and policymakers did know what the problems were, they could not devise solutions that would produce results which could help. Implementation problems thwarted efforts which showed great promise for easing industry difficulties.

The experience suggests the pessimistic conclusion that such government intervention has little chance of success. Nothing about the current difficulties of important industries or the governmental processes for handling the problems will keep the same factors from interfering with the effectiveness of programs. The failure of efforts to help suggests that government should aid troubled industry principally to ease the difficulties of the groups that have trouble adjusting to the change—workers, communities, and perhaps the owners of durable capital equipment. The aim of such aid should be to facilitate eventual adjustment to new economic conditions.

Even when government should not help on economic-efficiency grounds, political pressures will often compel intervention. Therefore, such government assistance ought to be more effective in solving industry problems to avoid wasting more public money. Jantscher's study suggests several ways to do so. Government should not subsidize a single factor of production. In the merchant marine, wage subsidies have promoted excessive use of shipboard labor and discouraged labor-saving innovation. Aid for one industry should not increase costs for another industry. Requirements that the maritime industry operate U.S.–built ships helped the shipbuilding industry, but burdened the merchant marine. Subsidies to a troubled industry should be subject to frequent review; legislation should include termination dates so that some positive action by Congress will be required to keep a program in existence.

More generally, the experience of government assistance for troubled industry and current appeals for help suggest that much more knowledge and analysis should contribute to the efforts to help. Government intervention must be based on a much better understanding of the reasons for the problems. Government cannot rely just on the industry's assessments of its own difficulties but must have some independent source of analysis. "Industry analysis" should accompany policy analysis to improve understanding of how an industry will respond to a program. The industry analysis should consider cultural, institutional, and political as well as economic factors. Policymakers should also analyze the implementation problems which programs may encounter and should redesign programs to increase chances of successful implementation.

Furthermore, industry analysis should be initiated before political pressures to help become overwhelming, in order to inform the design of later programs. The goal of the industry analysis should be to help reduce losses in efficiency while addressing critical equity issues.

GOVERNMENT AND HEALTHY INDUSTRIES

While the U.S. government has rarely tried explicitly to aid the growth of healthy industry, government policies have nevertheless influenced those industries' fortunes. Such government actions have constituted an unintended sectoral policy. The third session of the Humphrey conference looked at the experience of healthy industries. The chapters by Egan and by Erickson and Maitland detail the effects of government actions on the semiconductor industry and on commercial jet aircraft, computers, forest products, frozen foods, metal cans, and pharmaceuticals.[9]

The chapters suggest that the effects of government activity have been profound for some young industries. Government procurement has often been important in providing "thin specialty markets" for new industries. Buyers in such markets are willing to pay high premiums for superior performance in a few dimensions and to accommodate some performance deficiencies.[10] Procurement decisions have reflected no desire to choose future growth sectors. Instead, the creation of thin specialty markets has been the by-product of public actions directed at other goals, most commonly defense or NASA activities. For example, the military and NASA were the semiconductor companies' principal customers during the 1950s and early 1960s.

Even when government has not purchased the products of a new industry, its actions have occasionally spurred private sector demand and therefore given such industries an enormous advantage in making their products known and in earning revenues at early stages of product development. For example, food rationing during World War II increased the demand for new, relatively unrestricted frozen foods.

Government funding for research and development (R&D) has frequently accompanied government purchasing during the early growth of an industry. As Egan shows, the semiconductor companies received enormous amounts of R&D money from the military and from NASA in their early years.

For mature, healthy industries, the effects of government policy have been more diverse. The chapters have little praise for the effects of government activities. For instance, government procurement has imposed boom-and-bust cycles on some industries. Uncertainty about getting contracts and the short-term nature of contracts have caused problems for others. Trade policy has handicapped some industries. Tax policies have reduced the supply of capital to the semiconductor industry and therefore have inhibited vital innovation in that industry.

The history of the haphazard impact of government actions on these healthy industries suggests that government officials should develop systematic means for identifying the economic impacts of public policies and should find ways to moderate the injuries they inadvertently inflict. Accidental negative effects become too costly in an economy with slowing productivity.

.As in efforts to help troubled industry, government should have a better understanding of the character of industries. That means government should employ a contingent of industry analysts to make assessments of the problems that industries face and the ways that government policies affect them. In addition, government should institutionalize procedures for economic-impact analyses of proposed government actions. Policymakers would then look systematically at direct and indirect effects of their actions and might become more sensitive to the consequences for industry. Again, an industry's own assessment of its problems and of the effects of government activity are not reliable enough to be the only source of information.

INDUSTRIAL POLICY IN OTHER COUNTRIES

Other countries have tried policies now under debate in the United States. Advocates of government intervention to direct investment toward selected industries point to the Japanese efforts as the best example of what the United States has to do. West Germany sets another good example, many believe, although its experience has received less attention than Japan's. Great Britain's difficulties, in contrast, show what the United States should not do, the pitfalls this country should avoid. The chapters by Trezise, by Menden, and by Blank and Sacks examine the record of industrial policy in those countries.[11]

The most striking conclusion of these chapters is that the success of Japan's and Germany's economic growth cannot be attributed to their industrial policies. The Japanese government has not been able to pursue a consistent policy to direct capital and labor to certain industries and out of others. Trezise's review of the Japanese record of activities discloses that little attention has been paid to sectors with high growth potential. In West Germany, Menden feels, the keys to success have been a very productive manufacturing sector with strong exports in high-technology goods; a strong currency; liberal trade policies; and a disciplined, hard-working labor force.

In Japan, West Germany, and Great Britain, a great deal of aid has gone to troubled industries. Pressures to help declining sectors seem as inexorable there as in the United States. In Japan, the bulk of public investment in industry has gone to ailing but politically important sectors, and trade policies have protected weak, vulnerable sectors. In 1970 in West Germany, two-thirds of federal subsidies and tax allowances went to help declining industries.[12] In Great Britain, the major result of industrial policy has been a succession of bail-outs, despite proclaimed intentions to target growth sectors and regardless of the party in power.

Great Britain's industrial policy has more obviously failed in view of the chronic troubles of the British economy. That nation's experience in industry policy may be an even more relevant example for the United States than are those of Japan and West Germany, Blank and Sacks warn, because the United States and Britain share traditions of constraint in state intervention in the economy, a weak state role in directing private sector activities. That tradition may have been the source of some of the difficulties encountered by British industrial policy. The two countries also share a sense of the importance of preserving their world economic leadership; recapturing that role of preeminence or hanging on to it have been themes in both countries. Blank and Sacks argue that the effort to restore Britain's place in the international economy and particularly to defend the international reserve currency status of sterling has strained the economy and interfered with industrial policy.

Britain's experience suggests some problems that may be generic in implementing industrial policy. Efforts remained ad hoc; no institutional innovations occurred to make it possible for government to deal with problems consistently or for officials to learn from the past. Political goals predominated over economic ones. Although plans and goals were formulated, crises always came up to change the direction of policy. As domestic economic problems worsened, each new government reversed the policies of the old.

The experiences of all three countries suggest that the United States would not succeed in an industrial policy to direct investment toward winners and away from losers. Political realities would ensure that the major result of such an effort would be to help troubled industry on a larger scale than ever before because more government resources would be committed to the industrial policy effort.

IMPLICATIONS FOR INDUSTRIAL POLICY

The chapters show clearly that the United States has had a sectoral policy of sorts which has influenced investment and growth in some industrial sectors, disinvestment and decline in others. The components of that industrial policy have included fiscal and monetary measures, defense and NASA procurement, regulations to promote health and safety, trade policy, programs to help troubled industry, and many other government activities. This industrial policy has been ad hoc, accidental, and piecemeal.

Continuing the policies of the past would mean that the United States still had a sectoral policy, but an unsatisfactory, incoherent, and inadvertent one. Ineffective aid for troubled industry would be more expensive than before and more important politically, because larger industrial sectors are distressed. Aid to troubled industry would dominate sectoral policy. The accidental side effects of a variety of government policies would continue to have tremendous impacts on healthy industries, not necessarily in ways that encourage growth and productivity.

An implication of the chapters in this volume is that the United States should not try to pick "winners" toward which to direct investment. Government may or may not be capable of identifying the growth sectors of the future, but government certainly cannot conduct a consistent policy of directing investment toward those sectors. The approach would degenerate into helping losers. The United States has been very unsuccessful at helping ailing industries in the past and may do no better in the future.

Neither of these alternatives is satisfactory. Instead, the government needs to assist in the adjustment of troubled industries and the workers and communities affected by them to new economic conditions but should very rarely try to revitalize a distressed sector. Government's major role should be to cushion the impact of industrial decline on workers and communities so that the transition to new industries can be less painful. The government needs to understand more clearly the impact on industry of its many activities and should seek to reduce ill effects. Such a moderate approach which seeks to correct errors of the past but does not attempt a dramatically new solution would be consistent with political traditions in this country and be most likely to receive support over a long term.

NOTES

1. The White House, "Economic Growth for the 1980's" and "Fact Sheet: Economic Program for the Eighties," Aug. 28, 1980.
2. David A. Stockman and Jack Kemp, "Avoiding a GOP Economic Dunkirk," *Wall Street Journal*, Dec. 12, 1980, p. 28; Christopher Conte, "The U.S. Message for Ailing Industries," *Wall Street Journal*, April 6, 1981, p. 20.
3. Felix Rohatyn, "The State of the Nation's Industry—All Talk and No Action," *Washington Post*, July 20, 1980, p. G4; Lester C. Thurow, "The Productivity Problem," *Technology Review* 83, 2 (Nov./Dec. 1980): 40-51; Neal R. Peirce and Carol Steinbach, "Reindustrialization—A Foreign Word to Hard-Pressed American Workers," *National Journal*, Oct. 25, 1980, pp. 1786-88; Ezra F. Vogel, *Japan As Number One* (Cambridge, Mass.: Harvard University Press, 1979), pp. 232-33.
4. Conte, "The U.S. Message," p. 20; Timothy D. Schellhardt and Burt Schorr, "Reagan's Aides Stress Block Grants to States in Preparing '81 Agenda," *Wall Street Journal*, Aug. 21, 1981, p. 21; Kenneth H. Bacon, "Reagan Plans to Ease 34 Car Rules, Sees $1.4 Billion Industry Saving Over 5 Years," *Wall Street Journal*, April 7, 1981, p. 2; "Proposal to Give S&Ls Many Rights of Banks Is Favored By Reagan," *Wall Street Journal*, Aug. 4, 1981, p. 45.
5. See the work of the Office of Technology Assessment of the Congress and of the Office of Industry Policy, the Bureau of Industrial Economics, and the Office of Technology Strategy and Evaluation in the Department of Commerce.
6. Conte, "The U.S. Message," p. 20.
7. These conclusions benefited from the comments of Timothy J. Hauser, senior international

economist in the Office of Industry Policy, Department of Commerce, at the Humphrey conference.

8. Willard W. Cochrane of the Department of Agricultural and Applied Economics, University of Minnesota, discussed the agricultural aid program, and Margaret E. Dewar analyzed efforts to revitalize the fisheries.

9. These conclusions reflect in part the comments of Theodore W. Schlie, Office of Technology Strategy and Evaluation, Department of Commerce, at the Humphrey conference.

10. William J. Abernathy, "Innovation and the Regulatory Paradox: Toward a Theory of Thin Markets," in Douglas H. Ginsburg and William J. Abernathy, eds., *Government, Technology and the Automotive Future.*(New York: McGraw-Hill, 1980), pp. 38–61.

11. The conclusions draw in part on the comments of Ian Maitland of the School of Management, University of Minnesota, at the Humphrey conference.

12. George H. Küster, "Germany," in Raymond Vernon, ed., *Big Business and the State: Changing Relations in Western Europe* (Cambridge, Mass.: Harvard University Press, 1974), p. 74.

INDUSTRY VITALIZATION

Part I:
Industries in Trouble

1
Troubles and Opportunities in the United States Steel Industry

Joel S. Hirschhorn*

Revolutions are not always noticed while they are taking place. This is especially true when the shift in power is within an industry rather than an entire society, and when the profound change takes place during years rather than during days, weeks, or months. Such is the case for the United States steel industry. For the past ten years, small steelmakers, often called mini-mills, midimills, or market mills, have undergone phenomenal growth. Based on a strategy involving technology, marketing, and management changes relative to past practices, these successful firms have captured a significant portion (about 15 percent) of domestic production for steel products while making profits far higher than the well-known large integrated companies which still account for the majority of steel production. That this restructuring of the American steel industry has been taking place during a period when the poor performance of the large steelmakers has attracted considerable public and political attention, and the steel industry has been labeled sick, troubled, and a loser, may explain, in part, why the revolution has gone so unnoticed. But now when public policy associated with economic renewal and the revitalization and reindustrialization of American industry is being debated intensely, the need to recognize the pluralistic nature of the United States steel industry is urgent. The challenge for policymakers is to make public policy that is keyed to the future rather than the past, and to fostering the growth of successful companies rather than preserving the existence of firms with poor performance through often costly distortions of the marketplace.

The structure of my discussion consists of four elements. First, I will summarize important historical trends which describe the decay of the domestic steel industry viewed in aggregate and provide a brief description of

* The views expressed in this chapter are entirely those of the author and are not necessarily those of OTA.

the more recent restructuring of the industry explained in terms of three industry segments. Second, I will discuss the important and often controversial issues which arise in any attempt to explain the historical decline of the American steel industry. Third, I will discuss the present crisis facing the private and public sectors in terms of ideal solutions, emphasizing long-term strategies and policies. Fourth, I will review and compare a number of major policy approaches now under consideration for dealing with the domestic steel industry in a specific manner, as well as the potential for utilizing more broadly defined economic or industrial policies, perhaps in conjunction with sector-specific policies.

It would be easy to cite voluminous data about foreign and domestic steel industries, but since so many recent studies of the steel industry exist, I see no reason to do this. Instead, I will emphasize a conceptual policy-issue-oriented discussion. For those interested in more detailed and data-filled discussions, I recommend two recent studies, one by the domestic steel industry's major trade association, the American Iron and Steel Institute, entitled *Steel at the Crossroads: The American Steel Industry in the 1980s*,[1] and the other by the congressional Office of Technology Assessment (OTA) entitled *Technology and Steel Industry Competitiveness*.[2] The OTA report is used as a primary source for factual material (unless noted otherwise) for this chapter, although the opinions expressed are totally my own.

HISTORICAL TRENDS

Production and Trade

Up to and throughout World War II, the United States maintained an unapproachable lead in steel production and its technology was considered first rate. However, the postwar rebuilding stimulated the expansion of European and Japanese steel mills, and provided foreign producers with great competitive leverage. U.S. firms did not build enough new plants or expand existing capacity sufficiently to capture a portion of the rapidly rising world demand for steel.

The dramatic decline in the growth rate of the U.S. steel industry, compared to that of other countries, is revealed in world production figures. From 1956 to 1978, for example, the U.S. share of total world output of steel dropped from 37 to 17.5 percent and domestic production increased only 10 percent. During this period, Japan increased its production nearly tenfold. Japan and the European Economic Community (EEC) experienced a combined growth rate from 1950 to 1976 that was 10 times greater than that of the United States.

Steel exports from the United States have remained relatively constant during the past thirty years, even though worldwide exports increased more than tenfold during that time. In 1978, for example, the United States exported only 2.5 percent of its total domestic raw steel production, while West Germany exported 53.7 percent; Japan, 36.8 percent; Italy, 37.6 percent; and the United Kingdom, 21.5 percent. Many foreign industries built steelmaking capacity with the export market in mind, because their capacities far exceed the volumes needed to satisfy their domestic needs.

Steel imports into the United States since the late 1950s have grown at the rate of 10 percent per year. The average for the past decade is approximately 15 percent of domestic consumption. The increasing gap between domestic steel exports and imports has had a striking negative effect on the U.S. trade balance. Steel imports exceeded exports in dollar value for the first time during the late 1940s and in volume during the late 1950s. Since that time, imports have captured much of the growth in domestic steel consumption. Steel trade patterns have led to a very high annual trade deficit, second only to petroleum as a source of trade deficit (in terms of commodities). Although exports of ferrous scrap and coking coal have grown significantly, they reduce this trade deficit by a relatively small amount, and large amounts of imported iron ore and occasionally high levels of imported coke have contributed to the trade deficit associated with the steel industry.

Profitability and Investment

During the past several decades, the domestic steel industry has had a far better financial performance than major foreign steel industries. Only the smaller Canadian steel industry has consistently outperformed the U.S. steel industry. However, international profitability comparisons should be made with caution, since foreign government ownership and direct and indirect support by governments, all substantial for many foreign steel industries, make measures of profitability used for private domestic firms difficult to apply to all foreign firms. The interest paid to banks by the highly debt-leveraged Japanese steel firms makes comparisons to U.S. firms difficult.

In relation to other domestic industries, however, the situation is quite different. In only four years (1955–1957 and 1974) during the past twenty-five did profitability (aftertax profits as a percentage of stockholder equity) of the domestic steel industry exceed the average for all domestic manufacturing firms. Steel industry profitability has been lower than the prime interest rate for five years in the period 1967–1978. The real rate of industry net income has declined to very low levels, finally becoming negative during the past few years as inflation rates exceeded steel industry profit margins.

With regard to capital use, dividend payments have been surprisingly stable, however, even in years of very low profitability. In addition, capital expenditures as a percentage of net internally generated cash funds have been relatively high. The industry's long-term debt increased tenfold between 1950 and 1978. In the same period, stockholder's equity increased only by a factor of three. As a result, the debt-to-equity ratio increased from 11.2 percent in 1950 to 44.0 percent in 1978.

The relative profitability of the U.S. steel industry compared to foreign steel industries, the large size of the domestic market, the increasing costs to transport foreign steel to the United States, the existence of company stocks that are undervalued relative to book value, and, at times, exchange rates favorable to foreigners have made investments by foreign firms in the U.S. steel industry attractive. However, the increased foreign investment in recent years has taken place mostly in small steel firms and steel distributors rather than in the larger and least profitable integrated companies. About ten small domestic steelmakers are owned partially or entirely by foreign interests.

Steelmaking Costs

Through the 1950s the U.S. steel industry could easily claim to be the world's low-cost steel producer. In the 1960s, however, several European countries and Japan become lower-cost producers of steel. In more recent times, production costs have become more volatile and difficult to assess, in part because of the role of foreign governments, such as by eliminating debts. Since about 1973, the Japanese may have lost some of their cost advantage relative to the United States, and European producers lost their advantage altogether. But recent strengthening of the dollar has reversed this effect. Compared to other major steelmaking nations, U.S. raw material and employment costs per ton of steel are somewhat high and capital costs somewhat low. Several Third World, developing nations have relatively low production-cost steelmakers, but their capital costs are often high.

Widely fluctuating exchange rates and substantially different utilization rates among nations continue to make international cost comparisons difficult. Nevertheless, on the whole, the domestic steel industry is cost-competitive in most domestic markets, and for some types of steels, even cost-competitive in international markets. Coastal markets are most impacted by imports. It must be noted that the costs of exporting, including transportation costs, warehousing, sales, and marketing, are also relevant when making international cost comparisons. This is why, today, lower-cost foreign steelmakers may not be competitive in the domestic market, especially for inland markets inaccessible to low-cost water transportation. Moreover, a relatively low rate of capacity utilization substantially increases production costs, especially for large economy-of-scale-integrated plants such as those in Japan, which have been operating at about 70 percent of capacity for the past several years. But even at that level, they can be profitable. Domestic utilization rates have been higher. It cannot be emphasized enough, however, that this cost-competitiveness is on an aggregate basis for the domestic steel industry. Production costs vary substantially among domestic steelmakers because of wide differences in age and efficiency of facilities, plant management practices, local market conditions, product mixes, and variations in regional costs of basic inputs.

Much attention has been given to wages and labor costs in the domestic steel industry and to problems with productivity improvements. Abroad, steel industry wages are often higher than the all-manufacturing average, but less so than in the United States. In the United States, the gap between steel industry and manufacturing industry average wages narrowed during the late 1960s in response to increased import competition and reduced profitability in the steel industry; but in the 1970s and particularly since 1974, the lead held by steel industry wages again increased significantly. The 1974 steel labor settlement which took place in a booming market has been criticized by many for being too generous, including its cost-of-living-increase clause. Management was obviously eager to avoid any disruption of production. Since that time, steel industry wages have been much higher than the average for domestic manufacturing, and hourly employment costs in the steel industry have increased by 10 to 15 percent since 1960, on an annual basis, with higher-than-average increases during recent years.

The increases in wages have led to substantial increases in the contribution of labor toward the total costs of making steel, because such increases in hourly costs have been offset by labor productivity gains to only a small degree. For the period 1960 to 1978, the average rate of change in hourly compensation was nearly 11 percent annually in terms of actual dollars and 2.6 percent in terms of real dollars, while output per employee-hour increased at an average rate of 1.9 percent annually. Productivity, however, remains at a very high level for domestic steelworkers. Moreover, it must be noted that productivity is also a strong function of capacity utilization rate, which is very cyclic, and of the character of technology chosen by management. Labor productivity is greatest in the nonintegrated mills.

While low hourly wages in some developing nations are an advantage which is often combined with new plants, steel industries in industrialized nations have experienced increases in labor costs during the past decade that were greater than those in the United States because of currency changes and because of wage increases that exceeded those in the United States. From 1969 to 1978, West German and Japanese employment costs increased 345 and 299 percent, respectively, compared to 117 percent in the United States; and these two nations are generally considered to be the most effective and technologically modern in the world. Nevertheless, in 1978, U.S. hourly costs were still 30 percent higher than West German costs and 40 percent higher than Japanese costs, but annual employment-cost increases in local currencies were much lower than in dollars.

Technology, Innovation, and R&D

The two most striking aspects of technology that have changed during the past several decades for the domestic steel industry are an increase in the age of facilities and a reduction in the amount of advanced forms of technology in use as compared to foreign steel industries. Moreover, there is ample evidence to support the claim that the U.S. steel industry has not been an innovator in steelmaking technology, in the sense that it has not played a key role in developing and introducing into commercial use important new technologies—although, in fairness, it has done better in the steel product development area than in process technology. The generally held view is that the Japanese steel industry is the world's premier steel industry in terms of technology, even though it took many research results and new technologies from other nations, including the United States. Given large amounts of new steelmaking capacity, Japan, like some other nations, has been able to build on a base of foreign technology by constantly improving and innovating. Japan has become a major source of new steel technology for the entire world and it has shifted its interest to exporting technology rather than steel products to nations building their own steelmaking capacity.

Because the domestic steel industry has not built major new plants to the extent other nations have, the average ages of different types of equipment are relatively old. Estimates have indicated that 20 to 25 percent of steelmaking facilities in this country are technologically outmoded or obsolete, a much higher figure than for most industries. In several important categories of equipment, such as plate mills, hot strip mills, and cold strip mills, the average age is 20 or more years. Important recent advances in computer control and instrumentation which greatly influence quality control and productivity have not been widely adopted by the industry.

The record with regard to several important changes in technology varies. For example, the domestic steel industry is at the forefront of world industries for adoption of electric furnace steelmaking, up from 10 percent of steel production in 1964 to nearly 30 percent today. However, unlike most major steel industries, the domestic industry still has a significant amount of steel made in open hearth furnaces, while most other industries have few or none of these furnaces in use anymore. This is related to a low adoption rate for basic oxygen steelmaking.

More important, the United States has fallen behind in the adoption of continuous-casting technology, which has spurred cost savings, energy savings, improvements in productivity, and reduced environmental pollution by the rest of the world's steel industries. The use of continuous casting is also a major way to increase the efficiency or yield of steelmaking operations, that is, to increase the amount of finished steel products made from a given amount of raw steel. Japan now makes about 60 percent of its steel by continuous casting; the European Community, about one-third; but the United States makes only about 20 percent of its steel this way. And the Japanese are aggressively pursuing a goal of making 80 to 90 percent of their steel in this manner.

While several nations, notably Japan, have very large, modern, integrated steelworks employing all the newest technology, the United States has built only one major new steelworks in the past two decades, and even this has probably not matched the improvements made through incremental technological innovation that the Japanese have become proficient in.

The innovation process covers the spectrum from research and development through pilot testing and demonstration, and finally to introduction into the marketplace. The technological decline of the domestic steel industry includes a decline in R&D. R&D expenditures by the U.S. steel industry, as a percentage of sales, have declined in recent years and are lower than in most other basic industries in the United States. For example, the level of R&D spending by steel is about half that of the nonferrous industry and about one-seventh that of the chemicals industry. The industry's basic research effort is particularly small. Steel industry R&D has very little federal support compared to other industries and is complemented by only a limited amount of steel R&D carried out by the government and universities.

Foreign steel R&D, on the other hand, is generally in a more vigorous state because of large budgets, stronger government support, more positive attitudes toward future prospects for innovations in steelmaking, and more aggressive approaches toward export of steel technology. A number of foreign steel industries benefit also from greater cooperative efforts among firms and between firms, universities, and government facilities.

Industry Restructuring

The U.S. steel industry is no longer the homogeneous industry it once was. During the past decade, the industry has been undergoing permanent and important changes in the character and competitive positions of its constituent firms. Important aspects of this restructuring include changes in technology, product mixes, geographical patterns of company locations, costs of entry into the industry, and raw material use. The competition among three distinct segments of the industry may be more important than the competition from foreign steelmakers. The three industry segments are integrated, nonintegrated, and alloy/specialty steelmakers.

Integrated steelmakers (such as United States Steel Corp. and Bethlehem Steel Corp.) start with iron ore and coal to make iron and coke, and go on to make a large variety of steel products. These plants, based on coke ovens and blast furnaces, are what most people think of when steel plants are mentioned. There are twenty such companies in the United States, with an average of about 2.5 plants per firm. Generally, the plants make from two to six million metric tons of steel annually. Most steel made in this country (and the world) is made in integrated companies. The decline of the integrated segment of the United States steel industry is, in fact, bleaker than the preceding discussions indicate, since the historical aspects of the two other industry segments are quite positive in many respects. The decline of integrated firms, particularly in terms of financial performance, has led to considerable diversification, for some companies, out of steelmaking. Hall has presented an analysis of domestic integrated steel companies.[3] He has concluded that the diversification strategy has generally been unsuccessful for most steel companies because their efforts have been too small and have been managed in too conservative a fashion. The exception is Armco; they continue to reduce the contribution of steelmaking to their corporate efforts, and generally have the best financial performance of major integrated producers. Hall also notes that in steel and other basic manufacturing industries, it has been possible for firms to be quite successful by staying in their original line of business and becoming a low-cost producer. This has been the case for Inland Steel, whose financial performance in recent years has been relatively good, even compared to other types of companies perceived to be profitable and successful. Thus, the loss of market share by the domestic steel industry in recent years is accounted for by the integrated segment and, more importantly, by the least successful integrated companies who have reduced their steelmaking capacity.

Nonintegrated steelmakers, often called minimills, midimills, or market mills, start with ferrous scrap and make simpler, commodity items such as wire products and reinforcing bar. There are about fifty such companies in the United States; some of the more successful and better known firms are Nucor, Florida Steel, and Korf Steel. Nonintegrated steelmakers have increased their share of the domestic market from under 3 percent in 1968 to about 15 percent today. Much of that increase has come from penetration of markets formerly held by integrated producers and in some cases by being more competitive than steel imports. Many of the better-performing nonintegrated firms are the world's lowest-cost producers of steel. Nonintegrated producers have capitalized on locally available domestic ferrous scrap and are totally dependent on it as their source of iron, whereas integrated producers use a small percent of purchased scrap in their operations. The energy contained in such scrap enables scrap-based steelmakers to keep costs down. They use scrap from domestic and imported steel made in energy-intensive integrated steelmaking plants. Moreover, nonintegrated producers rely mostly on local markets served with low-cost transportation (although some are exporting and some are becoming more regional in character). They generally use nonunion labor because of their concentration in nonunionized regions of the country in the Sunbelt, and have capital costs per ton of annual capacity that are about 10 to 20 percent of those of new integrated plants.

Technologically, the nonintegrated steelmakers make use, for the most part, of a highly efficient combination of electric steelmaking furnaces, continuous casting, and a relatively narrow product line for any particular plant. They have spearheaded the development of a number of technological advances even though they have modest formal R&D programs. They are quick to adopt advances made available by equipment manufacturers and often do their own engineering and construction to keep capital costs down. Although many observers, particularly from the integrated steel producers, point to the potential problems with the quality and availability of ferrous scrap and possibly electricity, the nonintegrated firms continue to expand their capacity. They do this by building new plants more so than by expanding capacity at existing plants, although the latter is going on at the smaller plants. The optimum size of these nonintegrated plants appears to be about 500,000 tons of steelmaking capacity annually and is increasing. Several companies, however, now have total capacities in the 1-million-ton or more range. Many of these firms are expanding their relatively simple and narrow product mixes to include more costly, sophisticated, and higher-quality steel products.

Alloy/specialty steelmakers, such as Carpenter Technology, Lukens Steel, Cyclops, and Washington Steel, start with scrap or iron ore and make higher-priced, more technology-intensive steel products, such as stainless steels, tool steels, and high-alloy steels for aerospace and other demanding applications. From an international perspective, alloy/specialty steelmakers possess the best technology, have pioneered many manufacturing and product innovations, and have low production costs. The use of their steel products has been growing at a much faster rate than that for carbon steels. Some of these firms are beginning to capitalize on their ability to export. While these producers only account for a few percent of the domestic production of steel, the dollar value of their products is several times greater. Like integrated steelmakers, the alloy/specialty producers have often faced stiff and probably unfairly traded (below cost) imports; nevertheless, they have, for the most part, persevered with emphasis on new technology and capital investment to reduce costs.

Some comparative data on the three industry segments of the domestic steel industry are given in Table 1.1 for 1978. While there is significant variation among firms in all three segments, there is little debate that the nonintegrated and alloy/specialty segments exhibit far better financial and

Table 1.1. Summary Data on Steel Industry Segments, 1978

Characteristic	Integrated	Nonintegrated	Alloy/ Specialty
Steel Shipments			
1,000 tons	75,522	11,291	2,014
Percent	85	13	2
Return on Investment	6.9	12.3	11.1
Steel Only—Pretax Profit			
$/ton shipped	$9.60	$31.60	$81.33
Employment Costs			
$/ton shipped	$209	$138	$341
Percent Steel Continuously Cast	11.0	51.5	16.5

SOURCE: Office of Technology Assessment, *Technology and Steel Industry Competitiveness, 1980.*
NOTE: Tonnages are metric.

technical performance than the integrated segment. Similarly impressive financial comparative data for the past ten years are given in Table 1.2.

UNDERSTANDING THE PAST: CAUSES AND ISSUES

To explain the previously described historical trends for the United States steel industry, one must invoke many complex and often interrelated factors that frequently rest on subjective judgments rather than unequivocal facts.

Table 1.2. Comparative Financial Data for Industry Segments

Average	Nonintegrated + Alloy/Specialty Composite (14 firms)	Integrated (Six largest)	Dow Jones Industrials (30 stocks)	Shearson Manufac- turing Composite (180 firms)
Pretax Profit Margin (%)				
1975-1979	9.80	3.18	12.26	9.64
1970-1979	9.96	4.90	13.25	9.75
Net Return on Assets (%)				
1975-1979	7.54	3.06	6.92	7.78
1970-1979	7.17	3.74	6.97	7.52
Net Return on Equity (%)				
1975-1979	12.86	5.78	14.02	15.32
1970-1979	12.19	6.87	13.47	14.39

SOURCE: Joseph C. Wyman, *Steel Mini-Mills—An Investment Opportunity?* (New York: Shearson Loeb Rhoades Inc., Nov. 20, 1980).

To simplify and organize this discussion, I will use three basic types of explanations for each of the five areas of historical trends discussed previously. These three types of explanations are foreign actions and policies, steel industry management decisions, and federal policies. In this manner it is possible for government policymakers to understand those factors that they have little control over, that they must be aware of and may influence indirectly, and that they have direct control over, respectively.

As an introduction and overview of this discussion, I have summarized the major impacts of these three types of explanations on the five areas of historical trends in Table 1.3. This is useful if one asks the question: How important, for example, have been foreign actions and policies on the decline in profitability and investment in the domestic steel industry? And how do foreign activity and policies compare to federal policies or management decisions in explaining this decline? The answer, in this particular case, is that both management decisions and federal policies have been very important, while foreign activity and policies explain this decline in only a minor and indirect way.

I have also listed the five historical trends, in the order of decreasing importance, from the perspective of the domestic steel industry as manifested by their emphasis in recent years when they have brought their case to the public and political arenas. The industry (mostly through the American Iron and Steel Institute) generally emphasizes trade and import issues first, then their problems with declining profitability and ability to reinvest in steelmaking, and then costs, including the burden of regulatory costs. The areas of technology, innovation, and R&D and industry restructuring, for the most part, receive little attention by the industry. In examining Table 1.3, therefore, it is important to note that as one attempts to understand the causal factors for the five historical trends, going from top to bottom (from most to least important from the perspective of the industry), there is a shift from

Table 1.3. Summary Generalizations on Causes of Historical Trends

	Explanatory Power of Cause: +++ Very Important		
		++ Important	
		+ Minor and Indirect	
Historical Trend	Foreign Actions & Policies	Steel Industry Management Decisions	Federal Policies
Production & Trade	+++	+	++
Profitability & Investment	+	+++	+++
Steelmaking Costs (incl. regulatory costs)	+	+++	+
Technology, Innovation, R&D	+	+++	+
Industry Restructuring	+	+++	+

foreign actions and policies and federal policies to management decisions. In other words, the industry emphasizes those areas of difficulty for which they can externalize the causes. This is perfectly reasonable from the industry's perspective. However, from a public policy viewpoint, the consequence has been, in part due to the successful lobbying efforts of the industry, that federal policies have been much more responsive to problems facing the industry which have remedies outside the industry than to those problems or trends (positive in the case of industry restructuring) that are best understood in terms of the decisions made by industry management.

Production and Trade

Why has the United States steel industry, since the 1950s, experienced a substantial decrease in steel exports, a loss of domestic market share due to rising imports, and a loss in position in terms of fraction of total worldwide steel production and capacity? A combination of newly built steel industries in European nations whose steel industries were devastated in World War II and in Japan and Third World developing nations to meet both domestic needs and capture export markets is the answer.

Foreign steelmaking industries are generally viewed by their governments as strategically crucial to satisfy the immediate and long-term growth needs of industrial infrastructures. Moreover, steel exports have been viewed as a means to obtain foreign currencies, gain positive trade balances, maintain high levels of employment in domestic steel industries (particularly in times of slow domestic demand), facilitate the construction of large economy-of-scale steelworks, and in some cases to make greater use of domestic raw materials such as iron ore, coal, or natural gas. Major steel industries have also been used to spur the development of other industries that use steel, such as shipbuilding and automobiles, to develop a base of skilled workers and technical professionals, to develop technology for export and in a more vague way to gain national prestige and influence. Rarely have foreign steel industries been required or expected by owners to make profits in the sense that United States steelmakers are. And for the most part, foreign steel industries have not been profitable in terms of return on investment or equity, but they have served the goals noted above, even to the extent that they have often cost considerable money to their governments who, to a large extent, own or subsidize their steel industries.

Has the United States been singled out as an export market by foreign steel industries? Yes, to the extent that United States markets represent the single largest and one of the most open and highest priced markets in the world for steel products. In some ways there has been considerable restraint, particularly by the Japanese, not to fully utilize available capacity at times and deluge the American market with competitively priced steel. In summary, it is difficult to "blame" foreign steelmakers for their expansionist policies, for defining the value of steel industries in ways other than the United States has, and for taking advantage of legitimate export market opportunities. With the growth of steel industries in Third World developing nations—formerly lucrative export markets—there is increasing interest in exporting to the United States. Balancing this, however, is the inability of many nations (such as the United Kingdom) to continue to sustain large economic costs for maintaining steel industries with far more capacity and often with technologically inferior facilities than can be justified on the basis of domestic needs or other social benefits such as maintaining employment.

This brings us to the second most important cause of the problems of production and trade: federal policies. The issue is: To what extent have federal policies been responsible for increasing imports and, less importantly, for decreasing exports? With regard to imports, the industry's argument is that federal policies have been ineffective in preventing unfairly traded steel imports. The federal government has been responsive to steel industry arguments that steel imports have been unfairly traded by, for example, instituting the Trigger Price Mechanism to detect unfairly priced steel imports and by imposing quota restrictions in some cases. Reasonable evidence has been found to indicate that some products from some foreign industries during limited periods have been traded unfairly in the sense that they have been priced below costs or below market prices in the market of the foreign industry, but not for the majority of steel imports over past years. In particular, the bulk of the evidence suggests that Japanese imports have not been traded unfairly for the most part. However, the evidence (substantial firm losses) does indicate that a number of European steel industries have dumped steel in the United States at times. The federal government appears to have been relatively tolerant of European dumping of steel because of other international trade considerations (such as the positive net trade from the United States to Europe) and for political considerations. Considering the excess capacity of the Japanese steel industry that has often existed, however, it can be argued that even if unfairly traded European steel had been more effectively eliminated, the Japanese could have increased their penetration of the United States market.

With regard to exports of steel from the United States, there appears to be merit to the position that the government could have played a stronger role in promoting exports of those steel products for which the country is especially competitive. In particular, the inhibiting effect of antitrust laws on the formation of joint trading ventures, used effectively by other nations, appears valid. Finally, in regard to exports and the inability of domestic steelmakers to compete effectively in the domestic market with some foreign steel, Wyman[4] has presented a convincing argument for the negative impact of federal monetary policies, linked to overly rapid credit generation, growth of United States budget deficits, and an overvalued dollar, that have put domestic steelmakers at a disadvantage. With regard to imports, however, during 1974 to 1978, when the value of the dollar declined substantially against currencies of major trading partners, there was a significant rise in imports. This can be looked at as resulting from increased demand for imports leading to weakness of the dollar, or, as the industry looks at it, increasing unfair trade of steel.

To what extent have steel industry management decisions been the cause of the production, capacity, and trade decline? Considering that domestic steelworks survived World War II without damage, that the United States generally wanted both its allies and former enemies to rebuild their industrial infrastructures, and that it has been in the nation's best interests to maintain and promote free international trade, especially for United States exports, it is difficult to attribute much responsibility to steel industry management. At the most, it can be argued that management generally pursued relatively conservative strategies after World War II. They did not, but perhaps could not, respond to demographic shifts in the United States which moved steel demand away from the traditional Northeast to the West and South and created opportunities for import penetration. The settlements made with the steelworkers have been criticized, but previous strikes did create opportunities for import penetration.

Users of imported steel and foreign exporters of steel have often argued that domestic steelmakers have not reduced prices sufficiently during periods of worldwide sluggish demand to remain competitive. But since the domestic steel industry is far more profit-oriented and dependent on internally generated cash to sustain itself, this pricing strategy makes sense. After all, domestic steelmakers are not able to turn to the federal government for financial assistance in the same manner that many foreign steel industries can, particularly in Europe.

Profitability and Investment

Both steel industry management decisions and federal policies are chief causes of the decline in profitability and investment in the domestic steel industry. Management can be criticized for: (a) failing to make long-range strategic plans that would have allowed faster and more appropriate responses to changing market conditions, to available new technologies to reduce costs, to major changes in the costs of inputs, to the availability of low-cost ferrous scrap, and to a host of social and political changes such as the environmental and worker health and safety movements; (b) failing to rationalize steel plants to obtain a better and more efficient match between technology and a limited product mix, rather than competing across a broad mix in the same market areas; (c) developing a strategy based on attracting investors through high dividends rather than through appreciation of stock value without making equity investments attractive; (d) failing to emphasize cost reductions through technological innovation; (e) failing to take measures to reduce the capital costs of steelmaking facilities, such as doing more in-house engineering and construction of equipment and thus obtaining more productivity from their investment capital; (f) poor labor relations; and (g) poorly planned and executed diversification investments. Nonunionized, nonintegrated firms have demonstrated how union work rules can be quite detrimental.

The industry correctly has placed considerable blame on federal policies for its problems with declining profits and capital; however, it must also be noted that a few steelmakers operating within the same policy environment have performed markedly better than the industry average because of different management decisions, even without pursuing a diversification strategy. The federal influence on profits has mostly been caused by limitations placed on steel prices, often through informal jawboning at times when steelmaking costs were rising sharply. The steel industry has been selected as an industry for which price controls are especially important, due to the basic nature of steel and the influence on other domestic industries. However, while this logic may have been true at one time, it no longer is compelling. The intensity of steel consumption in the United States has declined and the contribution of steel costs to the total costs of products has decreased for many large-scale applications such as automobiles and consumer appliances.

Domestic steelmakers also argue that federal trade policies have contributed to the profit problem by allowing unfairly priced imports to force domestic prices down. And to a limited extent, this has some merit. But the recent Trigger Price Mechanism has provided a means to increase domestic prices.

On the investment side, capital formation has been hurt by overly long depreciation times. A number of nations have used short depreciation times to spur steel industry investment, particularly Canada.

The industry has maintained that federal regulations in the environmental area have led to high capital costs which have limited investment in steelmaking. While these costs have certainly not been trivial, neither can they be considered to have been a prime determinant of the decline in the industry's steelmaking investments. The data in figure 1.1 indicate that the changes in total and steelmaking capital investments and in long-term debt do not mirror the changes in capital investment for pollution control. In terms of a percentage of total capital spending, the pollution abatement costs for the steel industry, although high, have been only slightly greater than for some other domestic industries, such as chemicals and petroleum refining, and similar to those of the Japanese steel industry. The steel industry has often made considerably more note of its projections of pollution-abatement capi-

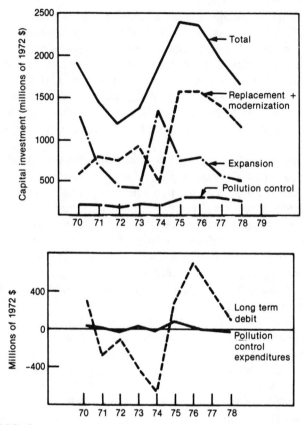

Fig. 1.1. TOP: Capital investment in constant dollars from 1970 to 1978 for domestic steel industry in three categories plus total. BOTTOM: Long-term debt and pollution control capital costs from 1970 to 1978 in constant dollars for domestic steel industry.

Source: P. Meier and S. Brown, "The Impact of Energy and Environmental Legislation on Industry: Problems of Regulatory Cost Assessment." (Paper delivered at 89th National Meeting of American Institute of Chemical Engineers, Portland, Oregon, August 1980.)

tal costs than its actual costs, and retrospective analyses have revealed that the actual costs have been markedly less than previous projections. For example, an analysis performed by A.D. Little in 1975 for the industry for the period 1975 to 1977 estimated capital costs of $(1972)2.92 billion, which would equal 25 percent of total industry capital spending, but the actual costs were $(1972)0.9 billion and 13.5 percent of the total.

The OTA study revealed that close to half of the industry's past pollution-abatement capital costs have been met through industrial development bond financing. This mitigates the cash flow problem and provides a low cost for the borrowing. Thus, federal policy has also reduced the burden of regulatory costs. However, there are a number of other types of regulatory costs which the steel industry has had to face, including the uncertainty of future OSHA standards and regulations.

Another example of federal policy which has contributed to the capital formation problem is the refusal to grant special energy-saving-investment tax credits for continuous casting facilities. Narrow bureaucratic interpretations appear to be the cause.

To the extent that there has been below-cost pricing by some foreign steel industries, foreign actions and policies may be blamed for a relatively small role in the decline of profitability and investment in the domestic steel industry.

Steelmaking Costs

The substantial rise in steelmaking costs, both production and other costs, must be viewed to be, within some limits, under the control of steel industry management. Perhaps the most controversial area is labor costs. The major steelworkers union has been singled out for unwarranted increases in hourly wages, but more realistically, it is management that decides to accept or reject such wages. Moreover, although there has been lagging productivity that explains increases in unit labor costs, there is little evidence to suggest that workers perform poorly. A stronger case can be made that for a number of plants, there has been poor labor-management relations. But better performing plants in regions with workers in the same union suggest that the problem is more on the management side. Moreover, labor productivity in steelmaking is largely determined by the equipment and technology that management chooses. Interestingly, some of the most profitable and low-cost steel plants that use nonunion labor pay the same total yearly compensation to workers that union workers receive, but the management style, work rules, and facilities are different.

Other than labor costs, technology also determines the costs of other factors of production such as energy and raw materials. Management can be criticized for inappropriate selection of new technology. Integrated companies can be criticized for slow investment in continuous casting and for not taking greater advantage of domestic supplies of ferrous scrap, for example.

For some firms and plants, there appears to have been an emphasis on maintaining production levels rather than on reducing costs and increasing total profitability even if it meant a reduction in tonnage of steel produced. As contrasted to Japanese steelworks, American steel plants have not emphasized cost cutting from the bottom up—that is, instituted through workers' suggestions that individually may appear small, but collectively are profoundly important. There are now enough examples in this country of plants in steel and other industries in which worker-based cost-cutting programs are successful to indicate that such an approach can and could have been used in the domestic steel industry pervasively.

Management can also be cited for placing more emphasis on technology and the use of technical personnel for product development rather than on steelmaking processes. Process technology appears to have been viewed in a static manner. The relationships between R&D personnel and plant management and personnel have not generally been structured to promote steady cost cutting through better use of technology and the use of the plant itself as, in limited ways, a laboratory for process improvement. One can see these preferred approaches in other domestic industries, such as chemicals, and in foreign steel industries.

To what extent can federal policies be accused of increasing costs? The industry has placed considerable emphasis on the high costs of federal regulations, particularly those in the environmental and worker-health-and-safety areas. Pollution-control costs have indeed been high for the domestic steel industry. But they have also been high for other domestic industries, such as nonferrous and cement, for example, in terms of energy requirements to run pollution-control equipment. Myers and Nakamura[5] find that the energy requirement as a percent of gross energy consumption for pollution control in 1976 was 2.1 percent at most for the steel industry, 2 percent at most for the cement industry, and 2.8 percent for the aluminum industry. The Japanese and a good part of the European steel industries have similar pollution-abatement costs. The contribution of pollution-abatement costs to production costs in the United States steel industry has been estimated by industry to be over 6 percent, while EPA has estimated it to be about 5 percent, including capital, operating, and maintenance costs for air and water pollution-abatement facilities. Considering the low profit margin for the industry, these costs are significant. To the extent that other domestic industries and some foreign steel industries do not incur such costs, the domestic steel industry has a competitive disadvantage.

A controversial issue is the extent to which federal policies have contributed to erratic and sometimes high prices for ferrous scrap, an important resource for the steel industry. The scrap industry maintains that a free market should exist in which foreign purchasers of scrap should have complete access to United States scrap, the world's largest supply. The steel industry's viewpoint is that export of ferrous scrap, which has been substantial (about 10 million tons per year), should be limited in ways similar to those used by other industrialized nations. They argue that ferrous scrap is a valuable national resource which is highly energy intensive, a means to ensure greater competitiveness for the domestic steel industry, and that it is used by government-subsidized foreign steel industries to make steel that is traded unfairly in our market. There is no doubt that exports of domestic scrap are substantial, but the link between export levels and domestic prices is difficult to quantify because, in part, prices vary considerably among different geographical regions. Nevertheless, there is some evidence to indicate that scrap exports do influence domestic prices (see figure 1.2). The government has moved to a limited degree to at least monitor scrap exports in order to assess unusual trade that might be detrimental to the United States.

Offsetting the above considerations is the fact, often noted by foreign steel industries, that the domestic steel industry has benefited in the past from artificially low prices for energy because of governmental price controls.

To argue that foreign actions and policies have been responsible for increases in the domestic costs of making steel is not particularly persuasive. The United States steel industry does import considerable iron ore, but there is no indication that unfair actions have increased the cost of iron ore. For relatively brief periods, the domestic steel industry has had to import coke to sustain integrated steelmaking, but here too there is little indication that anything other than market conditions influenced costs. Finally, the domestic steel industry is dependent on a number of foreign sources for alloying elements, such as chromium. In this case, there is evidence to suggest that at certain times foreign sources of domestically unavailable metals and minerals have taken advantage of their market position. However, the contribution to the bulk of the domestic steel industry has not been large.

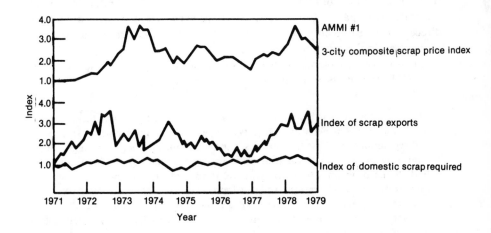

Fig. 1.2. Scrap: Price and Export Levels; Domestic Purchased Scrap Requirements, 1971–79.
SOURCE: *American Metal Market*, U.S. Bureau of Labor Statistics.

Technology, Innovation, and R&D

The general decline in the scientific and technological base of the industry must be attributed primarily to management decisions and attitudes. The industry's position, however, is that insufficient financial resources prevented whatever technological opportunities existed from being fully exploited. To some extent, as already discussed, factors outside the industry have contributed to declining financial resources. But other facts shift the chief responsibility to industry management. If the industry had greater financial resources, the evidence suggests, their emphasis would not have been on technology.

Here are two examples of such evidence. First, with regard to development and adoption of new technology as well as investment in R&D, it is possible to find companies within the domestic steel industry who performed in a manner counter to the general trend of the industry. What differed among companies were attitudes toward risk taking and the use of technology as a problem-solving tool. Management often used available capital for technology rather than for modernization or expansion based on older, well-proven technology, for diversification, or for dividends. Recent history for the nation's two largest steelmakers, Bethlehem Steel in 1977 and U.S. Steel in 1979, has shown that closing of inefficient plants can have a positive influence on company profitability. While such plant closings have gone on, other companies have opened new plants using more efficient technology.

Second, I cite the report by the American Iron and Steel Institute in 1980. In this major study and policy statement by the industry (albeit, representing integrated steelmakers for the most part), the executive summary contains no direct reference to technology and innovation or to R&D. In two appendices some attention is given to these topics.

The state of management has been well described by one of the industry's own R&D executives in an unusually candid statement:

> There is a trend toward more defense type research . . . more time being spent on shorter-range projects and projects designed to meet government mandates and regulations, and less time being spent on the kinds of long-term, high-risk, innovative projects which will lead to the new ways of making steel in the future. Part of the problem is that what we are doing with this money is not what everybody would call research and development . . . but is pointed more toward short-term objectives for a variety of reasons and not so much on the real innovative work and the fundamental research work that you might define as research and development.[6]

In addition to the nature of R&D changing in the industry, the amount of resources devoted to R&D declined. For example, in the 1960s, 0.7 percent of sales was spent on R&D, but by the late 1970s the level was only 0.5 percent, one of the lowest levels for any domestic industry. Historical data suggest that the industry viewed R&D as the lowest-priority discretionary spending of funds. In recent years the sum of money spent on diversification out of steelmaking and for dividends was about four times greater than the sum spent on R&D. The OTA study found a statistically significant relationship, with higher levels of pollution-abatement capital spending leading to lower levels of R&D spending.

Steel industry management seems to have convinced itself that economic arguments favor trading leadership in innovation for less risky follow-the-leader adoption of well-proven technology. They do not appear to follow a strategy of gaining technological advantage. Instead they seek, at best, parity. But while they argue that there is no knowledge gap between the domestic and foreign steel industries, because they have at least some of the latest technology in place, they miss the intrinsic advantages possessed by true innovators as well as the relationship between the source of innovation and the nature of the technology created.

Domestic steelmakers may be able to buy new technology, but whatever new technology is purchased from foreign sources still leaves the purchaser one step behind the originator. By the time all is learned about the innovation, the foreign source is well on its way to exploiting the next one by moving up on the learning curve for the generic technology. Knowledge about innovations is not equivalent to innovating. It takes years for new steelmaking facilities to be built, and those who innovate tend to stay ahead of their competitors, even those who purchase "new" technology. Moreover, domestic steelmakers undervalue the importance of developing unique process technologies which are responsive to domestic resource opportunities, regulatory requirements, existing plant facilities and layouts, and market opportunities. Domestic steelmakers often spend considerable sums to purchase foreign technology, and then still more money to adapt the technology to domestic needs and constraints. Thus, management's strategy to buy rather than develop technology is not necessarily optimum from either an economic or a technological viewpoint. It should be emphasized that development of process innovations requires considerable risk-taking by management, since very expensive pilot and demonstration testing of new process technologies is required to evaluate economic and technological costs and benefits. These risks and costs have not won out, in most cases, against the apparent safety and costs of purchasing innovative technology from foreign sources; nor has any competitive advantage been gained.

To what extent have federal policies contributed to the scientific and technological decline of the domestic steel industry? The most important area is direct federal funding of steel-related R&D. Historical data clearly show that for the past several decades, federal support for the ferrous area has been extremely small compared to other industrial areas. However, there is some correlation between the level of federal support and the level of R&D spending by industry itself. Thus, the argument can be made that the federal role has been one of partnership rather than unusual subsidies for selected industries.

The steel industry has also suggested that antitrust policies have reduced the opportunities for joint programs in high-cost process technology work. However, this has not appeared to have affected other basic industries, such as the chemicals industry.

To attribute some causality to foreign actions and policies for the decline in the scientific and technological base of the domestic steel industry is not easy. Neither the use of available information from the United States nor the sale of technology to the United States can be viewed as extraordinary or unreasonable. In a number of nations the role of government in fostering both basic science and technology of use to the steel industry is very strong. Comparatively, therefore, the domestic steel industry has had a disadvantage. Balancing this is the greater profitability exhibited by the domestic steel industry.

Industry Restructuring

The chief explanation for the decline of the integrated segment of the domestic steel industry as compared to the growth of the nonintegrated segment and the healthy posture of the alloy/specialty steelmakers is in the area of management decisions. Operating within the same domestic market—which accounts for most of the business of all three segments, the same set of government policies, the same labor pool, and the same sphere of technological opportunities—management made widely differing decisions and chose different marketing and technological strategies.

The impressive growth and profitability of the nonintegrated companies can be attributed to their fundamental decision to make greater use of domestically available scrap, to quickly adopt continuous casting, and to emphasize narrow product mixes for individual plants which take advantage of nearby market opportunities. These companies emphasize reduction of production costs to a far greater extent than integrated companies have. This has led to their being very competitive against both integrated producers and imports. Labor costs per ton of steel shipped are lower than for integrated producers because of greater productivity, not because of lower total labor costs resulting from mostly nonunionized labor being used. Even in a sluggish domestic market, nonintegrated firms have found particular niches to capitalize on. Low capital costs have resulted not only from the elimination of ironmaking, but also from astute management that has made use of internal design and manufacture of equipment and sometimes lower-cost equipment from foreign sources. A number of recent studies of how American manufacturing firms must adapt to changing economic, political, and social conditions can be applied to the nonintegrated companies to explain their success. It should be emphasized that no federal policies have contributed to their success.

The one characteristic of the alloy/specialty producers that stands out is their emphasis on technological innovations. In contrast to the integrated firms, who also have received various forms of trade protection in recent years, the alloy/specialty firms took advantage of the protection to greatly improve their cost and technological competitiveness. While the alloy/specialty producers have not exhibited the growth of the nonintegrated firms, they have been able both to maintain good profitabilities for the most part and to compete effectively with very aggressive imports attempting to move from carbon commodity steels to the more profitable and technology intensive alloy/specialty steels.

Industry restructuring must also be considered a consequence of the faults of integrated company management, already discussed. It is reasonable to argue that whatever nonintegrated and alloy/specialty firms have done to achieve success could also have been done by integrated companies. Indeed, the question has often been asked: Why didn't the integrated companies, for example, build nonintegrated plants pursuing the same strategies that nonintegrated companies have? For the most part, the answer is that integrated company managers did not assess the opportunities or the changing economic, political, and social climate in the nation correctly. There was and, to a large degree, still is a lethargy often associated with large corporations that makes management defensive and oriented to the past rather than forward looking and positively aggressive in attitude and style.

Have federal policies been responsible for the restructuring? I believe not. While it is true that a number of federal policies, ad hoc and poorly coordinated with each other, have presented serious problems to integrated companies, the success of the nonintegrated and alloy/specialty companies demonstrates that there were ways to cope with such policies. Technology, for example, could have been used more aggressively and enthusiastically to deal with the burden of environmental regulations, capital formation problems, and rising labor costs. The actions of Bethlehem Steel and U.S. Steel have demonstrated that closing of inefficient plants should have been done earlier.

It is equally difficult to seek foreign actions and policies which can truly be found to be the causes of the restructuring of the domestic steel industry. The pressures from imports could have been used as a stimulus by integrated steelmakers for reducing costs, improving steel product quality, and improving marketing and customer services. Mature domestic industries are indeed vulnerable to foreign competition, but the restructuring of the domestic steel industry has already demonstrated that there are ways to cope with such competition, as well as with slow growth in demand, other than seeking federal help or pursuing diversification.

IDEAL SOLUTIONS TO PRESENT PROBLEMS

Studies of the domestic steel industry, particularly those made by the industry itself, tend to speak of today's problems in terms of a crisis facing the industry. In reality, it should be noted that the trends which have been discussed do not reflect abrupt changes in the circumstances of the industry. Both the negative and positive developments have been taking place for the most part in a steady manner over many years. Crisis, however, is one effective way to get political attention. But there is not so much a crisis today for the domestic steel industry as there is a set of possibilities for the future which may lead to crisis conditions. There are, however, so many uncertainties about so many important variables that predictions of crises are highly speculative.

Ideally, what we need now, I believe, is a well-coordinated sector approach for the steel industry that addresses both public and private policies that are responsive to past trends, but aimed at long-range strategic plans for the future. Changes in federal policies which are macro in nature and oriented toward improving economic conditions in general and affecting all American industry are not likely to reverse negative trends in the steel industry. There must be industry-specific policies; but these do not necessarily imply, as some would think, that large-scale federal funding or extensive trade protection are required. It is more a question of responsiveness to particular problems being required, as well as systematic approaches and extensive coordination of policies. At the same time, it is foolish to think of improved and changed federal policies without also requiring changes in the industry itself, particularly in the policies, attitudes, and decisions of management and, to a lesser extent, in labor.

Long-range strategic planning is just as much needed in industry as in government. Ideally, government and industry must recognize common goals and needs, as well as those that are different. The federal government could provide: (1) the means to reach agreement on data and analyses upon which policy changes, both public and private, must be based; (2) a forum in which the various components of the steel industry, the government, and suppliers and consumers associated with the industry can come together to reach mutually acceptable goals for the industry and government; and (3) a context to relate steel-industry-specific policies to those of other industries and to economic and industrial policies of a more general nature.

Long-range strategic planning does not imply government intervention in the marketplace. While there has not been a free market system in the United

States in recent history, federal policies can be designed to facilitate *market forces* being the prime determinants of success *and failure* in the steel industry. Nor does long-range strategic planning imply that detailed and specific choices of a more operational or tactical nature are being made by government or by any consensus among corporations by themselves or in conjunction with other interests, such as labor. Planning on a macro (national or industry) level which reconciles the needs of both the private and public sectors can be compatible with freedom on micro (firm) levels.

The ideal solutions do not involve *saving* the steel industry. From whom is it to be saved—from itself, from the government, from foreign competition? Simplistic labels for industries have already done more damage than good. It is not a question of the domestic steel industry being sick, a loser or a winner. What is needed for the steel industry is a future-oriented, comprehensive approach that recognizes changing conditions in the industry itself, in the nation, and in the world, and one that is aimed at taking advantage of opportunities rather than preserving what objective analysis tells us is no longer effective, efficient, or useful. This of course means that there will likely be dislocations affecting companies, workers, and communities. But the goal should be to develop cost-effective ways to deal with the dislocations, rather than to fight the changes which lead to the dislocations. The United States steel industry of the future *will* be different from the one we have today, just as today's industry is different from the one which existed here twenty years ago.

Here is an analogy. For good personal health, it is reasonable to conclude that an individual needs so much of several basic kinds of food, and so much exercise, and so much work and play, for example. But it is not necessary for any institution or anyone else, or even the individual himself or herself, to determine what particular type of food in a broad category of protein, for example, or what particular type of exercise, and so on, is required for some specific time in the future. Setting some long-range plans for the steel industry by setting goals, agendas, and means reached through rational and equitable discussion among the interested and affected parties requires no abandonment of our economic, political, or social institutions and principles. The United States has in fact done it before with certain industries, usually in time of crisis. The challenge for the nation and the steel industry today is not to wait for such a crisis. The best reason for not waiting is that while crises have tended to come upon us faster than ever before, the time to actually build a steel plant or develop a commercially feasible innovative technology has not been dramatically reduced, and although we have learned how to use other materials for many applications, steel remains a most vital material to keep our society functioning in time of peace and war. And although we may speculate how much steel and from whom it may be available in the future, we have certainly learned about the risks involved in being overly dependent on foreign sources for things which are essential to the running of our society.

Having long-range strategic plans (such as for technology development and adoption, and restructuring) for the steel industry upon which public and private policies are based will not provide certainty for the future, but they would reduce major *un*certainties which are particularly debilitating for investment decisions, risk-taking innovations, and personal commitments. There are more than enough uncertainties thrust upon our nation from outside our borders. What is done for the steel industry could serve as an excellent case study of what is needed for other major domestic industries. It is a climate, a framework in which all the factors which by themselves are necessary but not sufficient to ensure health for the industry—such as technology, capital, skilled labor, technical personnel, and good management— can be focused on in a systematic way to make both a more efficient and a more profitable industry. However, it is also necessary to recognize that no matter how good are strategic plans and public and private policies for a specific industry, success still depends on the general economic climate in the nation and, to an increasingly greater extent, in the world. They too are necessary, but not sufficient for a healthy domestic steel industry.

Criteria for Evaluation of Policies

The preceding discussion provides a basis for developing several criteria which can be used to evaluate proposed policies or strategic plans for the domestic steel industry. The five criteria are discussed below.

1. *Comprehensiveness*. Does the policy plan address all major historical trends and chronic problems of the industry? It has become more recognized that to act in one functional area, such as trade, for example, without solving problems in other critical areas is not likely to be effective. I suggest that, at the minimum, there are six critical areas: capacity, trade, profitability, capital formation, cost (including regulatory), and technology. General national security and economic interests demand consideration for developing an understanding of a minimum acceptable level of domestic steelmaking capacity. The issue of unfairly traded imports and the potential for promoting more exports of technology-intensive steels remain important policy areas. Though capital formation is a major problem, declining profitability for many firms is just as important if capital is to be invested in steelmaking facilities. Reducing the costs of regulations must be balanced by goals of reducing production costs. The role of technology is crucial in improving the health of the industry in the long term, if the need for government assistance is to be minimized.

2. *Feasibility*. Is the policy approach designed in a politically and economically feasible way for obtaining both short- and long-term solutions to

fundamental causes, rather than short-term fixes for symptoms? There must be a pragmatic approach that recognizes current limitations for federal assistance and intervention. Wherever possible, policy instruments should not involve federal spending. Where federal spending is required, there should be some attempt at assessing costs and benefits. The relationship between steel-industry-specific policies and broader policies should be analyzed.

3. *Restructuring*. Does the policy strategy acknowledge and facilitate future restructuring of the industry because of the economic benefits offered? Recognizing the problem of dislocations in society, there must be effective policies to cope with the dislocations rather than impede worthwhile restructuring.

4. *Innovation*. Does the policy approach place emphasis on future technological innovation (often neglected for basic, mature industries) for the reduction of production and capital costs, and for domestic circumstances in order to improve economic and financial performance? There must be attempts to facilitate as well as to provide assistance for major innovative changes in technology which are responsive to the particular needs of the industry and domestic resources. Is innovation losing ground to diversification?

5. *Equity*. Does the policy package distribute costs and benefits equitably across all interested and affected parties in society? An effective approach requires broad public support. Analyses must reveal how particular policy measures are, in their totality, fair in all ways.

COMPARATIVE ANALYSIS OF AVAILABLE POLICY APPROACHES

Four Options Available

It is difficult to find an American industry which has been more studied than steel. Even though there is a vast literature on the steel industry, at present there are four policy studies which have been publicly disseminated during the past year or so and which still remain under discussion and available to policymakers. One is regarded as the plan proposed by the industry itself; it is the study by the American Iron and Steel Institute mentioned previously. The second is the OTA study already mentioned. Third is the set of findings of the Steel Tripartite Advisory Committee formed by President Carter.[7] These findings were submitted to President Carter and, to some extent, were adopted by him and used in his announced program for the steel industry. While the findings of the Tripartite Commission are likely to remain of interest, I do not believe that the presidential program remains viable; therefore, it is not included in the following discussion. Lastly, there is the most recent report by the General Accounting Office.[8]

There is of course a fifth option: that no new policy approach be pursued. This possibility is considered in both the OTA and AISI studies in the form of a scenario which paints a very bleak picture for the industry and for the nation in terms of lost employment and risky dependence on imports. Since the OTA study does not make recommendations, the status quo situation is treated as one of three scenarios. However, the other three studies take the position that a new policy approach should be taken by the federal government.

The four studies are difficult to describe and compare, for a number of reasons. First, each is, strictly speaking, not a policy study exclusively or even primarily. The studies attempt to analyze the problems and needs of the industry in varying degrees and from particular perspectives. In all cases, there is very little detailed analysis of specific policy instruments, options, or measures in a rigorous and quantitative manner. Rather, they attempt, for the most part, to speak in broad terms and critical policy choices or goals. Moreover, there is considerable detail which cannot be described here. Therefore, even though the four studies will be reviewed by discussing them in terms of the five criteria discussed previously, it should be emphasized that their shortcomings often stem from the lack of emphasis on policy, which is characteristic of the studies.

The AISI Study

On the basis of comprehensiveness, this study and its policy recommendations are deficient primarily in the area of technology. Its methodology is primarily assertion, rather than analysis. The study emphasizes the need for effective policy measures in three critical areas:

> Policies that would encourage and permit steel companies to achieve competitive rates of return, accompanied by provisions for accelerated capital recovery. Modifications of government-mandated regulatory programs (notably environmental) that would reduce non-income-producing capital demands. Firm assurances that imported steels, either by excessive volumes or unfair pricing, will not disrupt the domestic steel market, particularly during the industry's revitalization effort.[9]

The study also asks for removal of government interference in steel company pricing decisions. In an appendix there are recommendations for federal support of research in the areas of energy and environment, new steel products, and for development of formcoke processes.

In general, the political and economic feasibility of the proposed policy measures is good. There is attention to both the short and long terms, and a strong case is given for the need for some government costs, but the emphasis is on measures which do not involve outright spending by government. The orientation is more on removal of disincentives for investment, on removal of government interference in the marketplace, and on the needs of integrated firms.

Both restructuring of the industry and technological innovation are absent in the analyses and in the formulation of policy approaches. The issue of equity is not addressed directly, and the absence of a number of topics, such as what to do about high labor costs and adjustment to plant closings and declining employment, indicate that, not surprisingly, this industry-generated program did not delve into questions of equity.

The OTA Study

The central theme of this study was how technology might be used to improve the competitiveness of the industry. With regard to comprehensiveness, therefore, there is limited coverage on trade and a limiting perspective on most issues. The primary emphasis is clearly on technology and innovation and on those policy options (without giving recommendations) that can use these as a means to achieve other goals, or on policy options in other areas which could have an impact on technology and innovation. The policy options which are discussed and which "could be instrumental in improving the industry's competitiveness" are aimed at: increasing R&D and innovation, encouraging pilot- and demonstration- plant testing of new technologies, facilitating capital formation, reducing the adverse economic costs of regulatory compliance, improving the availability of scrap, and constraining steel imports and facilitating certain exports.

There is much attention to the potential benefits and risks of a steel industry sector policy by the federal government, as follows:

> The most critical policy option may be that of a governmental steel industry sector policy, that is, for a coherent set of specific policies designed to achieve prescribed goals. The present state of the industry and the need for a critical examination of policy options are, in large measure, a consequence of a long series of uncoordinated policies. These policies have not been properly related to each other or to a well-considered set of goals for the industry, goals that satisfy the needs of both the Nation and the industry. The lack of a sector policy and the designation of a lead agency to implement such a policy has led to policies that often conflict with one another, create an adversarial relationship between Government and industry, and fail to address critical issues. At pres-

ent, a large number of people and agencies in the Government deal with steel, but they do not reinforce each other's work nor do they provide an accessible source of expertise and guidance for the industry or facilitate its efficient inter- action with the Government.[10]

The report also emphasizes the need for comprehensiveness in policy by noting that "neither technology nor capital, alone, will solve the steel indus- try's problems. Substantial trade and tax issues exist with regard to the steel industry, and federal policies on these issues need examination."

Unlike the other studies, the OTA analysis emphasizes analysis of the advantages and disadvantages of various policy instruments to achieve cer- tain goals, such as greater capital formation. Table 1.4 from this study illustrates this approach for the case of several options for increasing capital formation; and table 1.5 presents its review of a number of regulatory changes.

As some of the above comments suggest, the OTA study gives consider- able attention to political and economic feasibility, to short- and long-term solutions, and to assessments of economic costs and benefits.

Perhaps more than any other study, there is substantial emphasis on in- dustry restructuring. There is a detailed analysis of the economic benefits of this restructuring—for example, in reducing future capital needs of the in-

Table 1.4. Features of Four Federal Options for Increasing Capital Formation in the Domestic Steel Industry

Federal option	Govern- ment cost	Adminis- trative burden	Bias against small firms	Promotion of new technology	Applies to steelmak- ing only
Accelerated depreciation					
Jones-Conable	High	Low	Yes	No	No
Certificate of necessity	Moderate	Low	Yes	No	Yes
Investment tax credit					
Increase capacity...........	Moderate	Low	No	No	Yes
Modernization	Moderate	Low	Yes	No	Yes
Innovation.................	Moderate	High	No	Yes	Yes
Loan guarantee					
Increase capacity...........	Slight	Moderate	Yes	Yes	Yes
Modernization	Slight	Moderate	Yes	Yes	Yes
Innovation.................	Moderate	High	Yes	Yes	Yes
Subsidized interest loan					
Increase capacity...........	Slight	Moderate	No	No	Yes
Modernization	Slight	Moderate	Yes	No	Yes
Innovation.................	Slight	High	No	Yes	Yes

Source: Office of Technology Assessment, *Technology and Steel Industry Competitiveness* (Washington, D.C., June 1980), p. 45.

Table 1.5. Regulatory Change: Policy Options and Consequences

Regulatory change	Social impact[a]	Promotion of new technology	Regulatory cost impact	Capacity
Bubble concept	Modest	Yes	Reduction	Facilitates replacement
Distributing cost of tradeoff requirements (offset policy)	None: increased equity among expanding firms in non-attainment areas	No	Reduction	Facilitates expansion
Extension of limited-life facilities policy while replacing steel facilities or otherwise providing for regional economic growth	Modest; at least partially offset by strengthening regional economy	Yes	Reduction	Replacement/ expansion
Fugitive emissions	High	No	Slow down growth rate	NA
Use of administrative penalty payments for environmental technology R&D fund	None, but goal change in favor of R&D	Yes	Transfer of costs	NA
Improved coordination of OSHA compliance deadlines	Modest	Yes, if given as condition for extended deadlines	None	NA
Improved coordination of EPA innovation waivers	Modest	Yes	None	NA
Cost/benefit analysis	Varies with cost-benefit tradeoff	No	Potential reduction	NA

SOURCE: Office of Technology Assessment, *Technology and Steel Industry Competitiveness* (Washington, D.C., June 1980), p. 51.
NA, not applicable.
[a] Social impact is defined as increased environmental degradation or occupational risk resulting from regulatory relaxation.

dustry. There is also a forecast for future shifts in market share among the three industry segments and on what factors this restructuring depends. Policy options are generally evaluated in terms of their impact on restructuring, and policies concerning ferrous scrap are dealt with in some detail because of the dependence of nonintegrated firms on scrap as a feedstock.

The need for technological innovation to improve competitiveness, and prospects for specific innovations, are focused on. The problem of meshing both government and private sector policies in order to achieve innovation is discussed. A strong case is made for greater support by government for pilot and demonstration plant testing of new steelmaking processes which can reduce capital and production costs, reduce pollution, and make greater use of domestic resources such as coal.

Equity issues are treated in a limited way. There is emphasis on dealing with the needs of industry as well as national needs. There is, however, no detailed analysis of dislocations and adjustment policies related to plant closings and the restructuring process.

The Tripartite Committee Findings

An added difficulty with discussing the policy approach contained in this report is that the consensus findings of various subcommittees did not always become the consensus conclusions and recommendations of the entire committee, but the latter are the ones described here. With regard to comprehensiveness, most major areas (with the notable exception of pricing) were considered, even though there were not original analyses performed by this group in all cases. The following were the major policy objectives recommended:

Modernizing our economic base

Modernization of the American steel industry must be regarded as a key part of a larger effort to revitalize our overall industrial base and to increase productivity within our economy. Government assistance for steel will be most effective if it is part of a program aimed at stimulating business investment in general. The Committee . . . endorsed tax changes that would encourage more rapid capital recovery.[11]

Reducing the burdens of adjustment

A central element in a steel program must . . . be aggressive programs to assist workers to retrain for new jobs or to relocate to areas where jobs are more plentiful. The programs must also attract new employers to those communities where steelmaking jobs have declined.[12]

Responding to unfair import competition

A steel industry program should, consistent with our overall trade policy objectives, work toward a situation in which trade in steel products is free of barriers, determined by economic costs—not government inducements—and conducted without injury attributable to dumping or subsidization. Our import competition laws are fully consistent with the obligations we have undertaken under the Multilateral Trade Agreements. The government must enforce these laws rigorously. The government should be prepared to administer them expeditiously.[13]

Environmental and safety and health improvement

To achieve compliance with environmental goals as well as to encourage modernization, government should find ways to allow the industry to make investments in steel production which will assure that both objectives can be attained. Government reexamination of the reasonableness of its regulatory procedures may be required, too. We should expect that industry, for its part, will use any funds that are saved through changes in regulatory requirements for investment in modernization and commit firmly to full and timely compliance with all environmental and occupational safety and health requirements.[14]

Adopting the best technology

It is not sufficient . . . for a steel program to aim at helping domestic producers match the extent to which foreign producers use the latest of available technology. Rather, the aim must be to assist our industry in the development and testing of the possibilities so that they are positioned to incorporate new technologies into their operations as soon as they are proven. The great share of research and development should properly be carried out and financed by the steel companies themselves. A steel industry program should set into motion multi-firm collaboration and industry-government cooperation in R&D to find solutions in these common problem areas.[15]

Competition should set capacity

The size of the industry should be determined by market forces. Government's role is to do all it can to assure open and fair competition at home and in the international marketplace.

An integrated long-term approach

A piecemeal approach to the steel industry will accomplish little. The problems of the industry cover a number of areas including capital formation, trade, environmental regulation, technology, and the adjustment of workers and communities to changing industry conditions. With or without Government assistance, measures directed only at one of these areas cannot set the industry on a new path. A coordinated and integrated set of initiatives, maintained for a 3 to 5 year period, or longer, is required to remedy the industry's situation.

A partnership commitment

A commitment by management, labor and Government to support and contribute to a steel industry program will be an absolute prerequisite for its success. Changes in Government policies alone cannot make the industry modern and competitive.[18]

Generally, the Tripartite policy recommendations rate high in terms of feasibility, innovation, and equity. However, there was little effort to focus attention on the restructuring of industry and the impact of various policies on that process and on steel consumers. This is due to the absence of representation from nonintegrated firms on the committee. For example, delayed compliance with the Clean Air Act and refundable tax credits promotes the existence of integrated firms with the poorest performance.

The GAO Report

While the GAO study included examination of most critical areas (with the exception of technology for which it referenced, for the most part, the OTA study) its policy recommendations are skewed toward one particular conclusion. GAO recommended "that Congress define a policy guidance performance objective for the domestic steel industry." Such an objective would be "in terms of efficient capacity." The purpose would be to "help determine appropriate Federal means toward achieving overall objective of a competitive industry." The rather unusual recommendation of asking the federal government to set a capacity level for a major industry was justified on the basis that in the absence of a generally agreed upon performance objective for the industry, "it is just not possible to judge the adequacy of the set of proposals for industry revitalization, nor be able to suggest how they might be usefully amended." There is, however, no detailed analysis to demonstrate that consideration was given to other measures of performance, in terms of efficiency or means, rather than mere level of output.

The report also deals with supportive policies which "ought to be formulated for a range of important peripheral activities":

—wage and compensation restraint and labor-management commitment to a
   sound revitalization strategy,
—measures to induce the entry and growth of new competitors,
—accelerating depreciation rates,

—improving administration of environmental regulation,

—eliminating discriminatory price restraints, and

—creating a trade policy yielding predictable and acceptable effects on imports with a minimum of inflation.[19]

The report also presents a case for "the likely need for new means of policy administration to insure that a necessarily interdepartmental, multi-faceted steel policy succeeds in promoting industry revitalization."

Although there are some very strong findings concerning the benefits of industry restructuring, there is little attempt to relate policy measures to this process. Since the report did not address technology, innovation is not covered. With regard to both feasibility and equity, there is substantial coverage, with the one important exception being the difficulty of the government setting a level of capacity for the industry, the study's main recommendation.

Agreement Among the Four Policy Approaches

It is important to recognize the impressive amount of agreement among the four studies described above, even though different methodologies were used and each study had different mandates or objectives. To recognize this agreement is crucial if within the near future there is to be a serious attempt at formulating and implementing a specific and detailed policy for the domestic steel industry.

First, in each of the four cases a strong case is made that the steel industry either can be or should be restored to a healthier state. Moreover, in each case there are specific measures which are believed to be capable and cost-effective to do this job. There is little despair or hopelessness exhibited. Rather, there is a sense of urgency in getting all interested parties to come to an agreed-upon strategy.

Second, there is agreement that the best policy approach is to deal in a comprehensive manner with a number of critical areas at the same time, and that to do otherwise would be ineffective and inefficient. Moreover, for the most part, there is agreement that changes in government policies must be accompanied by changes in the policies and attitudes among management and labor.

Third, there is considerable agreement on the need to deal with the problem of capital formation in order to modernize the industry, and to develop and implement innovative new technology in order to improve profitability and international competitiveness. Although accelerated depreciation has received the most attention and the highest level of endorsement, it is also generally recognized that by itself, this policy would not provide sufficient capital, even though there is some disagreement on the actual amount of capital needed in future years.

Fourth, with the exception of more federal spending on R&D and innovation activities, there is little support for direct federal spending on the industry, although significant spending is generally recommended for adjustment programs for workers and communities. Most policy measures which are supported involve removing existing regulations or disincentives and doing other things to achieve greater efficiencies in both the public and private sectors, and to let normal market forces operate with less interference by the government. There is, however, strong recognition for the need to have federal policies which in their own right are competitive with foreign policies toward steel industries.

Fifth, in the two studies (OTA and GAO) in which industry restructuring and the benefits and growth of nonintegrated companies were examined, there is strong agreement on the need to avoid obstacles to this restructuring if the overall competitiveness and health of the domestic steel industry are to be improved. OTA, for example, forecasts that by 1990 nonintegrated firms could account for 25 percent of domestic production.

Finally, although there are elements of each of the four studies that can be used in future policy work for the steel industry, there is also considerable need for more independent analysis and data gathering for precise policy formulations. There are important criticisms of past government efforts and a general consensus that a new administrative mechanism is needed both for analysis of the industry and for discussing, formulating, and implementing steel-industry-specific policies.

The Connection Between Steel Industry Policy and Industrial Policy

There remains the issue of how steel-industry-specific policy should be related to a broad federal industrial policy, if such a policy affecting all American industry was to be formulated, as so many have been advocating under the rubrics of revitalization, reindustrialization, and renewal. I will not review all the formulations of industrial policy presented. Some take the position that the policy levers for change should not be targeted to specific sectors or industries, while others focus on industry- or sector-specific means. What comes out of the four studies of the steel industry is a strong case for the need of a steel-industry-specific-policy approach. But this does not imply that by itself such an approach would actually work. Neither a steel-industry-specific policy nor some broad-based economic or industrial policy without targets would by itself be sufficient. Each is necessary, but not sufficient. Most of the objectives and quantitative analyses lead to the conclusion that broad-based, untargeted approaches would not provide an adequate solution to a particular problem, such as capital formation, or that specific problems would simply not be addressed.

A subset of those favoring the targeted approach of industrial policy prefer to label industries as winners or losers so that federal policy can facilitate the decline or promote the growth, respectively. An important consequence of the past studies of the steel industry should be the recognition that applying such labels is fraught with risk. In all cases that I have seen where such labeling has been done, even in those using rigorous, quantitative means, the steel industry is labeled a loser. This is inaccurate, because there is no recognition of restructuring, of the potential for technological rejuvenation, or of nonquantifiable reasons for wanting and needing the industry, such as national security considerations. Any targeted approach should simply be attuned to the opportunities and problems of an industry as well as to the need to reconcile public and private sector objectives.

I suggest that the lesson to be learned from the studies of the steel industry which could be of great value in the debate over industrial policy is that there are three fundamental rationales for government actions that affect industry.

Remedial. Past government policies have caused damage directly, or caused distortions or imperfections in the marketplace, or sent perverse signals to it, and these must be corrected.

Competitiveness. The actions and policies of foreign governments have caused distortions or imperfections in the international marketplace or sent perverse signals to it, and these have damaged our domestic industry and must be corrected by implementing federal policies which offset the damaging effects.

Efficiency. To borrow a metaphor from science, federal policies should play the role of a catalyst in making an industry reach desirable goals of improved performance for its own sake and the sake of the nation in the most efficient manner. A catalyst does not itself take part in a chemical reaction, but it makes the reaction take place with less energy, with less cost, and often with greater speed. Appropriate, catalytic federal policies, therefore, do *not* imply intervention in or subversion of the marketplace, or large amounts of spending. Rather, they offer the promise of smoother running institutions in the public and private sectors and more efficient and useful exchanges of information and resources across the many interfaces among these institutions. To paraphrase Abraham Lincoln, government cannot help industry permanently by doing for them what they could and should do for themselves. But that leaves a rich field of opportunities for government to act appropriately.

SUMMARY

Since World War II the United States steel industry has declined in terms of economic and technical performance criteria, and domestic steelmaking capacity has recently been decreasing as imports increased and firms properly (but belatedly) closed down older, inefficient plants. Creation and adoption of technological innovations have also lagged. But one bright spot in this otherwise dismal picture is that there has also been a significant restructuring of the industry which has instilled new vitality.

Steelmaking firms in the industry are not all alike. Dividing the industry up into three segments allows the restructuring to be examined. While integrated steelmakers have received the most attention by policymakers and the media, and indeed have undergone serious declines in virtually all measures of industrial health, the nonintegrated and alloy/specialty steelmakers have, for the most part, experienced much higher levels of profitability, growth, and technological competitiveness. The decline in market share of the integrated companies is in contrast to the rapid growth of nonintegrated firms, which will likely continue to provide a source of competition to domestic integrated producers, a source perhaps more significant than foreign competition.

The present challenge to policymakers is to decide whether to let the domestic steel industry drift along as it has been under a set of federal policies which have been of an ad hoc, uncoordinated nature and often inattentive to serious problems, or whether to make use of a number of recent major studies of the industry which offer many suggestions for a more comprehensive and future-oriented policy strategy for the industry. There appears to be a consensus that the domestic steel industry should and can exist in a more profitable, competitive, and technologically innovative form than it presently does. Because steel is so critical for the functioning of our society, the domestic steel industry, most studies conclude, should receive special policy attention and probably requires industry-specific policies for its survival and renewal.

NOTES

1. American Iron and Steel Institute, *Steel at the Crossroads: The American Steel Industry in the 1980's* (Washington, D.C., January 1980).
2. U.S. Office of Technology Assessment, *Technology and Steel Industry Competitiveness* (Washington, D.C., June 1980).
3. William K. Hall, "Survival Strategies in a Hostile Environment," *Harvard Business Review*, September-October, 1980, pp. 75-85.
4. Joseph C. Wyman, *Gold, Technology and Steel* (New York: Shearson Hayden Stone, Inc., February 21, 1979).
5. J. Myers and L. Nakamura, *Saving Energy in Manufacturing: The Post Embargo Record* (Cambridge, Mass.: Ballinger, 1978).
6. N. A. Robbins, in American Iron and Steel Institute, *The American Steel Industry in the 1980's—The Crucial Decade* (Washington, D.C., 1979).

7. "Report to the President by the Steel Tripartite Advisory Committee on the United States Steel Industry," mimeographed (Washington, D.C., September 25, 1980).
8. U.S. General Accounting Office, *New Strategy Required for Aiding Distressed Steel Industry* (Washington, D.C., January 8, 1981).
9. American Iron and Steel Institute, *Steel at the Crossroads*, p. 3.
10. U.S. Office of Technology Assessment, *Technology and Steel Industry Competitiveness*, pp. 33-34.
11. "Report to the President by the Steel Tripartite Advisory Committee," pp. 5, 10.
12. Ibid., p. 5.
13. Ibid.
14. Ibid., p. 6.
15. Ibid.
16. Ibid.
17. Ibid., pp. 6-7.
18. Ibid., p. 7.
19. U.S. General Accounting Office, *New Strategy Required*, p. viii.

2

The Men's Clothing Industry

Vera Miller

An evaluation of the current condition of the men's clothing industry and its prospects for the future calls for an understanding of its evolution and the significant factors in its development. In some relevant respects, the men's clothing industry differs from most other manufacturing industries. With a collective bargaining relationship, on an industrial union basis, going back seventy years in an industry characterized by relatively low economic concentration, industrial changes often resulted from the union's initiative and were, in any case, the outcome of a dynamic interaction of the employers and the union—and in certain periods, with government, a third important stream in this evolutionary development.

At the outset, one must be clear about the definition of this industry. It is *not* the one found in dictionaries, which define clothing as "garments in general." Nor is it synonymous with the word "apparel." In the menswear field, the men's (and boys') clothing industry—or the tailored clothing industry, as it is also called—produces primarily men's and boys' suits, overcoats and topcoats, tailored dress and sport coats (jackets), and tailored uniforms. The *Standard Industrial Classification Manual* of the Office of Management and Budget lists it as industry number 2311—men's, youths', and boys' suits, coats, and overcoats. The Bureau of Labor Statistics of the U.S. Department of Labor reports it as men's and boys' suits and coats. It was not until 1939 that data for this industry, as defined above, began to be issued. For earlier years, the industry group was broader and included producers of other items of male apparel. Thus, data on this industry are not available for the years prior to 1939, and later suit and coat data are not comparable with the data available for the years prior to 1939 for the broader male-apparel category.

HISTORICAL BACKGROUND

Let us begin with a glimpse at what the men's clothing industry was like when unionism began to be a major factor, soon after the turn of the century. The industry employed perhaps 120,000 workers, primarily in such large cities as New York, Chicago, Philadelphia, Rochester, Baltimore, Cleve-

42

land, Boston, Cincinnati, and Saint Louis. There were some large producers, but also many small operators, often contractors. The business was easy to enter, requiring only a small capital investment, and piece goods and equipment were usually available on credit.

There was considerable division of labor, with more than 150 separate operations. Many of the jobs were semiskilled and suitable for the employment of the masses of immigrants then flooding into the country—especially suitable for the women among the "greenhorns," as they were called.

The piece-rate and quota systems were already established and generally overseen by harsh foremen. The relentless pressure for more production was in part the result of the extreme competitiveness of the business, since any small change in a cost element led to the shifting of work from shop to shop and from market to market. In addition, since the demand for men's clothing was elastic and seasonal, production and employment were irregular. Because of these elements, the industry at that time could be characterized by a word: *instability.*

It was because of such conditions and the fact that they were often ramshackle workplaces that the smaller shops became known as "sweatshops." But whether in small lofts or large, (then) modern factories, the workers toiled in an atmosphere of constant pressure for more production, cuts in rates, fines, irregular employment, arbitrary firings, and long hours—"If you don't come in Sunday, don't come in Monday." They had no recourse for the multiplicity of festering grievances. The union in the field, the United Garment Workers of America, was craft-oriented and interested only in the clothing cutters, although it also had some following in the work-clothing field. There were several spontaneous outbreaks involving thousands of clothing workers in major markets such as New York and Chicago.

In 1910, at the Chicago firm of Hart Schaffner & Marx, still another rate cut provoked a walkout of the company's 8,000 workers. The strike soon spread throughout Chicago's clothing industry with its 40,000 workers and lasted four months. Although the strike itself failed, it had two consequences of the utmost significance: the establishment of the principle of the arbitration of disputes, an important step toward industrial stability; and the emergence of a group of leaders, such as Sidney Hillman and Frank Rosenblum, who, together with the New York group, were to form the Amalgamated Clothing Workers of America in 1914, firmly grounded on the precept of industrial unionism.

In the next fifteen years, the major clothing centers were unionized—New York, Chicago, Baltimore, Boston, Rochester, Cincinnati, Cleveland, Saint Louis, Montreal, and, finally, Philadelphia. These were very bitter and often protracted struggles. Some "country shops"—L. Greif & Bro., J. Schoeneman, The Palm Beach Company, and Haspel Brothers—were brought under contract in the 1950s.

Apart from the principle of arbitration, a number of other basic concepts were developed in the early years to deal with the instability that plagued the industry. Some of these are now established practices, but fifty or sixty years ago they were remarkable in a mass-production industry. A number of them—equal division of work (work sharing); maximum hours with time and a half for overtime; and the protection of workers when new machinery was introduced—emanated from the Chicago arbitrators before 1912. Others were initiated by the union and accepted by the employers: employment exchanges (1922), which not only curbed abuses such as bribery, discrimination, favoritism, and sexual intimidation by crude foremen, but also aided the employers in periods of rapid expansion; unemployment insurance (1923), which lessened turnover and was a forerunner of the federal system set up under the Social Security Act thirteen years later; and dismissal wage or severance pay (1926). In these years also, the manufacturer's responsibility for his contractors' payrolls was established, and the union participated in some of management's functions, such as the setting of piece rates, before the days when the clothing manufacturers began using industrial engineers.

It was in the early 1930s that the federal government became a primary factor in the industrial situation. The nation was in the depth of the Great Depression, with nationwide unemployment at crisis levels. Soon after Franklin D. Roosevelt took office in 1933, he called Sidney Hillman, the union's first president, to Washington to serve on the Labor Advisory Board of the National Recovery Administration. Under the NRA, companies in different industries were to form associations to develop codes of fair competition. Two of the concepts that had been operating in the men's clothing industry—work sharing and maximum hours—were adopted to spread employment. Other measures, such as minimum wages and the right of workers to organize, were also part of this program. Although the NRA was declared illegal by the Supreme Court in 1935, some of its essential elements were enacted as individual statutes.

Because of its experience in the men's clothing industry, the union was able to make an important contribution to national industrial policy in this period. At the same time, however, the formulation and functioning of the NRA men's clothing code provided the basis for the establishment, in 1937, of industry-wide collective bargaining between the union and the Clothing Manufacturers Association of the United States of America. This development was of the greatest significance. Industry-wide bargaining had a generally stabilizing influence, since the same increases were negotiated for all markets. It also made possible the insurance and retirement programs in the early 1940s on a basis that afforded protection for the workers even if they moved from shop to shop and which was funded by the same percentage of payroll contribution for every employer.[1]

STATISTICAL TRENDS

Establishment Data

Official statistics very clearly chart the course of the tailored clothing industry over the years. Table 2.1 presents data on the number of establishments and number of production workers, as well as the calculation of the average size of establishment, for the census of manufactures from 1939 through 1977. Except for a slight upturn in 1958, the number of establishments declined steadily from 1,848 in 1939 to 737 in 1977, a drop of 60.1 percent. The number of production workers rose from 116,900 in 1939 to 133,200 in 1947, when the industry was still meeting the demand pent up during the war years. The trend then fluctuated, but since 1967, it has been downward, reaching 86,200 in 1977, a figure 26.3 percent lower than in 1939 and 35.3 percent lower than in the peak year of 1947. The average size of establishment, however, increased, doubling between 1939 and 1972, and, at 117 in 1977, 85.7 percent higher than the average size of 63 in 1939.

Employment and Manhours

The Bureau of Labor Statistics of the U.S. Department of Labor has, since 1939, been reporting production worker employment data which supplement the census data. The BLS data are annual and are available for the years

Table 2.1. Number of Establishments, Number of Production Workers, and Average Size of Establishment in the Men's and Boys' Suit and Coat Industry, 1939-1977

Year	Number of Establishments	Number of Production Workers	Average Size of Establishment[a]
1939	1,848	116,900	63
1947	1,814	133,200	73
1954	1,310	106,700	81
1958	1,365	107,200	79
1963	1,112	109,000	98
1967	1,003	119,900	120
1972	856	108,300	127
1977	737	86,200	117

SOURCE: U.S. Department of Commerce, Bureau of the Census, *Census of Manufactures, Vol. 11, Industry Statistics, 1958* and *1977*.
[a] Calculated from the census data.

after 1977, the latest census year. In addition, from the BLS data on employment and hours, it is possible to calculate average weekly manhours. This measure is of some importance since work sharing is an established practice in this industry. Table 2.2 presents these BLS data on production worker employment and average weekly manhours. Employment fluctuated during each decade, but, apart from the Second World War and the immediate postwar years, there has clearly been a downward trend, with a marked drop in the 1970s and especially from 1975 through 1980. The preliminary figure of 68,700 production workers in 1980 is only 57.3 percent of the 1939 employment level. The trend of average weekly manhours, for which data are available only since 1947, is roughly the same, with average weekly manhours of 2,467,000 in 1980, only 46.7 percent of the 1947 level.

Table 2.2. Production Worker Employment and Average Weekly Manhours in the Men's and Boys' Suit and Coat Industry, 1939-1980 (in thousands).

Year	Production Worker Employment	Average Weekly Manhours[a]
1939	119.9	n.a.
1940	124.3	n.a.
1941	154.2	n.a.
1942	156.8	n.a.
1943	141.2	n.a.
1944	129.3	n.a.
1945	119.4	n.a.
1946	125.0	n.a.
1947	136.5	5,283
1948	137.0	5,151
1949	123.2	4,386
1950	127.4	4,816
1951	126.4	4,652
1952	115.3	4,139
1953	118.2	4,480
1954	107.0	3,799
1955	108.5	4,058
1956	114.4	4,313
1957	111.3	4,074
1958	102.6	3,581
1959	105.9	3,950
1960	107.2	3,956
1961	102.4	3,615
1962	104.3	3,880
1963	102.9	3,776
1964	102.6	3,724
1965	107.0	4,055
1966	111.5	4,270

Table 2.2. (*Continued*)

Year	Production Worker Employment	Average Weekly Manhours[a]
1967	113.1	4,230
1968	115.2	4,355
1969	115.8	4,354
1970	103.7	3,630
1971	95.0	3,335
1972	99.0	3,604
1973	100.5	3,658
1974	92.4	3,216
1975	76.1	2,587
1976	79.0	2,852
1977	79.8	2,865
1978	78.6	2,822
1979	70.4	2,478
1980[b]	68.7	2,467

SOURCE: U.S. Department of Labor, Bureau of Labor Statistics, *Employment and Earnings, United States, 1909-1978*, Bulletin 1312-11, 1979; *Supplement to Employment and Earnings, Revised Establishment Data*, Aug. 1981; and *Employment and Earnings*, Monthly Series.

[a] Calculated from the BLS data on employment and hours.
[b] Average for January-November (November data preliminary).
n.a. = not available.

Production

Data on the production of major items of men's and boys' tailored clothing from 1947 through 1979 are reported in table 2.3. The general decline of tailored suits, the mainstay product of this industry, is evident, and overcoats, topcoats, and stormcoats have also lost out. Tailored dress and sport jackets and dress and sport trousers, on the other hand, have moved upward on the whole, reflecting the long-run shift to casual wear. Jackets peaked in 1973 and slid downward thereafter; trousers peaked in 1971, and dropped markedly by 1979. Preliminary 1980 data, reported only for men's items, indicate that output of tailored dress and sport coats and overcoats, topcoats, and stormcoats increased over 1979 levels.

Since their introduction in the mid-1970s, leisure or casual suits and casual suit-type sport coats have also been a factor in the market for men's and boys' clothing. Production of leisure suits expanded very rapidly until 1975, when output peaked at 13.2 million, and then subsided just about as quickly. Only 900,000 leisure suits were cut in 1979. Output of leisure jackets reached a high of 11.1 million in 1976, but by 1979 had fallen to 3.0 million.

Table 2.3. Production of Major Items of Men's and Boys'
Tailored Clothing, 1947-1979[a] (in thousands of units)

Year	Tailored Suits	Overcoats, Top-coats, and Stormcoats[b]	Tailored Dress and Sport Jackets	Dress and Sport Trousers[c]
1947	28,337[d]	7,683[d]	5,186[d]	59,775[d]
1948	26,120	—[e]	5,885	53,927
1949	22,437	6,463	7,300	58,603
1950	27,145	7,384	8,855	65,819
1951	22,110	6,154	8,361	59,562
1952	22,248	6,284	10,809	67,638
1953	24,069[d]	6,380[d]	9,936[d]	77,531[d]
1954	22,204	5,886	8,337	77,184
1955	23,857	7,007	10,234	98,924
1956	24,256	8,144	11,390	109,776
1957	23,481	6,516	11,847	114,827
1958	21,464	6,233	11,589	113,808
1959	25,689	7,703	13,594	144,926
1960	26,419	6,979	14,203	157,639
1961	24,326	6,228	13,484	158,490
1962	26,678	5,794	15,259	188,682
1963	26,573	5,346	14,775	192,300
1964	26,628	4,964	14,187	200,218
1965	27,712	5,225	16,327	200,071
1966	25,807	5,155	17,957	204,596
1967	24,367	5,192	17,456	201,992
1968	25,444	5,242	18,941	224,598
1969	25,572	4,790	18,748	221,831
1970	22,356	5,225	16,081	227,088
1971	20,261	4,304	18,476	234,321
1972	22,221	4,091	24,336	213,140
1973	19,645	5,624	25,300	214,869
1974	19,651[f]	5,458	21,054[f]	196,219
1975	16,234	5,076	13,193	153,631
1976	18,234	5,147	13,569	160,682
1977	20,669	5,452	15,886	147,715
1978	21,767[g]	4,471	15,019	144,415
1979	19,835[g]	3,658	15,764	140,359

SOURCE: U.S. Department of Commerce, Bureau of the Census, *Facts for Industry*, Series M67B, and *Current Industrial Reports, Apparel*, Series M23A.

[a] Excludes men's uniform suits, coats, jackets, and trousers; boys' uniform items are included in all years.

[b] Excludes men's stormcoats, 1947-1953.

[c] Excludes men's and boys' shorts.

[d] Annual figure adjusted to a 52-week basis for purposes of comparison.

[e] Data for boys' garments not available; 6,194,000 men's overcoats and top-coats were cut in 1948.

[f] Includes some casual (nontailored) items and is not comparable to figures for other years.

[g] Includes boys' casual suits.

Imports

Imports of men's and boys' tailored wool and man-made fabric suits increased dramatically between 1964 and 1978, as shown in table 2.4. The climb was erratic, with years of moderate growth and even decreases interspersed with periods of sudden and rapid surges in the quantities of offshore goods entering the country. By 1973 total suit imports had increased to 2.0 million, from only 117,000 in 1964. Between 1973 and 1977, the upward pace in imports of tailored suits continued, though the magnitude of that growth was distorted by the sharp rise and subsequent decline in popularity of leisure suits, which, until 1978, were counted in the same import

Table 2.4. General Imports and the United States Market for Men's and Boys' Suits,[a] 1964-1979

| Year | Type of Suit[b] | Suits (in thousands) | | | General Imports as a Percent of the U.S. Market[c] |
		Total	Domestic Production	General Imports	
1964	Tailored	26,063	25,946	117	0.4%
1965	Tailored	27,954	27,712	242	0.9%
1966	Tailored	26,074	25,807	267	1.0%
1967	Tailored	24,633	24,367	266	1.1%
1968	Tailored	25,923	25,444	479	1.8%
1969	Tailored	26,524	25,572	952	3.6%
1970	Tailored	23,851	22,356	1,495	6.3%
1971	Tailored	21,537	20,261	1,276	5.9%
1972	Tailored	24,206	22,221	1,985	8.2%
1973	Tailored	21,687	19,645	2,042	9.4%
1974	Tailored and Leisure	21,802	19,651	2,151	9.9%
1975	Tailored and Leisure	32,594	29,429	3,165	9.7%
	Tailored	n.a.	16,234	n.a.	n.a.
	Leisure	n.a.	13,195	n.a.	n.a.
1976	Tailored and Leisure	29,001	25,367	3,634	12.5%
	Tailored	n.a.	18,234	n.a.	n.a.
	Leisure	n.a.	7,133	n.a.	n.a.
1977	Tailored and Leisure	26,118	22,826[d]	3,292	12.6%
	Tailored	n.a.	20,669[d]	n.a.	n.a.
	Leisure	n.a.	2,157[d]	n.a.	n.a.
1978	Tailored and Leisure	26,480	22,580[d]	3,900	14.7%
	Tailored	25,489	21,767[d]	3,722	14.6%
	Leisure	991	813[d]	178	18.0%

Continued on p. 50

Table 2.4. (*Continued*)

Year	Type of Suit[b]	Suits (in thousands)			General Imports as a Percent of the U.S. Market[c]
		Total	Domestic Production	General Imports	
1979	Tailored and				
	Leisure	24,102	20,769[d]	3,333	13.8%
	Tailored	23,067	19,835[d]	3,232	14.0%
	Leisure	1,035	934[d]	101	9.8%
1980	Tailored and				
	Leisure	n.a.	n.a.	2,488	n.a.
	Tailored	n.a.	n.a.	2,430	n.a.
	Leisure	n.a.	n.a.	58	n.a.

SOURCE: U.S. Department of Commerce, Bureau of the Census, *Current Industrial Reports, Apparel Survey*, Series MA-23A, and *U.S. Imports for Consumption and General Imports*, FT 246 and IM 145-X.

[a] Domestic production data are for suits of all fabrics (in which wool and man-made predominate). Import data are exclusively for wool and man-made fabric suits. Cotton suits were not counted as suits in the years 1964-1977. The jackets of cotton suits were counted as jackets and the pants as pants. Since import data for cotton suits are available only for 1978 and 1979, they have not been included in the import data in this table.

[b] Leisure suits did not figure prominently as an item of men's and boys' apparel until 1974. In 1974, an unknown quantity of leisure suits was included in the domestic production data. In the import data, unknown quantities of leisure suits were counted in the tailored suit categories in the years 1974-1977.

[c] General imports and domestic production combined.

[d] 1977-1979 data are not strictly comparable with earlier years because of the addition of new establishments to the survey.

n.a. = not available.

categories as tailored suits. By 1978, imports of tailored suits were at an all-time high of 3.7 million units, exceeding the 1973 level by 1.7 million. The level of tailored suit imports declined by over a third during the next two years, however, and in 1980 was at a six-year low of 2.4 million.

The 117,000 suits imported in 1964 were a negligible 0.4 percent of the total United States market (the sum of domestic production and imports). Exports of United States suits have never totaled more than 200,000. Imports of tailored suits grew much more rapidly than the total market between 1964 and 1973, when their share of that market increased to 9.4 percent. Market penetration by tailored suit imports cannot be separated from the figures for the combined tailored and leisure suit market between 1974 and 1977. By 1978, however, the share of the tailored suit market claimed by imports had grown to 14.6 percent. In 1979, the penetration rate dropped, although the decline was not as great as the drop in the level of imports because domestic production also fell off. In 1979 the share of the tailored suit market going to imports was 14.0 percent. A comparable figure for 1980 will not be available until final domestic production data for 1980 are released.

Imports of men's and boys' suit-type sport coats and jackets followed a steady upward course from 1964 through 1976, interrupted by only two years of relatively mild decline, 1971 and 1974, as reported in table 2.5. Over the twelve years, imports soared from 271,000 to 6.9 million. Wide swings in import levels have characterized the subsequent years—down 19.2 percent between 1976 and 1977; up 38.9 percent between 1977 and 1978; down 32.0 percent between 1978 and 1979. A further decline of 16.7 percent from 1979 to 1980 brought the level of imports to a nine-year low of 4.4 million.

The share of the United States market for men's and boys' suit-type sport coats and jackets taken by imports increased tenfold from 1.9 percent in 1964 to 19.0 percent in 1974. The penetration rate remained relatively stable for the next three years, but then jumped to 29.6 percent in 1978. The following year, it fell back to 21.9 percent, and was probably lower still in 1980.

Table 2.5. General Imports and the United States Market for Men's and Boys' Suit-Type Sport Coats and Jackets, 1964-1980

Year	Type of Suit-Type Sport Coat and Jacket[a]	Suit-Type Sport Coats and Jackets (in thousands)			General Imports as a Percent of the U.S. Market[c]
		Total	Domestic Production	General Imports[b]	
1964	Tailored	14,458	14,187	271	1.9%
1965	Tailored	16,776	16,327	449	2.7%
1966	Tailored	18,753	17,957	796	4.2%
1967	Tailored	18,329	17,456	873	4.8%
1968	Tailored	20,717	18,941	1,776	8.6%
1969	Tailored	20,877	18,748	2,129	10.2%
1970	Tailored	19,198	16,081	3,117	16.2%
1971	Tailored	21,323	18,476	2,847	13.4%
1972	Tailored	28,780	24,336	4,444[d]	15.4%
1973	Tailored	30,611	25,300	5,311[d]	17.3%
1974	Tailored and Leisure	26,004	21,054	4,950[d]	19.0%
1975	Tailored and Leisure	27,901	22,397	5,504	19.7%
	Tailored	n.a.	13,193	n.a.	n.a.
	Leisure	n.a.	9,204	n.a.	n.a.
1976	Tailored and Leisure	31,573	24,686	6,887	21.8%
	Tailored	n.a.	13,569	n.a.	n.a.
	Leisure	n.a.	11,117	n.a.	n.a.

Continued on p. 52

Table 2.5. (*Continued*)

Year	Type of Suit-Type Sport Coat and Jacket[a]	Suit-Type Sport Coats and Jackets (in thousands)			General Imports as a Percent of the U.S. Market[c]
		Total	Domestic Production	General Imports[b]	
1977	Tailored and				
	Leisure	26,934	21,371[e]	5,563	20.7%
	Tailored	n.a.	15,886[e]	n.a.	n.a.
	Leisure	n.a.	5,485[e]	n.a.	n.a.
1978	Tailored and				
	Leisure	26,159	18,429[e]	7,730	29.6%
	Tailored	n.a.	15,019[e]	n.a.	n.a.
	Leisure	n.a.	3,410[e]	n.a.	n.a.
1979	Tailored and				
	Leisure	23,971	18,715[e]	5,256	21.9%
	Tailored	n.a.	15,764[e]	n.a.	n.a.
	Leisure	n.a.	2,951[e]	n.a.	n.a.
1980	Tailored and				
	Leisure	n.a.	n.a.	4,379	n.a.

SOURCE: U.S. Department of Commerce, Bureau of the Census, *Current Industrial Reports, Apparel Survey*, Series MA-23A, and *U.S. Imports for Consumption and General Imports*, FT 246 and IM 145-X.

[a] Leisure jackets did not figure prominently as an item of men's and boys' apparel until 1974. In 1974, an unknown quantity of leisure jackets was included in the domestic production data on jackets, and there has been a separate count for leisure jackets in the subsequent years. The import data have never distinguished between tailored and casual jackets, although quantities of casual jackets have probably been imported in all the years from 1970 on.

[b] Includes cotton jackets imported as parts of suits. There were 1,416,684 such jackets in 1978 and 1,106,256 in 1979. For earlier years, this breakdown is not available.

[c] General imports and domestic production combined.

[d] Data include an estimate for man-made knit items, made by the Research Department, ACTWU.

[e] 1977-1979 data are not strictly comparable with earlier years because of the addition of new establishments to the survey.

n.a. = not available.

Since 1974 leisure jackets have been a significant portion of the total United States market for suit-type coats and jackets. Because leisure jackets are not separated from tailored items in the import counts, the penetration rates from 1974 onward are for the combined leisure and tailored jacket market. In 1976, leisure items accounted for a third to a half of the total jacket market, and it is not clear whether the penetration rate for the combined market is a reliable indication of the effect of imports on the tailored jacket market. By 1979, however, the significance of leisure jackets had declined substantially, making it more likely that the penetration rate for the combined market is an adequate proxy for market penetration in tailored jackets for that year.

Table 2.6. Average Hourly Earnings in the Men's and Boys' Suit and Coat Industry, All Manufacturing Industries, and Nondurable Goods Manufacturing Industries, 1947-1980

	Average Hourly Earnings					
Year	All Manufac-turing Industries	Men's/Boys' Suit/Coat Industry	Difference	Nondurable Goods Manufac-turing Industries	Men's/Boys' Suit/Coat Industry	Difference
1947	$1.216	$1.258	+$ .042	$1.145	$1.258	+$ .113
1948	$1.327	$1.346	+$ .019	$1.250	$1.346	+$ .096
1949	$1.376	$1.322	−$ .054	$1.295	$1.322	+$ .027
1950	$1.439	$1.338	−$ .101	$1.347	$1.338	−$ .009
1951	$1.56	$1.45	−$ .11	$1.44	$1.45	+$ .01
1952	$1.64	$1.46	−$ .18	$1.51	$1.46	−$ .05
1953	$1.74	$1.53	−$ .21	$1.58	$1.53	−$ .05
1954	$1.78	$1.58	−$ .20	$1.62	$1.58	−$ .04
1955	$1.85	$1.61	−$ .24	$1.67	$1.61	−$ .06
1956	$1.95	$1.69	−$ .26	$1.77	$1.69	−$ .08
1957	$2.04	$1.74	−$ .30	$1.85	$1.74	−$ .11
1958	$2.10	$1.73	−$ .37	$1.92	$1.73	−$ .19
1959	$2.19	$1.75	−$ .44	$1.98	$1.75	−$ .23
1960	$2.26	$1.85	−$ .41	$2.05	$1.85	−$ .20
1961	$2.32	$1.92	−$ .40	$2.11	$1.92	−$ .19
1962	$2.39	$1.95	−$ .44	$2.17	$1.95	−$ .22
1963	$2.45	$2.04	−$ .41	$2.22	$2.04	−$ .18
1964	$2.53	$2.10	−$ .43	$2.29	$2.10	−$ .19
1965	$2.61	$2.16	−$ .45	$2.36	$2.16	−$ .20
1966	$2.71	$2.24	−$ .47	$2.45	$2.24	−$ .21
1967	$2.82	$2.37	−$ .45	$2.57	$2.37	−$ .20
1968	$3.01	$2.58	−$ .43	$2.74	$2.58	−$ .16
1969	$3.19	$2.77	−$ .42	$2.91	$2.77	−$ .14
1970	$3.35	$2.91	−$ .44	$3.08	$2.91	−$ .17
1971	$3.57	$3.05	−$ .52	$3.27	$3.05	−$ .22
1972	$3.82	$3.20	−$ .62	$3.48	$3.20	−$ .28
1973	$4.09	$3.41	−$ .68	$3.70	$3.41	−$ .29
1974	$4.42	$3.60	−$ .82	$4.01	$3.60	−$ .41
1975	$4.83	$3.84	−$ .99	$4.37	$3.84	−$ .53
1976	$5.22	$4.10	−$1.12	$4.70	$4.10	−$ .60
1977	$5.68	$4.41	−$1.27	$5.11	$4.41	−$ .70
1978	$6.17	$4.79	−$1.38	$5.53	$4.79	−$ .74
1979	$6.69	$5.11	−$1.58	$6.00	$5.11	−$ .89
1980[a]	$7.23	$5.34	−$1.89	$6.50	$5.34	−$1.16

SOURCE: U.S. Department of Labor, Bureau of Labor Statistics, *Employment and Earnings, United States, 1909-1978*, Bulletin 1312-11, 1979; *Supplement to Employment and Earnings, Revised Establishment Data*, Aug. 1981; and *Employment and Earnings*, Monthly Series.
[a] Average for January-November (November data preliminary).

Comparison of Earnings

A comparison of average hourly earnings of production workers in the suit and coat industry, in all manufacturing industries, and in nondurable goods manufacturing industries since 1947 gives a compelling indication of what has happened to the relative position of the clothing workers over time. As shown in table 2.6, in 1947 the clothing workers' average hourly earnings were 4¢ higher than earnings of all manufacturing workers and 11¢ higher than earnings of nondurable goods manufacturing workers. This relationship was short-lived, and from the early 1950s onward, the trend has been steadily downward so that by 1980 clothing workers were averaging $1.89 less than all manufacturing workers and $1.16 less than nondurable goods manufacturing workers. There are, to be sure, many reasons for this trend: the clothing industry is labor intensive, very competitive, with few large producers, and with profit margins lower than some other mass production industries. The earlier favorable position in relation to average hourly earnings of production workers probably also reflected, in part, the fact that this industry was almost totally unionized before there was extensive unionization in other mass production industries.

Other Characteristics

From the industry wage surveys of the men's and boys' suit and coat industry made periodically by the Bureau of Labor Statistics since 1963, other interesting shifts over the period of 1963 through 1979 can be discerned.[2]

The proportion of production workers who were women increased from 67.3 percent to 78.7 percent. The proportion of production workers in nonmetropolitan areas increased slightly, from 18.9 perecent to 21.9 percent. The proportion of production workers in the Middle Atlantic states declined from 55.2 percent to 44.1 percent. The proportion of production workers in the Southeast was 6.5 percent in 1963 and was 25.9 percent in the Southeast and Southwest in 1979 (none were reported in the Southwest in 1963). The proportion of production workers unionized decreased from 90.0 percent to 80.7 percent.

FACTORS IN THE CHANGING FORTUNES
OF THE INDUSTRY

There have been a number of factors, of varying nature, involved in the changing fortunes of the men's clothing industry. Among them are changes in demand, technological developments, imports, and, to a lesser extent, changes in the management of companies and the leadership of the union.

Changes in Demand

Before the Second World War, the usual attire of males who were not blue-collar workers was a suit or perhaps a tailored sport jacket and slacks. Once the pent-up demand for apparel of the 12 million men discharged from the armed forces in 1945-1946 was met, the demand for tailored clothing was affected by major socioeconomic changes in living patterns.

Because of the housing shortage and new family formation, there was a shift to and expansion of the suburbs. A larger portion of consumer income was being used for housing, home appliances, and automobiles, and suburban living itself called for more informal attire. With the prevalence by then of the five-day workweek, longer vacations, and paid holidays, there was more time for activities away from the job—sports, gardening, do-it-yourself projects, and outdoor entertaining. This led in the 1950s to greater shifts from suits to sport jackets and slacks; from overcoats and topcoats to suburban coats and car coats; from dress shirts to sport shirts; and to the proliferation of a broad variety of outerwear and leisurewear.

The impact of the high birthrate of the immediate postwar years was felt resoundingly in the 1960s and early 1970s. For teenagers and young people, and not a few adults, it was the time of the counterculture and the so-called jeaning of America. Standard dress was rejected and extreme informality dominated, with put-togethers of bottoms and tops of all kinds, ethnic influences, and some unisex garments. The appeal of casualness in menswear was reflected in the popularity of the leisure suit in 1974-1975 and in leisure jackets and sportswear. In this period also, wash-and-wear and easy-care apparel was developed. Knits found favor for a brief period, but did not last.

One overall point on demand should be noted. The demand for apparel has always been elastic. It is not as essential as food and shelter, and is always competing with other consumer goods.

Technological Developments

The technology of the men's clothing industry has not been very complex. It consists essentially of cutting, sewing, and pressing, with about 150 sewing and pressing operations. Early changes were largely the shifting to machine work of operations that had formerly been done by hand—buttonholes, pockets, and lapels. There was also some de-skilling through attachments. In recent years, automatic cutting devices and computer-directed marker-makers have been developed.

In terms of impact on the men's clothing industry, the most significant innovation may have been the development of fusing in the 1960s. Suit coat fronts had been made of cloth, lining, and interlining, and required great skill in basting these together to shape the coat front. Fusing is a process utilizing heat to glue the interlining to the cloth, and requires relatively little skill. The manufacturers making the most expensive suits continued to make coat fronts as before, by basting the cloth, lining, and interlining together to shape the coat front. The popular-priced and cheapest lines were made by fusing the entire coat front. In the in-between lines, the lower part of the facing was fused and the rest used a floating chest piece made of canvas, which was basted.

In the short run, fusing was a problem because it resulted in the displacement of the basters and canvas makers. It had even more fundamental and lasting significance, however, in that it made it possible for many companies which had never made suits to make suits, which were called leisure suits. With their so-called semiconstructed or unconstructed jackets, they were more like shirts than tailored suit coats in their fabrication.

Leisure suits and leisure jackets met a demand for more informal apparel and could be produced at cheaper prices than tailored clothing because they called for less skill and had lower labor content. Traditional industry lines began to break down as major work-clothing and pants houses and some outerwear companies began making leisure suits and leisure jackets. Some of these were companies which had achieved or consolidated national prominence in the period of the mass adoption of jeans—such as Levi Strauss and Haggar. Many of them were nonunion or only partly unionized.

Although the leisure-suit fad has passed, these companies have remained in the suit field. Their products do not compare with tailored suits, but they are meeting a need—at a price.

Imports

Male apparel imports, primarily of cotton garments, began to be a problem in 1955. Systematic collection of data on quantities of apparel imports was not begun until 1964. These data on suits and suit-type coats and jackets were presented earlier. In brief, from 117,000 imported tailored suits, representing only 0.4 percent of the United States market in 1964, tailored-suit imports reached a peak of 3.7 million in 1978, when they constituted 14.6 percent of the market. The trend of suit-type coats and jackets is roughly similar, although the quantities and the penetration rates have been consistently higher.

The apparel industries have been particularly vulnerable to imports. To begin with, they are labor intensive. The tailored clothing industry, for instance, had fixed assets of only $2,952 per production worker in 1976, compared with $18,575 in textile mill products and $84,174 in basic steel.[3] The apparel industries' technology, production methods, and merchandising techniques proved to be easily and quickly internationalized, and there was little to offset the advantage that came from the low wages of foreign producers, particularly those in the Far East. At first, imported men's clothing was of relatively poor quality and in the lower price lines. In time, however, quality improved and, partly in response to import quotas in the United States, there was upgrading to higher-price lines. Imports also began coming from other countries, and in 1980 three European countries (Poland, France, and Romania) were among the top four foreign suppliers of suits. It seems likely that the People's Republic of China may soon claim its share of the market, competing on an altogether different basis than most foreign suppliers.

The quantity of imports at any given time is affected by a number of factors, including an estimate of the state of the United States market in the light of current economic conditions, the relationship of the dollar to any given foreign currency, and the degree to which quotas on particular items are being filled. But whatever fluctuations have resulted from these and perhaps other factors, there is no question that since 1964, imports of tailored men's clothing have increased substantially and now claim a significant part of the United States market.

The resulting liquidation and contraction of companies and the heavy job losses have been a primary concern of the men's clothing industry and the union. From the year ending September 30, 1976 to September 30, 1980, almost 16,000 workers under 137 petitions from men's clothing companies were certified for trade adjustment assistance under the Trade Act of 1974.[4] These figures represent only a portion of the jobs lost because of imports and, of course, do not reflect at all work time lost because of imports by workers still employed.

Changes in Management in the Industry and Leadership in the Union

In the early period of unionization, many clothing companies were family-held. In the smaller companies, the employers often had backgrounds similar to those of their workers and, as likely as not, had begun as workers in the industry. The close working quarters and common backgrounds sometimes made for a bond of understanding not to be found in the larger firms.

In the larger family-held companies, as well as in the smaller firms, the sons of the founders, especially those who were immigrants, did not usually enter the family businesses. Among some of the immigrant employers, it was a matter of pride, albeit sometimes rueful, that their sons would become doctors, lawyers, or other professionals. Such companies were ripe for acquisition when the first generation of management either died or reached retirement age.

In the 1950s and 1960s, a number of major companies were acquired by conglomerates: J. Schoeneman by Cluett, Peabody & Co., Inc.; L. Greif &

Bro. and Phoenix Clothes, Inc. by Genesco; Joseph H. Cohen and Cross Country Clothes by Rapid-American Corporation; Louis Goldsmith, Inc. by Kayser-Roth Corporation, in turn acquired by Gulf + Western, Inc.; and The Joseph & Feiss Company by Phillips–Van Heusen Corporation. Except for Cluett, Peabody & Co., Inc., most of the acquiring companies had many nonunion components or were antiunion. In any case, they were more remote from the direct operation of the clothing companies and did not have the same direct interest in the companies, the workers, or the communities in which the plants were located. Their emphasis was on the "bottom line," and they did not hesitate to liquidate a company if the figures on that bottom line were red.

Changes also took place in the leadership of the union. Originally confined to the men's clothing industry, its jurisdiction grew to include shirt, pants, outerwear, glove, and other male-apparel workers; laundries and cleaning and dyeing establishments; retail trade; and office and related equipment makers (primarily Xerox Corporation). In 1976, the Textile Workers Union of America merged with the Amalgamated Clothing Workers of America, and the organization was renamed Amalgamated Clothing and Textile Workers Union (ACTWU). In 1979, the United Shoe Workers of America merged into ACTWU.

When the union's first president, Sidney Hillman, died in 1946, the leadership—Jacob S. Potofsky, Frank Rosenblum, and Hyman Blumberg—were of the founding generation. There was a continuity, not only of tradition, but also in the collective bargaining relationship, since, in most of the years of their tenure, many of the manufacturers were still individuals known to them over the years. At the time of the retirement of Potofsky and Rosenblum in 1972 (Blumberg having died in 1968), and their succession by Murray H. Finley and Jacob Sheinkman, the industry was besieged by many problems, including imports, and conglomerates were something of a factor on the management side. It was a time of testing for the new leadership of the union, and the 1974 collective bargaining agreement was arrived at only after a one-week nationwide strike, the first in the clothing industry since the organizing strikes in the earliest years.

THE RESPONSES OF THE UNION AND THE INDUSTRY TO MAJOR PROBLEMS AND THE ROLE OF GOVERNMENT

The problem of imports has been one in which there has been a high degree of labor-management cooperation over many years and in which the federal government has played an important role.

Initially, male apparel imports were in cotton garments. Japan, then a major producer of these garments for import into the United States, adopted a voluntary five-year program of restraints in 1957 to forestall more stringent quotas by the United States. The union and the apparel industries with which it dealt were aware of the threat of imports to the job security of the members and the stability of the industries. They initiated a program which varied in emphasis in different periods and included such activities as repeated joint (labor-management) representations to the Congress and to the administration in office; concentrated and sometimes nationwide demonstrations by Amalgamated members; and consumer and retailer educational activities. The position maintained throughout was *not* one *against* free trade but *for* fair trade—not to prohibit imports, but to regulate their volume so that imports would be orderly and not disruptive of the domestic industry.

In 1961, under the Kennedy administration, the Short-Term Cotton Textile Arrangement was negotiated, followed by the Long-Term Cotton Textile Arrangement in 1962, under which the United States negotiated bilateral agreements with Japan and other countries beginning in 1963. There was no provision for wool and man-made fiber imports, however, and, as the quantities mounted, the need for such coverage became more urgent. The Nixon administration was sympathetic to the southern textile manufacturers, and in 1974, the Multi-Fiber Arrangement Regarding International Trade in Textiles (MFA) that was negotiated included wool and man-made products. At the end of 1977, the MFA was renewed for four years. So far, the United States has negotiated twenty-one bilateral agreements under the MFA. The previously mentioned Trade Act of 1974 provided for trade adjustment assistance to aid workers, companies, and communities injured by imports. In 1978, an effort was made to minimize tariff reductions for the products of the apparel industries under the General Agreement on Tariffs and Trade (GATT). Representatives of labor and industry have served as advisers to the government representatives negotiating the arrangements and agreements dealing with imports.

Recently, public concern has focused on the serious threat of imports to such basic industries as steel and auto. In the earlier period, imports affected primarily the textile-apparel group, electronic products such as radios and television sets, and shoes. Of that earlier period, it can probably be said that the federal government was most responsive in those situations in which there were strong cooperative labor-management efforts.

As reported before, the problems of technology and changes in work methods were raised in the earliest years, with the protection of workers on the introduction of new machinery being the result of an arbitration award in the Chicago market. This became, and remains, a basic clause in the collective bargaining agreement, with provision for mutual resolution in such cases.

In recent years, the issue of technology has come to the fore again. Tailored clothing manufacturers were obliged to become more competitive because of the surge in imports and the entry into the market for suits and sport coats of companies in other branches of the male-apparel industries—work clothing, outerwear, and pants—a situation made possible by the development of fusing and the popularity in the mid-1970s of the leisure, or casual, suit and jacket.

However, relatively few men's clothing manufacturers are large enough to have the resources for research and development or even for the purchase of expensive new equipment. Being privately held and unable to raise capital through selling shares, most of them are limited to borrowing from banks. In periods of high interest rates, all but the largest companies have difficulty in borrowing, and pay a very high price to sustain their current level of operations, let alone to purchase costly new equipment.

But the need to become more competitive was clear, and when the Carter administration indicated that it would be more sympathetic to pleas for protection from imports from industries willing to help themselves, the union and the men's clothing industry developed a number of programs toward this end. In 1978, the union and the Clothing Manufacturers Association of the United States of America founded Joint Job Training & Research, Inc. (JTR) as a nonprofit corporation to assist the industry to become more competitive. Two of its major projects have been a training program and a research and development program.

The training program, funded by the Employment and Training Administration of the U.S. Department of Labor, had two primary objects: first, to provide training and jobs for the disadvantaged and to provide trained workers for the industry; and second, to yield relevant findings, for both JTR and the Department of Labor, about such training programs and the potential utilization of private industry for bringing the disadvantaged into the mainstream of the nation's economic life. All the training was on-the-job training. In the first two years of its operation, more than 2,600 workers were placed in permanent jobs, and at the end of 1980, an additional 1,100 were enrolled in the program in eighty plants throughout the country.

The research and development program is funded by the Economic Development Administration of the U.S. Department of Commerce. Several projects are currently under way or completed. Completed projects include the development of a supervisor training package for use throughout the industry and a study to determine test methods to improve the durability of fused coat fronts in normal use. Projects under way include the development of an automated production planning and control system; the construction of a statistical quality control system; and the creation of a data base for industry forecasting.

Recently, ACTWU and the tailored clothing companies undertook another program to assist the industry to become more competitive by establishing the Tailored Clothing Technology Corporation. Under the aegis of John T. Dunlop of Harvard University, and with funds from the government, the companies, and the union, the corporation will deal with research, development, and the application of new machinery and technology, as well as with methods and procedures such as material handling and assembly.

The foregoing section has dealt with joint labor-management responses to major changes in the industry. Some of the men's-clothing manufacturers attempted to meet the demand for casual wear and the competition from the work-clothing, outerwear, and pants companies in various ways. Some began producing suits that were leisure suits in terms of styling but were tailored and generally of better quality fabric. Some began making "duos" and "trios," which were combinations of sport coats and slacks with a more informal look. On the whole, being tailored-clothing manufacturers, they could not easily shift their lines to the cheaper suits produced by some work-clothing, pants, and outerwear companies. This would have required a re-engineering of their plants to produce for a low-end market in which they were not established. Many of them had had a product "image" and clearly identified brands for more than fifty years, which could not be sacrificed to produce an unfamiliar product. One major manufacturer, which did re-engineer a plant to produce less-constructed suits to compete with those of Levi Strauss and Haggar, found the market already preempted by work clothing, pants, and outerwear manufacturers well known in this low-end market, and discontinued the line, closing the factory.

THE OUTLOOK

Population trends indicate that there will be substantial increases in the number of males five years old and older and even greater proportionate increases in those in the prime apparel-buying ages of twenty-five to forty-four. Projected increases from 1980 are shown in table 2.7. Occupational trends suggest that in the foreseeable future, the products of the tailored clothing industry will still be the customary attire at work of certain occupational groups.

It is clear that the market for male apparel of all types will continue to grow, but the share of it that will go to the tailored clothing industry, as distinct from the work-clothing, pants, and outerwear industries, will depend on a number of factors. Primary among these will be the industry's ability to compete with other male-apparel companies now producing tailored clothing items and with imports. Both of these depend on the narrowing of cost differentials, not only through increased productivity in the industry, but also through the greater unionization of the major domestic nonunion competitors and the raising of international labor standards. The ability to compete with imports is also related to the extent to which the government will

Table 2.7. Projections of U.S.
Population from 1980

	5 Years and Older	25-44 Years Old
1985	3.7%	15.2%
1990	8.5%	25.6%
2000	17.4%	22.4%

SOURCE: Based on U.S. Department of Commerce, Bureau of the Census, *Projections of the Population of the United States: 1977 to 2050, Current Population Reports*, Series P-25, No. 704, July 1977.

regularize the quantity of imports from all countries producing these products and adhere to trade and tariff policies that will not be destructive of the domestic industry. Given the nature of the industry, recent experience has shown that the government can play a positive role in assisting it to increase its productivity.

This is not to suggest that there will not be many tailored-clothing firms that will go out of business. Those which survive, however, should be able to look forward to moderate growth. In all probability, the total industry will be smaller, with the larger firms most likely to survive. But with a degree of nurturing such as that indicated, the industry should be healthier.

COMMENTS ON NATIONAL INDUSTRIAL POLICY

Some of the background material in this chapter serves to remind us that there was, indeed, a time in this nation's history when there was a comprehensive and cohesive national industrial policy. There were actually two such periods, both under the administrations of Franklin D. Roosevelt—the New Deal and the Second World War. In both of these situations—the Great Depression and the war—there was overriding public involvement with and concern about the problems, together with the morale necessary to mobilize the public for the national policies.

In the depression of the 1930s, the overwhelming issue was mass unemployment and the need to get America's factories back to work. The New Deal constituted a national industrial policy toward that end. It encompassed such elements as minimum wages and maximum hours, unemployment insurance, the right of workers to organize, work projects, public works programs, and old-age benefits. Some of these which had been formu-

lated under the NRA were embodied in individual statutes after it was inval-
idated; others were enacted by themselves. Many of them remain as basic
underpinnings of our industrial life, although others have been altered significantly by subsequent legislation (for example, the National Labor Relations
Act, as amended by the Taft-Hartley Act and the Landrum-Griffin Act), and
still others, such as public works programs, have had varying courses under
different administrations.

During the first half of the 1940s, national industrial policy was directed
primarily toward maximizing production for, first, the defense effort, then
the war effort. Shortly after the fall of France in 1940, the National Defense
Advisory Commission was set up to plan arms production for defense. Early
in 1941, it was succeeded by the Office of Production Management for the
purpose of ensuring an adequate flow of capital and labor to defense industries. It was headed by the Amalgamated's first president, Sidney Hillman,
and by William S. Knudsen, president of General Motors. A National Defense Mediation Board was established to settle labor disputes that were a
threat to defense production. After the U.S. entry into the war, the powers of
OPM were strengthened, and it was reorganized as the War Production
Board, under the direction of one individual. Its labor division became the
War Manpower Commission. The National Defense Mediation Board became the War Labor Board, whose functions were broadened, as inflation
became an issue, to include the determination of wage policies to restrain
inflation, and the Office of Price Administration was established to control
prices, under an Office of Economic Stabilization. There was also a consumer rationing system covering such things as gasoline and food items.

Subsequent programs to apply wage-and-price controls were instituted
during the Korean conflict in the 1950s and under President Nixon in the
early 1970s. The Carter administration's wage and price guidelines were in
operation from October 1978 until the end of 1980.

But, apart from these wage-price components, we have not had national
industrial policies comparable in scope to those that were established during
the New Deal and the Second World War. The fact is that the United States
has had no traditional policy of economic planning—which, to be effective,
requires a degree of control over the allocation of resources that has been
viewed as inconsistent with the American system of "free private enterprise."
President Reagan is a strong proponent of private enterprise, and to the
extent that it can be said that he has a national industrial policy, it is one that
minimizes the role of federal government and calls for the deregulation of
industry and commerce. His economic program would also eliminate or
weaken important elements of the broad body of economic and social legislation that has been built up over a period of almost fifty years.

Recently, there has been some advocacy of an overly simplified and crude
approach to national industrial policy. It proposes that we back "winners"

and not "losers," that we support "sunrise" and not "sunset" industries or regions of our country, that production should flow to where it can be carried on at the lowest cost. This view suggests that we are obliged to engage in industrial triage. "Triage," as a term, received currency on the battlefield, where it meant that one had to choose who to help on the basis of a decision as to who was more likely to survive—a practice that strained more than a few consciences. As serious as our economic situation is, it is not yet comparable to a battlefield, and such an extreme measure as triage is, fortunately, not appropriate. Nor would it be in the best interests of the balanced growth of our national economy.

In view of the political philosophy of the Reagan administration, the influence on the Congress of well-financed special-interest groups, the lack of a tradition of economic planning in this country, the absence of a crisis as grave and broadly affecting as either the Great Depression or the Second World War, and the meager basis at this time for the kind of labor-management cooperation that the war effort evoked, it is difficult to contemplate the likelihood of a constructive national industrial policy or what its elements might be.

With regard to the winner-loser, sunrise-sunset theorists, I suggest, as a trade unionist, that economic blueprints should not determine our society, but that our societal needs and traditionally humane social values should determine our industrial policies. In such a context, there should be room for consideration of an industry, such as the tailored clothing industry, and its potential for continuing to function as a positive sector of our economy.

NOTES

1. The regular members of CMA are represented by it for collective bargaining and other labor relations with ACTWU. However, a few clothing manufacturers under contract with ACTWU are not members of CMA. The CMA contract sets the pattern for the dominant, unionized sector of the men's clothing industry.
2. U.S. Department of Labor, Bureau of Labor Statistics, *Industry Wage Survey, Men's and Boys' Suits and Coats*, October 1963, Bulletin 1424, and *Employee Earnings and Supplementary Benefits, Men's and Boys' Suit and Coat Manufacturing*, April 1979, Summary 80-2.
3. U.S. Department of Commerce, Bureau of the Census, *Annual Survey of Manufactures, 1976, Industry Profiles*.
4. U.S. Department of Labor, Bureau of International Labor Affairs, Office of Trade Adjustment Assistance.

3

Public Policy
and the Auto Industry

Sheldon Friedman*

It is no secret that the auto industry and auto workers are in the midst of the gravest period of difficulty since the 1930s. The current situation, in some ways, may be more serious even than that. At least after the Great Depression and World War II, the domestic auto industry enjoyed a robust recovery. The market grew rapidly, and for three decades virtually all of that growth was supplied by North American production. Neither of these happy circumstances can be counted on today, with replacement demand approaching 85 percent of total demand in the United States and the import share skyrocketing toward 30 percent—with no permanent upper limit in sight.

Though both the industry and auto workers are feeling the impact of the current difficulties, the effects are quite different for different companies, and very different for the companies than for workers. The difficulty facing the industry, quite simply, is this: during 1980 it experienced an enormous loss, at a time of great need to generate funds to finance major restructuring. Though GM returned to profitability in the fourth quarter of 1980, followed by Ford and Chrysler in the second quarter of 1981, the industry is not yet "out of the woods." Ford has been feeling the pinch much more sharply than General Motors; Chrysler was saved from bankruptcy twice, only by extraordinary action; even Volkswagen of America was in the red for 1980; and American Motors probably was headed for severe financial difficulty, but for the infusion of capital—and acquisition of effective control—by Renault. Numerous supplier companies also felt the pinch to varying degrees, up to and including bankruptcy in many instances.

The difficulties experienced by auto workers, by contrast, include loss of job and income security, literal destruction (or risk of destruction) of many of their communities, and massive loss of employment. Those lucky enough to remain at work face actual or potential erosion of living standards.

* The author wishes to thank several UAW Research Department colleagues who commented helpfully on an earlier draft of this paper, including Bruce DeCastro, Lydia Fischer, Dan Luria, Lee Price, and George Schwartz. The chapter also benefited from Margaret Dewar's suggestions.

Given the size and importance of the auto industry, its critical linkages to other sectors of the economy and the heavy regional dependency upon auto, it is hardly surprising that the crisis has emerged as a significant domestic policy concern. Over the last two years, this has confronted elected officials in Congress and two successive administrations with an uncomfortable quandary: what should they do? Do nothing? With the notable exception of assistance to Chrysler—and actions which led indirectly to Japan's recent announcement of mild, temporary export restraints—the "do-nothing" approach has pretty much been followed to date. A second possible approach would be to initiate policies to help solve the companies' difficulties. This course of action has been widely advocated, and support for it appears to be gathering momentum. A third approach would be to take steps to mitigate the difficulties facing auto workers. Though it is widely assumed that steps to solve the industry's problems and the workers' are identical, in fact these two courses of action may overlap, but certainly are not the same. Depending on what policies are chosen, helping the industry may do little to save jobs. Auto employment is caught in the jaws of a vise: the skyrocketing import share has cost literally thousands of jobs, while some of the steps being taken by the domestic industry to forestall further increases in import share will eliminate thousands more. Though some of these steps—such as further improvements in productivity—are necessary and inevitable, it clearly cannot be assumed that every set of policies to help the industry will automatically preserve employment.

Many believe that the "do-nothing" alternative runs the risk of transforming the U.S. auto industry, which for more than seventy years until 1980 was by far the largest in the world, into a mere shell of its former self, nearly overnight. At least one knowledgeable outside observer thinks that if nothing is done, the industry may virtually disappear within a decade or at most two.[1] That is probably alarmist, but there is every indication that a passive public auto policy runs a serious risk of massive, permanent reductions in domestic vehicle production and employment, with possible further shrinkage in the number of major domestic producers—and probable prolongation and deepening of the severe regional depression afflicting key auto states. Despite this, many influential government officials, legislators, and academics appear to believe that doing nothing is the most appropriate policy response. Given the high stakes if they are wrong, it is questionable whether even an administration as conservative as the present one will find it possible to follow such a course.

The second alternative would be to assist the companies, in effect by "throwing money" to ease their financing problems. Approaches taken could be sector-specific, or economy-wide, or more likely some combination of both. Untargeted corporate tax cuts, regulatory relief, "jawboned" or mandated wage reductions, and overall tax and social spending reductions for the alleged purpose of stimulating "noninflationary growth" are among the public policies favored by various proponents of this view. Advocates of this position tend to be free-marketeers who might otherwise favor doing nothing for auto, except they believe the industry's difficulties stem partly or largely from past government policy errors. On grounds of national defense and economic strength, they are also reluctant to allow decline in the country's industrial base of the magnitude which the auto industry's abrupt demise would cause.

The policies advocated by this group could ultimately restore some domestic production, but in the end they may do as much to finance the auto industry's internationalization and global restructuring as to preserve domestic employment. Such policies also represent, in some cases, an unfortunate sacrifice of other valid social goals. For example, several of the policies advocated under this rubric to assist industry will actually worsen the impact of the auto crisis on workers—including cutbacks in programs like unemployment insurance and trade adjustment assistance.

A third alternative would be to develop and implement policies which explicitly help auto workers and other workers dependent on the auto industry. Proponents of this view believe that the goals of "industrial policy" must go beyond enhancing "competitiveness" of the domestic economy, to explicitly encompass employment stabilization and community preservation objectives. In the case of auto, the goals of such an approach would be to preserve a reasonable level of domestic auto industry employment; assure a "soft landing" by limiting employment shrinkage to a rate which can be accommodated by natural attrition; and prevent regional depression by targeting new investment and job creation by other industries—backed up by a comprehensive set of other adjustment programs—to offset the severe local and regional impacts and tragic human costs of the auto industry's restructuring.

To articulate and defend the full set of public policies necessary to achieve the valid objectives of this "third approach" is beyond the scope of this chapter. Rather, the purpose of this chapter is to present an historical and economic overview of the motor vehicle industry, in the United States and elsewhere, with emphasis on broad trends which have shaped its development. In the process, the industry's rise to a position of prominence in the economies of the United States and other developed countries is documented, as are the origins, dimensions, and consequences of the U.S. industry's present crisis.

Though the full range of policies necessary to implement the worker- and community-oriented "third approach" to solving the auto crisis is not elaborated, the concluding section of the chapter spells out a new and admittedly controversial international trade policy for auto, which is of necessity an essential element of that approach.

OVERVIEW OF THE INDUSTRY

For the purpose of providing a framework, it is helpful to begin by defining the industry. It is, first of all, the motor vehicle industry, engaged in the manufacture of cars, buses, and trucks. Based on widely accepted usage, the motor vehicle industry consists of three "core" segments; there is also a closely linked set of supplier industries.[2] The "core" segments include, first, manufacture and assembly of complete motor vehicles; second, a much smaller segment engaged in the manufacture of bodies and trailers, mainly for trucks and buses; and third, a large and diverse sector engaged in the manufacture of motor vehicle parts and accessories, including engines, clutches, gears, transmissions, brakes, frames, wheels, and the rest. In the United States, these core sectors correspond more or less to SIC codes 3711, 3713/5, and 3714, respectively. Supplementing these "core" industries is another array of closely linked suppliers in such industries as rubber (tires), glass (automotive glass), textiles (automotive fabrics), and electrical equipment (batteries).

Further down the chain of production, the industry is an important consumer of other basic commodities. In 1978, for example, the auto industry consumed 22 percent of the nation's steel, 17 percent of aluminum, 53 percent of malleable iron, 57 percent of synthetic rubber, and 30 percent of zinc.[3] The radical product changes in which the auto industry has been engaged since the mid-1970s accordingly are fraught with potential for substantial dislocations in these and other supplier industries. The impact of weight reduction alone is illustrated in table 3.1. Extending forward in the production chain, there is the extensive network of dealers and service and repair shops.

Table 3.1. Estimated Material Consumption per Car

Material	Pounds Per Car		Percent Change
	1980	1976	
High strength steel	175	120	+45.8%
Aluminum	130	85.5	+52.0
Plastics	195	162.5	+20.0
Zinc die castings	20	44	−54.5
Iron	484	562	−13.9
Plain carbon steel	1737	2075	−16.3

SOURCE: *Ward's Automotive Yearbook, 1980*, p. 64.

Impact of the Automobile

The private automobile has long been the centerpiece of our system of personal transportation and a symbol of much that is American in the eyes of the world. The automobile has transformed the face of modern society, largely ending rural isolation and providing unprecedented mobility. It has not been an unmixed blessing, to be sure; many critics point to the safety hazards, pollution, profligate resource use, urban congestion, suburban flight, and the automobile's alleged contribution to the alienating character of modern life.

Yet, like it or not, the automobile is the dominant mode of personal transport—and the truck the dominant of commercial transport. Indeed, the dependency of our system of transportation upon motor vehicles now and for the foreseeable future is virtually complete. According to the latest figures (1977), over 87 percent of all U.S. households owned one or more motor vehicles, and these privately owned vehicles were used that year for 84 percent of all "person-trips," including 88 percent of all home-to-work trips. We rely for these trips on a fleet of some 154 million motor vehicles—including 120 million cars (one for every 1.9 persons—by far the highest ratio of cars to people in the world), plus 34 million trucks and buses. We have a bit over 5 percent of the world's population, but nearly two-fifths of the world's total motor vehicle fleet. The fleet, moreover, is five times the size of the nation's 31-million-unit 1945 figure. This remarkable increase was a significant factor in the nation's nearly three-decade-long robust postwar economic expansion.

Salient Features

The industry has a number of salient features which are important to keep in mind in order to better understand its current structure and historical development. Among these features are extreme and growing concentration at the level of the "prime" manufacturers, enormous capital requirements, long lead times, powerful economies of scale, and a relationship of dominance with suppliers and—until the UAW was organized—with workers as well. Early and continuing regional concentration and dependency, early and growing internationalization of the industry, a relentless drive to cut costs, raise productivity, and increase manufacturing efficiency, plus a strong role of government policy relative to the development and course of the industry in virtually every auto producing country, should also be added to this list—as should the tendency for competitive position to shift rapidly among companies and major producing regions; extreme cyclical instability of production and employment; the onset of maturity if not outright old age in the world's three major consuming and producing areas; and extreme vulnerability to external "shocks," notably regarding the price and availability of petroleum. Several other important features, related to the others, are auto's historically high profitability and rate of return on stockholders' investment, at least in North America, relative to other manufacturing industries; extreme *inequality* of profitability among "prime" manufacturers; and extreme sensitivity of profitability to the volume of production and rate of capacity utilization.

From the United Auto Workers' (UAW) standpoint, the above factors historically have dictated a strategy of "pattern bargaining" to remove labor costs as a factor in competition; emphasis on the struggle to maintain workers' dignity on the shop floor against what in the past at least was a relentless management assault; a high priority on job and income security to offset the impact of extreme cyclicality, competitive shifts and other factors on stability of employment; and acceptance of increased productivity, provided workers were compensated accordingly and work time was reduced to provide increased leisure time and to offset reductions in the number of jobs. Instability of income and employment gave rise to the UAW's pioneering supplemental unemployment benefits (S.U.B.) program in the 1950s. The early 1970s saw achievement of the "30 and out" early retirement program, a long-standing UAW proposal rooted in the physically demanding nature of so many auto industry jobs. The UAW's activism in collective bargaining has long been matched by its activism on a broad range of economic and social policy fronts.

THE INDUSTRY'S RISE TO ECONOMIC PROMINENCE

Despite significant pauses and interruptions, from the dawn of the auto age through at least 1973, worldwide motor vehicle production was characterized by extremely rapid growth. The industry was established in the decade after 1898; in 1900 total worldwide production was an estimated 9,500 units, mostly in France and the United States. In 1908 world production exceeded 100,000 for the first time; in 1915, the one-million-vehicle production threshold was crossed; and in the year 1919, over two million vehicles were built, By 1929, world output reached 6.3 million cars and trucks—a record which stood until after World War II.

Output plummeted to a depression low of 1.9 million in 1932. The postwar period saw a renewed takeoff of worldwide production, which nearly quadrupled from 10.5 million units in 1950 to 39.1 million in 1973. Subsequently, worldwide production fell substantially in 1974/1975, then recovered by 1978 to over the 42-million mark, then declined slightly in 1979 and again in 1980. By the end of 1978, the world's stock of motor vehicles totaled an

estimated 380 million cars, buses, and trucks, compared with 70 million at
the end of 1950—and a ninefold increase compared with 38 million at the
end of 1945.

Early U.S. Dominance

From virtually the dawn of the auto age through 1979, the United States was
far and away the world's leading motor vehicle producer. Though the auto
was not invented in the United States, the industry's real "takeoff" occurred
in this country and the automobile quickly became a worldwide symbol of
American culture, wealth, and industrial might. The industry rose rapidly
from eighth place among U.S. manufacturing industries in 1914, ranked by
value of output, to third place the following year, and to first place in 1923.
It has remained solidly entrenched as the nation's largest manufacturing
industry ever since.

As recently as 1950, over three-quarters of the motor vehicles built worldwide were produced in the United States. Despite relatively rapid U.S. output growth, that share slipped with the rise of European and later of Japanese production; nevertheless, as recently as 1974 fully half of the world's
eight decades of cumulative output of motor vehicles had been built in the
United States.

Not only has the United States traditionally been the leading motor vehicle producing nation; auto companies based in the United States have traditionally been dominant—or at least highly significant—in virtually every
corner of the globe. Ford's early dominance was so strong that in 1921 that
corporation alone produced 58 percent of *world* motor vehicle output. GM,
Ford, and Chrysler were all thoroughly international by the 1930s, and
between them accounted for three-quarters of worldwide production by the
middle of that decade. Ford opened a plant in Manchester, England, in 1911,
in Bordeaux, France, in 1913, and in Buenos Aires in 1916. By 1926, Brazil,
Mexico, South Africa, Malaya, Japan, Australia, and most larger European
countries had Ford plants. Not to be outdone, General Motors acquired
Vauxhall in 1925, and by 1938 accounted for 10 percent of U.K. auto output.
Opel was acquired in 1929; this became the largest pre–World War II car
firm in Germany, with a 35 percent share of the German market by 1937.
GM opened an assembly plant in Osaka, Japan, in 1926.

The U.S.-based auto multinationals had significant competition in few
parts of the world until the mid-1950s. In 1955, only two non–U.S. companies, BMC and VW, had over a 2 percent share of world output. Though by
1973 a total of eight significant foreign competitors had emerged,[4] the U.S.-
based Big Three still dominated the global industry. That year, 30 percent of
Ford's production was outside North America, as was 21 percent of GM's
and 34 percent of Chrysler's. In addition to controlling 100 percent of North

American production, in 1973 U.S.–based corporations controlled 26 percent of Western Europe's; 46 percent of Latin America's; and 60 percent of Australia's and South Africa's. The only significant producing or market area from which the Big Three were effectively excluded, apart from Eastern Europe and the Soviet Union, was Japan. European-based multinationals, for their part, controlled the remaining 74 percent of West European production; 53 percent of Latin America's; and 23 percent of Australia's and South Africa's.

Regional Dependency

Auto's concentration in the Great Lakes states dates back even further than its emergence as the nation's largest industry. Already in 1904, the five contiguous states of Michigan, Ohio, Indiana, Illinois, and Wisconsin produced 72 percent of the nation's motor vehicles and provided 58 percent of the nation's motor vehicle jobs. By 1914, Detroit was solidly entrenched as the "motor city"—as home base for nine of the nation's fifteen largest automotive corporations and producer of fully 69 percent of that year's national output of cars and trucks. There was some geographic dispersal of the industry in the decades which followed, but no diminution of the Great Lakes states' dependency on it. In 1977, 28 percent of all manufacturing employment in Michigan—307,000 jobs—was *directly* provided by the motor vehicle industry (SIC 371). Including primary metals, fabricated metal products, and nonelectrical machinery, much of which in Michigan is closely linked to auto, the proportion of the state's manufacturing employment that was "auto-related" rose to 55 percent—679,000 out of 1,100,000 manufacturing jobs.

The "auto dependency" of the Detroit SMSA (standard metropolitan statistical area) is even greater than for the state as a whole. In 1979, the motor vehicle and equipment industry accounted for 230,800 jobs in the SMSA—40 percent of all manufacturing employment. Compared with 1970, the SMSA's auto dependency actually increased; in that earlier year, the comparable figure was 37 percent. Including the auto-related sectors—primary metals, fabricated metal products, and nonelectrical machinery—"auto-related" employment is a staggering 65 percent of Detroit SMSA manufacturing employment.

Economic Importance

As to the industry's overall economic importance, estimates and measurements vary, but all point to auto's tremendous significance to the total economy and as a generator of employment. In national income accounting terms, auto and truck production and services account for 8½ percent of GNP, more than 25 percent of the nation's retail sales, and have held a remarkably steady 12 percent share of personal consumption expenditures over a long period of time. Direct employment in the industry (SIC 371) topped out at nearly one million production and nonproduction workers in 1978. Supplier industry employment is conservatively estimated at 1.4 million, including over 100,000 engaged in tire production, 91,000 engaged in building motors and generators to supply the industry, 60,000 producing electrical engine equipment, 57,000 workers in gray iron foundries, and many, many more. Altogether these 2.4 million manufacturing jobs in the auto industry and its suppliers account for one manufacturing job in nine nationwide.

As a result of the industry's geographic concentration, this huge manufacturing infrastructure constitutes the economic base of hundreds of communities, principally though not exclusively throughout much of the Midwest. It is in many cases the linchpin of the local economy, upon which countless service establishments—and the muncipal tax base—often depend. Just the "prime" manufacturers alone presently operate some ninety-six car and truck assembly plants in thirty-one states, and 248 parts plants in twenty-seven states.

SOME RECENT TRENDS

As noted earlier, long lead times, enormous capital requirements, and powerful economies of scale have long characterized the auto industry and continue to do so. Though there is considerable debate—and little hard evidence—a number of outside observers have agreed that for a variety of technological and economic reasons, to remain viable, the minimum production of a worldwide auto company must be in the neighborhood of 2 million units per year. This view is consistent with the global shake-out which is well under way, as smaller and financially weaker firms seek mergers, joint ventures, and/or government assistance in a desperate effort to avoid further deterioration of their competitive position and possible extinction. The trail is already littered with the corpses of those who did not succeed. As Gerald Meyers, chief executive of AMC, put it, "Few companies have the resources, transnational marketing strength and in-depth technical capability to be totally independent. Cooperation will grow and will cross oceans and national boundaries . . . there will be alliances, joint ventures and other mutual projects on a wide scale."[5] There are market "niches" which create the possibility for significant exceptions, but the overriding tendency will be continuing shake-out and further concentration.

Another important set of ingredients in the industry's competitive equation is international standardization of product, internationalization of sourcing, rationalization of production on a global scale, and, most important of all, intensification of global competition, linked first and foremost to the meteoric rise of the Japanese industry in a period of relatively slow total worldwide market growth. Though, as noted earlier, the industry has been thoroughly multinational in outlook from the very beginning, until comparatively recently there was relatively little rationalization across international boundaries, even among different subsidiaries of the same parent company. A notable exception was in North America, where the United States and Canada took a quantum leap toward becoming a single integrated auto market with the signing of the Auto Pact in 1965. Elsewhere, however, geographic fragmentation was the rule. In some cases, distinct products were produced by each major national subsidiary, and often there was relatively little international sourcing—frustrating the achievement of scale economies.

This will no longer be the case in the future; as befits the world's first auto multinational, Ford has pioneered the "world car." Its European Escort is being assembled in England and West Germany, from components produced by many different companies in seventeen countries of Europe, Asia, and North America. Table 3.2 provides a dramatic illustration.

Table 3.2. European Escort Car Component Sourcing

Country	Components
Austria	Radiator and Heater Hoses, Tires
Belgium	Hood-in Trim, Seat Pads, Tires, Brakes Tubes
Canada	Glass, Radios
Denmark	Fan Belts
France	Seat Pads, Sealers, Tires, Underbody Coating, Weatherstrips, Seat Frames, Heaters, Brakes, Master Cylinders, Ventilation Units, Hardware, Steering Shaft and Joints, Front Seat Cushions, Suspension Bushes, Hose Clamps, Alternators, Clutch Release Bearings
Italy	Defroster Nozzles and Grills, Glass, Hardware Lamps.
Japan	W S Washer Pumps, Cone and Roller Bearings, Alternators, Starters
Netherlands	Paints, Tires, Hardware
Norway	Tires, Muffler Flanges
Spain	Radiator and Heater Hoses, Air Cleaners, Wiring Harness, Batteries, Fork Clutch Releases, Mirrors
Sweden	Hardware, Exhaust Down Pipes, Pressings, Hose Clamps
Switzerland	Speedometer Gears, Underbody Coatings
U.S.	Wrench Wheel Nuts, Glass, EGR Valves
England, Germany	Muffler Ass'y, Pipe Ass'y, Fuel Tank Filler
England	Steering Wheel

Table 3.2. (*Continued*)

Country	Components
England, Germany	Tube Ass'y Steering Column, Lock Ass'y, Steering and Ignition
England, France	Heater Ass'y
England, Germany	Heater Blower Ass'y, Heater Control Quadrant Ass'y
England, Italy	Nozzle Windshield Defroster
England, Germany	Cable Ass'y Speedometer
Germany	Cable Ass'y Battery to Starter
England, Germany	Turn Signal Switch Ass'y, Light Wiper Switch Ass'y, Headlamp Ass'y, Bilux, Lamp Ass'y, Front Turn Signal
England, Italy	Lamp Ass'y Turn Signal Side, Rear Lamp Ass'y (inc. Fog Lamp), Rear Lamp Ass'y
England, Germany	Weatherstrip Door Opening, Main Wire Ass'y Tires, Battery, Windshield Glass, Back Window Glass, Door Window Glass, Constant Velocity Joints
France, Germany	Transmission Cases, Clutch Cases
England, Germany	Rear Wheel Spindles
Germany	Front Wheel Knuckle
England, Germany	Front Disc
England, France, Italy	Cylinder Head
England, Germany	Distributor
USA	Hydraulic Tappet
England, Germany	Rocker Arm
England	Oil Pump
Germany	Pistons
England	Intake Manifold
England, Germany	Clutch
Germany	Cyclinder Head Gasket
Eng., Germ., Swe.	Cylinder Bolt
N. Ireland, Italy	Carburetors
England	Flywheel Ring Gear

Steel (body steel and forging barstock) from U.K., Germany, Belgium, France, Italy, Austria (sheet), and Finland (bar).

SOURCE: U.S. Department of Transportation, *The U.S. Automobile Industry, 1980; Report to the President* (Washington, D.C.: Jan. 1981), p. 57.

North American producers have also announced extensive long-lead commitments, unprecedented in scope, to purchase foreign-made components for use in the domestic production of cars and trucks. A partial list of such announced arrangements is presented in table 3.3. Note that the purchase arrangements involve both foreign subsidiaries and affiliates of the "prime" manufacturers, as well as independent foreign suppliers.

All of this means that the lot of literally thousands of domestic auto supplier companies—which has always been characterized by extreme insta-

Table 3.3. Selected Known 1977-1981 Commitments by Major U.S. Automobile Manufacturers to Purchase Foreign-Made Major Components for Use in Domestic Nameplate Vehicles

Manu-facturer	Component	Intended For	Source	Approximate Number of Components	Delivery Begin-ning
GM	2.8 liter V-6	Cars	GM de Mexico	400,000/year	1982
	2.0 liter L-4 with transmission	Mini trucks	Isuzu (Japan)	100,000/year	1981
	1.8 liter diesel L-4	Chevette	Isuzu	small numbers	1981
	1.3 liter diesel L-4	S-Cars	Isuzu	n.a.	1983
	1.8 liter L-4	J-Cars	GM de Brazil	250,000/year	1979
	THM 180 Automatic transmission	Chevette	Gm Strasbourg (France)	250,000/year	1979
	Manual transmissions	J-Cars	Isuzu	250,000/year	1981
Ford	2.2 liter L-4	Cars	Ford-Mexico	400,000/year	1983
	Diesel L-4	Cars	Toyo Kogyo (Japan)	150,000/year	1983
	2.0 liter L-4	Mini trucks	Toyo Kogyo	100,000 year	1982
	2.3 liter L-4	Cars	Ford de Brazil	50,000/year	1979
	Diesel 6 cyl.	Cars	BMW/Steyr (W. Ger./Austria)	190,000/year	1983
	Diesel 4 cyl.	Cars	BMW/Steyr (W. Ger./Austria)	n.a.	1985
	Manual transaxles	Front drive cars	Toyo Kogyo	100,000 year	1980

	Component	Application	Supplier	Quantity	Year
	Aluminum cylinder heads	1.6 liter L-4	Europe, Mexico	n.a.	1980
	Accessory motors	Cars, trucks	Ford-Singapore	n.a.	1984
	Electronic engine control devices		Toshiba	100,000+/year	1978
	Ball joints	Cars	Musashi Seimibu	1,000,000/year	1980
Chrysler	L-6 and V-8 engines	Cars	Chrysler de Mexico	100,000/year	1982
	2.2 liter L-4	K-body	Chrysler de Mexico	270,000/year	1981
	2.6 liter L-4	K-body	Mitsubishi (Japan)	1 million	1981
	1.7 liter L-4	Omni/Horizon	Volkswagen (W. Ger.)	1.2 million	1978
	Manual transmission	Omni/Horizon	Volkswagen	500,000	1978
	1.6 liter L-4	L-body	Talbot (Peugeot)	400,000 total	1982
	2.0 liter diesel V-6	K-body	Peugeot (France)	100,000/year	1982
	1.4 liter L-4	A-body (Omni replacement)	Mitsubishi	300,000/year	1984
	L-4 engines	Cars	Peugeot	n.a.	1985
	Aluminum cylinder heads	2.2 liter L-4	Fiat (Italy)	n.a.	1984
AMC	Car components and power train	AMC-Renault	Renault in France and Mexico	300,000/year	1982
VWA	Radiators, stampings	Rabbit	VW de Mexico	250,000/year	1979
	L-4 diesel and gas engines	Cars	VW de Mexico	300,000+/year	1982

SOURCE: U.S. Department of Transportation, *The U.S. Automobile Industry, 1980: Report to the President* (Washington, D.C., Jan. 1981). p. 56 (updated).
n.a. = Figure not available.

77

bility and subservience to the needs of the prime manufacturers—will be-
cöme even less stable in the years ahead. For the workers in that sector,
hundreds of thousands of whom are members of the UAW and other unions,
insecure employment of times past may give way in many cases to nonexistent employment in the future. This is not to suggest that internationalization
of sourcing will not become a two-way street. In some areas of component
producing, U.S. manufacturers may well have a strong competitive position
and accordingly should benefit from increased access to world markets—
unless our government continues to stand idly by when other nations limit
efficiently produced U.S. exports. Moreover, even if internationalization becomes a two-way street, there will be substantial dislocations—including
wrenching geographic employment shifts—along the way.

Rationalization and Efficiency

The auto industry early on evolved a distinctive pattern of production and
work relations. Ever since Henry Ford introduced the assembly line, the
industry has been synonymous with mass production, cost cutting, and high
productivity. Consumers for years were conditioned, and willing, to pay a
price in terms of "craftsmanship" in exchange for the cost savings that
resulted from high-volume, highly rationalized mass production.

   This emphasis of corporate management was reflected in relationships
with employees. As early as the 1920s, well before formation of the UAW,
work in the auto industry came to symbolize "high wage alienation," with
minute subdivision of tasks, enormous pressure for production, and rigid,
authoritarian discipline. Add to this a not-so-benevolent paternalism, arbi-
trariness and favoritism by plant management, extreme job insecurity, and
the callous tendency of management to discharge older workers who could
no longer maintain the pace, and it is easy to see why the auto industry
became a seedbed of militant industrial unionism. The upsurge came comparatively late, but was all the stronger for having been pent up so long, and
swept the industry like a rising tide.

   In the years which followed, the union established a proud record. On the
shop floor, management abuses were significantly curbed; in place of arbitrary supervision, due process in the administration of work rules and other
important steps toward industrial democracy were instituted. On the economic front, significant gains in job and income security and steady improvement in workers' living standards were achieved, including a long list
of pioneering collective-bargaining breakthroughs which shone like a bea-
con to workers in other sectors of the economy. In its bargaining, however,
the union also prided itself on exercising restraint and responsibility, in spite
of the superprofits of the industry in most years and its remarkable record of
productivity growth. Indeed, the more objective of our critics are forced to

admit that their opposition to high levels of auto-worker compensation stems, not from the fact that auto workers don't earn it, but because auto workers' gains put "inflationary thoughts" into other workers' heads. A clear statement of this "liberal"—but decidedly antiworker—position has been made by Charles Schultze:

> The problem with the large wage and fringe increases in the auto industry is not solely or even principally the higher auto prices they lead to. *Indeed, because of faster-than-average productivity gains auto prices in the past 10 to 15 years have risen less than those of other products*. Rather, the problem of the outsized wage gains lie in their effect on the rate of wage increase in other industries.[6]

The "outsized wage gains" to which Schultze refers consist primarily of cost-of-living increases, which, when added to modest (3 percent) annual increases, has meant that over the last two years, auto workers' purchasing power has eroded only about 2 percent, in contrast to the considerably sharper reduction experienced by workers without cost-of-living protection.

Those who may still believe that the level of auto workers' compensation is a significant factor in the industry's current problems should read no less an authority than Philip Caldwell, Board Chairman and Chief Executive Officer of Ford: "Relative to most areas of the world, the U.S. is a *low-cost* producer, even with the high compensation U.S. workers enjoy. In autos, unit costs in the U.S. are generally better than in Europe and most Third World areas. With the decline of the yen after the Iranian crisis, Japan has been the outstanding exception."[7]

As a proportion of company sales revenues, total compensation of U.S. auto workers (wages plus fringe benefits) has long remained essentially stable. This ratio increases very slightly in years when sales decline, and correspondingly decreases when sales pick up; but over quite a long period of time, it has exhibited no trend. Table 3.4 illustrates this point vividly in the case of General Motors.

It is true that the Japanese manufacturers enjoy a substantial labor cost advantage relative to their U.S. and several European competitors. Indeed, based on unpublished Bureau of Labor Statistics comparisons, as of mid-1980 the total hourly compensation of Japanese autoworkers (including fringe benefits) was well below the level of Italy, and roughly on a par with Spain. Rather than U.S. and European auto workers being overpaid, it is widely believed in Europe that Japanese auto workers are *underpaid* relative to their productivity. According to Eugene Loderer, president of West Germany's largest trade union, I. G. Metall,

> We must all guard against adopting Japan's socio-political structures as our own. They are unequivocally behind the times. They operate at the expense of

Table 3.4. GM Total Hourly Compensation Costs as Percent
of U.S. Sales, 1969-1979

Year	U.S. Sales (millions)	Total Hourly Comp. Cost—U.S.* (millions)	Hourly Compensation Cost as a % of Sales
1979	$55,014.8	$14,325	26.0
1978	53,498.8	13,370.6	25.0
1977	47,551.0	12,155.9	25.6
1976	39,784.7	9,907.6	24.9
1975	28,917.8	7,404.7	25.6
1974	26,016.0	7,148.4	27.5
1973	30,371.8	7,700.5	25.4
1972	25,921.9	6,569.0	25.3
1971	24,594.6	6,013.5	24.5
1970	15,478.9	4,303.5	27.8
1969	21,216.5	5,109.8	24.1

SOURCE: UAW Research Department estimates based on company
annual reports.
* Includes wages plus all fringe benefit costs, including "statutory"
costs.

the worker, which naturally creates an advantage for industry. This is possible
in a backward social system such as Japan's. . . .
Japanese are no more efficient than Americans or Germans, but they work
longer hours. They have a system of self-perpetuating clans of lifelong workers. . . . This is a form of discrimination within the working class in favor of one
part of the workforce.[8]

The Auto and the Postwar Expansion

In the United States, "automobilization" proceeded rapidly after World
War II, under the stimulus of favorable government policy, and provided in
turn much of the impetus for a prolonged period of relatively robust economic growth. Extensive highway construction, cheap and abundant gas,
and the availability of FHA mortgages in the suburbs were among the
significant stimulative factors. Nearly three times more cars and trucks were
built in the United States during the thirty years after World War II than
during the previous fifty years—roughly 275 million between 1949 and 1979,
as against 100 million up through 1948. As a result of this prodigious production, the fleet of vehicles, as noted earlier, was up nearly fivefold, from
31 million at the end of 1945 to 154 million at the end of 1978.

The trend of annual production, though it was by no means uniform,
generally tended to be up, until 1973—and even established a new, slightly

higher all-time peak in 1978. Despite massive productivity growth, the increase in output—coupled with significant increases in complexity per unit—was such that until 1978, employment also tended to slightly increase. The figures are presented in table 3.5.

A sawtooth pattern is readily evident, indicating the extreme cyclicality of auto production—and hence employment—even in a period of relatively rapid growth. Though motor vehicle production in record year 1978 was up 61 percent compared with 1950, year-to-year output declines were sustained

Table 3.5. Production and Employment—U.S. Motor Vehicles Industry

Year	U.S. Production (millions)			SIC 371 Employment (thousands)
	Cars	Trucks	Total Motor Vehicles	
1980	6.4	1.6	8.0	773.8
1979	8.4	3.0	11.5	982.8
1978	9.2	3.7	12.9	997.2
1977	9.2	3.5	12.7	942.0
1976	8.5	3.0	11.5	881.0
1975	6.7	2.3	9.0	792.4
1974	7.3	2.7	10.1	907.7
1973	9.7	3.0	12.7	976.5
1972	8.8	2.5	11.3	874.8
1971	8.6	2.1	10.7	848.5
1970	6.6	1.7	8.3	799.0
1969	8.2	2.0	10.2	911.4
1968	8.8	2.0	10.8	873.7
1967	7.4	1.6	9.0	815.8
1966	8.6	1.8	10.4	861.6
1965	9.3	1.8	11.1	842.7
1964	7.7	1.6	9.3	752.9
1963	7.6	1.5	9.1	741.3
1962	6.9	1.3	8.2	691.7
1961	5.5	1.1	6.7	632.3
1960	6.7	1.2	7.9	724.1
1959	5.6	1.1	6.7	692.3
1958	4.2	.9	5.1	606.5
1957	6.1	1.1	7.2	769.3
1956	5.8	1.1	6.9	792.5
1955	8.0	1.3	9.2	891.2
1954			6.5	765.7
1953			7.3	917.3
1952			5.6	777.5
1951			6.8	833.3
1950			8.0	816.2

SOURCE: *MVMA Motor Vehicle Facts and Figures, '81*, p. 8; U.S. Bureau of Labor Statistics, *Employment and Earnings, United States, 1909-78* (Washington, D.C., 1979), pp. 351-352; *Supplement to Employment and Earnings, Revised Establishment Data* (Aug. 1981), pp. 125-126.

in no less than twelve of the intervening twenty-seven years. Indeed, the 1950 production level was not exceeded until 1955; the 1955 level, not until 1964; and the 1965 level, not until 1973.

Subsequent declines from each of these peaks have in all cases been substantial, and since 1965 have progressively increased. Between the 1965 peak and 1967 trough, production declined 19 percent, but this was mild compared with the 29 percent drop between 1973 and 1975. Between 1978 and 1980—which we cannot yet say for sure will turn out to be the trough—production fell a staggering 38 percent.

The brakes on the postwar expansion of the industry's output resulted chiefly from the interplay of three factors: market maturity, hastened after 1973 by doubts as to the price and availability of gasoline; skyrocketing imports from Japan, due partly to the same energy concerns; and the overall slowdown of economic growth in the 1970s, exacerbated in the last two years by the Federal Reserve Board's disastrous monetarist experiment. Put differently, there has been a steady and by now quite marked slowdown in the growth of the total market, while the import share of that market has soared. The first of these points is illustrated, for cars, in table 3.6.

This means that in 1978 more than eight cars in ten were "replacements" for cars which had been scrapped—up from three in ten in 1948. This ratio has steadily increased throughout the postwar period, and there is every reason to believe that it will continue to increase. Since the replacement of an auto is generally postponable, not only will market growth continue to slow as the stock of vehicles levels off, but the industry's historic cyclicality may well become even more pronounced.

What modest growth there may be in the U.S. market will be more than captured by imports, if recent trends continue. Sparked by skyrocketing imports from Japan, imports took a record 26.7 percent of the total U.S. auto market in 1980 and 19.4 percent of the truck market, as table 3.7 indicates.

Imports of Japanese autos rose from 381,000 in 1970 to 1.9 million in 1980. Comparing these two years, the total car market increased only about

Table 3.6. Scrappage and Market Growth

Year	Cars in Use Percent Increase Over Prior Year	Scrappage as % of New Cars Registered
1948	9.2	30.6
1958	4.9	53.5
1968	4.2	66.9
1978	1.7	84.4

SOURCE: *Ward's Automotive Yearbook, 1980,* p. 169.

Table 3.7. Growth in Import Share, 1955-1980

Year	Auto Import Share* Japan	Auto Import Share* Total	Truck Import Share*
1980	21.3%	26.7%	19.4%
1979	15.2	21.7	13.5
1978	11.9	17.0	8.2
1977	12.0	18.5	8.8
1976	9.2	14.8	7.5
1975	9.3	18.3	9.3
1974	6.7	15.8	6.6
1973	6.5	15.2	7.4
1972	5.6	14.4	5.4
1971	5.2	14.9	4.1
1970	3.7	14.7	3.6
1969		11.7	1.7
1968		10.7	1.3
1967		7.2	1.4
1965		6.1	0.9
1960		7.5	3.8
1955		0.8	0.8

* "Imports" exclude vehicles built in Canada.

600,000 units (8.9 million versus 8.3 million). During 1980, the import share in the trend-setting state of California exceeded 50 percent.

Productivity, Profitability, and Capacity Utilization

Throughout most of the postwar period, auto has been an exceptionally high-productivity and high-profit industry; and both productivity and profitability have been very sensitive to capacity utilization and output fluctuations. Between 1957, when the BLS first started to measure the industry's productivity, and 1979, output per employee-hour rose at an average annual rate of 3.4 percent in the motor vehicles and equipment industry. The comparable figure for all manufacturing was 2.8 percent. Over the entire period, auto productivity greatly outstripped the manufacturing norm by over 31 percent. Moreover, due to the way BLS measures hours paid but not worked, these official figures probably understate auto's productivity increase. With advances in robotics and other new manufacturing technology, future strides in auto industry productivity could be even more rapid than in the past. The happy circumstance—for employment—of output plus vehicle complexity growing even faster than productivity, however, is extremely unlikely to continue. Unfortunately, just the opposite is more likely.

Table 3.8. Capacity Utilization, Productivity, and Return on Investment

	1	II		III	
		Increase (Decrease in Productivity, Comapred with Prior Year		After-Tax Profits as a % of Beginning-of-Year Net Worth	
	Auto Industry Capacity	Mtr. Veh.	All Manufac-	Mtr. Veh.	All Manu-
Year	Utilization	& Equip.	turing	& Equip.	facturing
1980	58.2%	n.a.	(0.3%)	(8.6%)	15.1%
1979	80.9	(3.7%)	1.0	11.5	17.5
1978	89.4	(0.8)	0.9	18.4	15.9
1977	89.2	6.7	2.4	20.1	14.8
1976	82.7	7.0	4.4	18.4	14.8
1975	66.6	7.0	3.1	6.1	11.9
1974	79.1	(4.1)	(2.4)	7.0	16.0
1973	95.3	1.5	5.4	16.1	13.6
1972	90.7	3.3	4.9	15.3	11.2
1971	81.4	16.2	6.0	13.4	10.1
1970	65.3	(4.2)	(0.1)	6.2	9.6
1969	86.1	(1.9)	1.7	13.0	12.2
1968	91.8	8.3	3.4	15.8	12.6
1967	79.0	0.5	0.0	12.1	12.2
1966		0.5	0.8	16.6	14.2
1965		6.6	3.3	20.9	13.5
1964		1.1	4.6	18.0	12.1
1963		3.9	7.0	17.8	10.6
1962		9.7	4.2	17.3	10.1
1961		1.3	2.7	11.8	9.1
1960		8.6	0.7	14.2	9.5
1959		9.5	4.6	16.0	10.9
1958		(2.8)	(0.3)	8.3	8.9
1957				14.8	11.5
1956				13.8	13.1
1955				24.6	13.1
1954				14.9	10.3
1953				14.5	10.8
1952				14.4	10.7
1951				14.9	13.8
1950				28.2	16.3
1949				24.4	12.1
1948				21.9	17.2
1947				17.5	16.7

SOURCE: Capacity Utilization, Federal Reserve Board; Productivity, Bureau of Labor Statistics; Returns on Investment, Federal Trade Commission/Securities and Exchange Commission.

n.a. = not available.

Auto industry profitability has also been extremely high throughout most of the postwar period. The industry's rate of return on stockholders' investment outstripped the U.S. all-manufacturing average in all but seven of the last thirty-five years, usually by a substantial margin. These industry figures mask considerable variation among companies; suffice it to say that in every recent year, General Motors has been far and away the most profitable auto corporation.

Aside from strike-affected 1970, industry returns on investment dipped below the all-manufacturing average only in years of severe sales slumps—1958, 1967, 1974, 1975, 1979, and—in a loss year for the industry for the first time since the Great Depression—1980. For details, see table 3.8.

The key factor in 1980's loss is the fact that the industry's rate of capacity utilization in 1980 plunged to 58.2 percent—substantially lower than in 1975, and by far the lowest level since the Great Depression.

SETTING THE STAGE FOR THE CURRENT CRISIS

As rapidly as "automobilization" proceeded in the United States after World War II, its relative pace in many other parts of the world—starting from a much smaller base—was even more brisk. First Western Europe, and later Japan, reached the "takeoff point" with respect to motor vehicle production.

Unlike production of other commodities that has become dispersed more widely among developing countries, these three highly developed, industrialized areas—North America, Western Europe, and Japan—remain by far the world's dominant auto markets and account for the nearly all of total worldwide production. Historically, the lower wages available in other parts of the globe have been less enticing to auto manufacturers than the industrial infrastructure, economies of scale, technology, and pool of skills which only the highly industrialized regions have heretofore been able to provide. In 1979, for example, North America, Japan, and Europe (including Eastern Europe and the Soviet Union) produced a combined total of 95 percent of the world's motor vehicle output. Of the ten nations which produced over a million vehicles in 1979, only one—Brazil, with production of 1.1 million—could be classified as a developing country.[9] After this "club of ten," there was a large drop to the next tier of producers, none of which had output in excess of 500,000. This second tier included such countries as Australia (461,000), Mexico (444,000), Poland (429,000), and Sweden (355,000).

While this may change and conceivably could change quite rapidly in the future, for now the overwhelming bulk of the world's motor vehicle production takes place in North America, Europe, and Japan. To the extent that this does change, government policy in various countries of the world will be the decisive factor in initially overcoming the powerful advantages of the currently dominant producing areas. Already this was the case with Brazil, Spain, and Mexico. Local content, export performance requirements, stiff quotas and tariffs, and a range of investment incentives have been and will be widely used to encourage establishment of auto production when such production would not otherwise take place based on the multinationals' unguided investment decisions. Given the probable eventual diffusion of technology, industrial infrastructure, and skilled labor pool, this means that in the future any major producing country not willing to take affirmative steps to preserve its domestic auto industry must be prepared to see its home market targeted by subsidized exports and its domestic auto capital drained away. The magnitude of the shifts involved and the rapidity with which they will take place could be stunning. Among all the major auto-producing nations of the world and all the developing nations which aspire to become producers, only the United States appears willing to tolerate this uncertain situation.

A sampling of the measures taken by other industrial and developing countries to protect or stimulate domestic auto production is presented in table 3.9.

Meteoric Rise of the Japanese Auto Industry

Though the three major producing areas continue to account for the great bulk of world motor vehicle production, there has been a radical shift in their relative shares over the last thirty years.

Table 3.9. Measures Taken to Protect or Stimulate Domestic Auto Production[a]

Australia	Auto import duty 35-57%; stringent local content.
Belgium[b]	Quota on Japanese imports.
France[b]	Japanese limited to 3% market share.
Italy[b]	Formal quota on Japanese imports (2,200 cars!).
Spain[b]	55% local content; 68% tariff on non-EC/EFTA imports.
UK[b]	Voluntary limit on Japanese imports, 10.8% of market.
Andean Pact	70% local content; 115% tariff.
Argentina	90-93% local content; 55% tariff.
Brazil	Local content, negotiated individually with companies; imports presently *embargoed*; normally, tariff 185-205%.
India	Local content; 100-140% tariff.
Mexico	Local content; 75% cars/85% trucks, offset by export performance requirements. Imports normally not allowed; when they are, duty 35-100%.

SOURCE: U.S. Congress, House, Committee on Ways and Means, Subcommittee on Trade, *Auto Situation: 1980*, Report, 96th Cong., 2nd sess., June 6, 1980, pp. 94-100.

[a] Recent additions include W. Germany and Canada, in the wake of Japan's announcement of temporary U.S. export restraints. Canada already had a 14.9% tariff in place even before acting, while Germany limited growth in Japanese imports to 10% of the increase in its total market.

[b] In addition, EC tariff is 10.8%, vs. 2.9% U.S.

In 1950 the three major producing regions together accounted for 99.8 percent of world motor vehicle production—including North America, 79.4 percent; Europe, 20.1 percent; and Japan, barely on the charts with 0.3 percent. By 1979, some twenty-nine years later, there was a dramatic shift. The "Big Three" producing areas still accounted for 94.5 percent of world production, but North America's share had dropped to 31.6 percent; Europe's had nearly doubled to 39.4 percent; and Japan's had skyrocketed to 23.5 percent. The following year, Japan surpassed the United States as the leading motor-vehicle-producing nation for the first time since the dawn of the auto age, as Japanese production rose 13 percent over 1979 to a record 11 million units, while U.S. output plunged to 8 million units, the lowest level since 1961—a decline of 30 percent from 1979 and a drop of 38 percent compared with record 1978.

Details on the shift in shares of world production by major producing area, and the remarkable growth of the Japanese industry, can be seen in table 3.10.

As the figures in table 3.10 indicate, Europe remains the largest single producing area, but its share of world production actually peaked in 1958. The 1970s witnessed a marked tapering off in the growth of European production, while Japanese output, apart from a dip in 1974, continued to surge.

In fostering the spectacular development of the Japanese auto industry, the role of government policy is widely acknowledged to have been significant and quite possibly decisive.[10] The twin objectives in promoting development of the industry have been to preserve the home market exclusively for domestic producers and to foster the export potential of the industry. With respect to achievement of both aims, Japanese auto policy has been remarkably successful.

With regard to the first objective of preserving the home market for domestic producers, Japan twice moved decisively to restrict imports and to curb investment by foreign-based producers. In 1936 the Auto Manufacturing Law effectively closed the industry to foreign corporations, for military and nationalist reasons.[11]

The industry's postwar recovery was slow at first. Production levels of 1940/1941 were not surpassed until the 1953 Korean War boom, which fueled demand principally for trucks. By the early 1950s the Japanese government had implemented an impressive array of policies to protect and nurture the domestic industry. According to a 1972 U.S. Department of Commerce memorandum, "the structure of protection measures . . . was comprehensive and imposing." The 1951 Foreign Investment Law required specific government approval of all proposed foreign investments in the auto industry. This gave the government comprehensive control over foreign investment. The law was administered in such a way as to facilitate acquisition of foreign automotive technology on favorable terms; to bar marketing investments by foreign producers; and in general to foster development of the

Table 3.10. World Motor Vehicle Production (millions of cars and trucks)

Year	United States		North America		Europe*		Japan		North America, Europe and Japan Combined	
	No.	% of Total	No.	% of Total	No.	% of Total	No.	% of Total	% of Total	World Total
1980	8.0	20.9	9.4	24.5	15.5	40.5	11.0	28.8	93.7	38.4
1979	11.5	27.7	13.1	31.6	16.4	39.4	9.7	23.5	94.5	41.5
1978	12.9	30.5	14.7	34.8	16.2	38.3	9.4	22.1	95.2	42.3
1977	12.7	31.0	14.5	35.4	16.0	39.0	8.6	21.0	95.4	40.9
1976	11.5	30.0	3.1	34.3	15.3	39.9	7.9	20.7	94.9	38.3
1975	9.0	27.2	10.4	31.6	13.6	39.1	7.0	20.2	90.9	33.0
1974	10.1	29.0	11.6	33.4	14.5	41.8	6.6	19.1	94.3	34.7
1973	12.7	32.6	14.3	36.7	15.7	40.3	7.2	18.4	95.4	38.9
1972	11.3	31.8	12.7	35.8	14.8	41.7	6.4	18.0	95.5	35.5
1971	10.7	31.9	12.0	36.0	14.0	41.8	6.0	18.0	95.8	33.4
1970	8.3	28.3	9.5	32.4	13.2	44.9	5.4	18.3	95.6	29.3
1969	10.2	34.2	11.5	38.7	12.4	41.5	4.8	15.9	96.1	29.8
1968	10.8	38.2	12.0	42.2	11.2	39.6	4.2	14.7	96.5	28.4

Year										
1967	9.0	37.6	9.9	41.4	10.0	41.5	3.2	13.4	96.3	24.0
1966	10.4	41.8	11.3	45.3	10.4	41.7	2.4	9.5	96.5	24.9
1965	11.1	45.9	12.0	49.4	9.5	39.3	1.9	8.0	96.7	24.3
1964	9.3	42.8	10.0	45.9	9.2	42.4	1.8	8.1	96.4	21.8
1963	9.1	44.7	9.7	47.8	8.6	42.4	1.3	6.6	96.8	20.4
1962	8.2	45.5	8.7	48.4	7.7	42.2	1.0	5.8	96.4	18.0
1961	6.7	43.7	7.0	46.2	6.6	43.2	1.1	6.9	96.3	15.2
1960	7.9	47.9	8.3	50.4	6.8	41.4	.8	4.9	96.7	16.5
1959	6.7	48.3	7.1	51.0	6.2	44.9	.5	3.3	99.2	13.9
1958	5.1	45.4	5.5	48.5	5.4	47.9	.3	2.8	99.2	11.3
1957	7.2	58.2	7.6	61.6	4.3	34.8	.2	2.6	99.0	12.4
1956	6.9	59.3	7.4	63.3	3.9	33.3	.2	2.1	98.7	11.7
1955	9.2	67.5	10.0	70.9	3.7	27.5	.2	1.2	99.6	13.6
1954	6.5	63.2	6.9	66.6	3.2	31.3	.2	1.6	99.5	10.3
1953	7.3	70.4	7.8	75.1	2.4	23.1	.1	1.4	99.6	10.4
1952	5.6	66.8	6.0	72.0	2.2	26.0	.1	1.2	99.2	8.3
1951	6.8	72.2	7.2	76.7	2.1	22.6	—	0.4	99.7	9.4
1950	8.0	76.2	8.4	79.4	2.1	20.1	—	0.3	99.8	10.6

SOURCE: *MVMA Motor Vehicle Facts and Figures '81*, p. 7.
* Including Eastern Europe and the Soviet Union.

domestic industry. Strict controls over foreign investment were not liberalized until 1971.

Almost immediately, Chrysler acquired a 15 percent equity investment in Mitsubishi. Later in 1971, GM purchased a 34.2 percent stake in Isuzu, just below the newly liberalized 35 percent foreign ownership cap. Ford's link came a few years later, with Toyo Kogyo (Mazda)—a company which, ironically, was saved from bankruptcy in 1975 only by extraordinary assistance from a consortium of major banks, under the government's watchful and approving eye. Here, the parallels with Chrysler stop; the incredible divisiveness which clouded and nearly torpedoed the Chrysler assistance effort had no counterpart in this earlier episode in Japan. Moreover, unlike the Chrysler case, neither pay cuts nor layoffs were a condition for receiving financial assistance.

As a result of strict controls over foreign investment, the course of development of the Japanese auto industry was dramatically altered. Unregulated penetration by the U.S. companies probably would have led to development of an industry limited mainly or exclusively to serving the Japanese and Far Eastern markets, consistent with the general pattern of development of the Big Three's European and other foreign operations.

In addition to controlling foreign investment, the Japanese strictly protected their home market through a combination of quotas, stiff tariffs, and commodity taxes. Tariffs remained high until 1971; even today, a widely acknowledged array of formidable nontariff trade barriers remains in place.

Financial assistance was also a critical factor underlying the industry's postwar development. Auto was designated by the Ministry of International Trade and Industry (MITI) as one of the four "critical postwar reconstruction industries"; as such, MITI recommended loans to auto producers by the Japan Development Bank until 1955. This was the signal to the private banking system that auto should be financed; according to the 1972 U.S. Department of Commerce memo, MITI's recommendation had a "favorable impact on the auto producers' access" to private capital. To facilitate its rapid plant and equipment expansion, the industry also benefited from special accelerated depreciation rules reportedly far more liberal than those in the United States.

Most of the Japanese auto industry's recent capacity expansion is "targeted for export," as the ITC staff has acknowledged.[12] Much of this expansion in export capacity is geared to the U.S. market.

ENERGY CRISIS TRIGGERS IMPORT SURGE AND CURRENT SLUMP

Perhaps more than any other single factor, the availability of relatively cheap gas made North America a historically distinctive auto market. In contrast to most of the rest of the world, over most of the postwar period in the United States, the relative retail price of gasoline actually declined (see figure 3.1). As a result, cars produced and sold here tended to be much larger, heavier, and more powerful than those produced or sold in any other major region of the world—a trend which increased throughout the 1960s and into the early 1970s. By 1973, fully 95.6 percent of cars manufactured in the United States were equipped with engines with greater than 2,000 cc displacement—as against 2.3 percent of cars built in Japan, and 0.4 percent of Italian-made cars.

The emphasis on large, powerful cars was attributed by many observers to the auto companies' lust for profits. "Mini cars mean mini profits," Henry Ford reportedly said. But, truth be told, though the import share increased starting in the late 1960s, the bulk of the car-buying public apparently had little interest in smaller cars as long as gasoline remained inexpensive and abundant.

The oil shock of late 1973 triggered the worst auto slump and general economic downturn since the Great Depression. Needless to say, the auto slump was much worse here than in producing countries long accustomed to

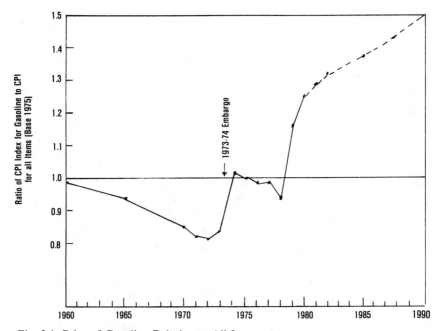

Fig. 3.1. Price of Gasoline Relative to All Items.
SOURCE: U.S. Department of Transportation, *The U.S. Automobile Industry, 1980; Report to the President* (Washington, D.C., Jan. 1981), p. 23.

small cars and expensive gas. Layoffs swelled to more than 270,000 at the Big Four alone. From peak month to trough, employment of auto workers fell 32 percent, while auto sales nose-dived 48 percent.

At the same time, there was a significant shift in the mix of cars sold. Subcompacts increased sharply as a proportion of total car sales, while the share of full-size makes correspondingly fell. Although import sales fell sharply, there *was* a significant increase in the import share. But except for the Japanese, foreign small car manufacturers were unable to capitalize on their sudden advantage. VW, in particular, was plagued by high German costs and a strengthening currency.

Following the slump, Congress reaffirmed its commitment to unrealistically cheap gas. The relative price of fuel again began to fall, and continued to fall until late 1978. Memories of gas lines faded. Mainly on the strength of renewed demand for large cars and explosive growth in sales of light trucks, the auto industry experienced a robust recovery in 1976, 1977, and 1978. In 1976 and again in 1978, the import share declined below the share of 1975.

Meanwhile, among the auto companies, GM took the lead in a major effort to reduce weight and improve mileage across its full line of cars, under the prodding of fuel economy standards mandated by Congress—and enacted with UAW support. The impact of the industry's "downsizing" program is summarized in table 3.11.

"Downsizing" might have worked, but for the events of early 1979. Since the United States was the only major petroleum-importing nation with oil price controls, it is hardly surprising in retrospect that the oil companies allocated to the United States as much as they could of the temporary worldwide oil shortage that followed the overthrow of the Shah. This sent the auto market into a horrendous tailspin from which it has yet to recover. Compounding the problem was restrictive monetary policy and, later on, general economic recession.

Unlike 1973, this time the foreign auto companies were ready, willing, and eager to accommodate the American consumers' wish to buy small cars. Import penetration increased from 17 percent in 1978, to 21.7 percent in 1979, and to 26.7 percent in 1980. Over the same period, Japanese imports soared from 11.9 percent of the total U.S. market to 15.2 percent and to 21.3 percent. Even among sales of domestic makes, the subcompact share skyrocketed from 13 percent in 1978 to 21.2 percent the following year and 25.4 percent in 1980.

By and large, with low costs and the benefit of a weakening yen, it was the Japanese producers who were positioned best to capitalize on the small-car surge. The result stood in marked contrast to the post-1973 slump, when in the early stages import sales in absolute terms were hit nearly as hard as sales of domestic makes. From the late 1978 peak to the May 1980 trough, sales of domestic makes plunged 45 percent, while imports *rose* 31 percent. In the

Table 3.11. Domestic New Car Trends in Physical Characteristics, Historical and Projected (1975-1985)

Model Year	1975	1976	1977	1978	1979	1980	1985
Average Dry Weight	3,970 lbs	3,900 lbs	3,830 lbs	3,440 lbs	3,330 lbs	3,080 lbs	2,400 lbs
Average Fuel Economy	14.7 mpg	16.5 mpg	17.1 mpg	18.6 mpg	19.0 mpg	21.2 mpg	31.0 mpg
Vehicle Mix[a]							
large (I + L)	60%	61%	65%	63%	55%	49%	33%
small (SC + C)	40%	39%	35%	37%	45%	51%	67%
Engine Type Mix[b]							
SI	100%	100%	100%	99%	98%	97%	85%
diesel	0%	0%	0%	1%	2%	3%	15%
Engine Size Mix							
8 cylinder	72%	69%	76%	66%	59%	37%	0%
6 cylinder (%)	19	21	18	24	24	36	35
4 cylinder (%)	9	10	6	10	17	27	62
less than 4 cylinder (%)	0	0	0	0	0	0	3
Average Engine Displacement[c]							
CID	329	318	316	286	273	238	140
CC	5,400	5,200	5,200	4,700	4,500	3,900	2,300
Power Train Configuration Mix[d]							
RWD	100%	100%	100%	98%	88%	82%	20%
FWD	0%	0%	0%	2%	12%	18%	80%

SOURCE: U.S. Department of Transportation, *The U.S. Automobile Industry, 1980: Report to the President* (Washington, D.C.: Jan. 1981), p. 24.

[a] L = Large, wheelbase over 119 inches

I = Intermediate, wheelbase between 112 and 118 inches

C = Compact, wheelbase between 101 and 111 inches

SC = Subcompact, wheelbase less than 100 inches

[b] SI = Spark Ignition Engine

[c] CID = Cubic Inch Displacement, CC = Cubic Centimeters

[d] RWD = Rear Wheel Drive, FWD = Front Wheel Drive

United States, auto-worker employment dropped 37 percent, while in Japan auto plants worked heavy overtime to fuel the export surge.

The Current Slump

For more than twenty-four months, the U.S. auto industry has been in a dismal state. In 1980 sales of domestic makes fell to the lowest level in nineteen years. The industry was awash in red ink, having lost $4.2 billion in 1980.

Though the companies have subsequently improved their "bottom lines," from the workers' standpoint there has been little respite from conditions as bad as are usually encountered only in the worst three or four months of a really severe slump, and no significant improvement is in sight. According to Department of Transportation (DOT) estimates, auto-related unemployment was in the range of 650,000 to 950,000 during 1980, including well over 300,000 laid-off employees of the Big Four, plus another 350,000 to 650,000 supplier, dealer, and other auto-related employees. By the summer of 1980, fully 32 percent of the Big Four's U.S. hourly workforce was on indefinite layoff. As of March 1981, the DOT estimated that auto-related unemployment was still 600,000, and Big Four layoffs alone still totaled 191,000. Part of the decline from the 300,000-plus layoff peak represented recalls to fill attritional openings rather any rebound in employment.

Upwards of 190 auto and supplier plants have closed permanently since the onset of the current slump, and some 2,400 auto dealerships have gone out of business. Unemployment rates in auto-dependent areas reached depression levels. There were 585,000 unemployed in Michigan in January 1981—13.7 percent of the labor force. Unemployment insurance benefit exhaustions in the state have been running at more than 20,000 per month. In metropolitan Detroit alone, there were 290,500 officially counted unemployed in January; the unemployment rate was 14.4 percent.

Like other auto-dependent cities, Detroit is in the midst of an acute fiscal crisis. This has led to cutbacks in vital services, with worse to come. Major crimes in Detroit increased 15 percent in 1980 over 1979, and 15 percent in January 1981 over January 1980. The year-to-year increase in burglaries was 25 percent.

The DOT estimates the public cost of an unemployed autoworker at $16,000 per year, including lost taxes plus various forms of public assistance. Supplier workers ineligible for Trade Readjustment Allowances "cost" somewhat less, about $10,000 in round numbers. Applying these factors to the 600,000 recently estimated to be in the pool of auto-related unemployed, the cost to the treasury of this staggering and tragic human and social waste will be $7.2 billion this year alone. Add in the multibillion-dollar reduction in corporate income taxes that would normally be paid, and a $10 billion 1981 public price tag for the slump looks like a conservative estimate.

Following Dr. Harvey Brenner, it can be predicted that this 600,000 group of unemployed, and their families, will experience a statistically significant increase in morbidity, social pathology, and death—all of which eludes the above $10 billion figure.

CONCLUSION

Though the U.S. auto industry is beset by stiff challenges and enormous problems—compounded by past and continuing hurtful U.S. government policies—it is hopefully clear from its long pre-1979 high-productivity, high-profit history that to permanently write off auto as a "sunset industry" would be grossly premature. The industry's resources and resourcefulness—and those of its workers—should not be underestimated. Given the right set of public policies, the key U.S.-based auto multinationals possess the internal capacity to restructure in order to effectively compete. What *is* in doubt is the level and geographic distribution of U.S. auto and auto-related manufacturing employment at the end of this restructuring process.

The key unknown is whether or not the United States will add its name to the list which already includes every other producing country and take steps to influence the investment and sourcing decisions of the auto multinationals to preserve domestic employment. In every other country which produces autos or aspires to do so, the need for such government policies is widely accepted. In the United States, by contrast, the desirability of taking steps to protect domestic auto-related employment is not a subject of national consensus, but rather is one of intense debate.

During the course of this seemingly interminable debate, auto workers have been squeezed ever-tighter in the jaws of the vise: imports surged while domestic production and employment plummeted; meanwhile, the domestic industry, operating under the assumption that its investment and sourcing decisions will be free of employment-oriented government constraints, lays unchallenged plans to eliminate more thousands of jobs.

What is most needed to achieve the necessary influence over the multinationals' investment and sourcing decisions is properly crafted North American content legislation. Phased in over a period of years, this would require all manufacturers who sell in high volume in this country to achieve a target level of domestic labor content in their product mix by a specified date. In view of the integration of U.S. and Canadian auto markets, the content requirements should be designed so as not to interfere with the flow of U.S.-Canadian automotive trade. Other refinements could be added, such as allowing higher foreign content to the extent that it is offset by automotive exports, but this is the basic proposal. Such legislation would have the effect of factoring a significant measure of concern over domestic employment into future auto company investment and sourcing decisions, regardless of the shifting sands of international competitive position.

Local content has numerous advantages over other forms of long-term domestic market protection. Rather than bar foreign manufacturers from access to our market, it would instead induce them to invest and source here, to provide jobs as a condition of access. We would get the benefit of their technology and methods; consumers would continue to have the opportunity to purchase their cars. Domestic manufacturers would continue to get a strong dose of much-needed competition. The benefits of international rationalization and sourcing would continue, provided there is a two-way street. Manufacturers would compete on the basis of product quality and efficiency—instead of on the basis of who can pay their workers less.

Some domestic manufacturers may not like this approach. They would rather not have the competition at their doorstep, and they are certainly not interested in employment-oriented constraints on their investment and sourcing decisions.

Given the extensive and growing worldwide interdependencies, it would be desirable for the details of local content to be determined through multilateral, international negotiations. This would take time, and once devised, could not be implemented quickly; hence there is an urgent, temporary need for a quicker fix. The U.S. manufacturers and beleaguered auto workers alike need a respite as the domestic industry completes its massive retooling and new-product programs.

It is ironic that those who argue against this course, primarily on grounds that the consumer comes first and that "cheapest is best," completely ignore the massive social cost of failure to take these steps—a cost which the general public, not the import-buying consumer, pays.

Trade restrictions, even in the form of domestic content requirements, admittedly are controversial. It is time to recognize, however, that there is really no such thing as "free trade" in motor vehicles and there has not been for some time. Virtually every other industrialized country, and every developing country which aspires to become a vehicle producer, has barriers to "free trade" much more formidable than ours. Apart from local content requirements, nothing else holds much hope of inducing the domestic industry to restructure in a way that will not cause massive losses of jobs. Nothing else offers significant hope of keeping within potentially manageable bounds the enormous dislocation which can be predicted to result from the interplay of a mature auto market, an uncertain energy outlook, international standardization of product, and rapid future productivity growth.

This conclusion, that local content requirements are vital if preservation of auto employment is to be assured, gives pause to many—on the left, right, and center of the political spectrum—who would otherwise be sympathetic, but adhere to a "free trade" philosophy. Yet it would seem that the burden is on those "free traders" who claim to care about employment to come forward with a coherent alternative plan for how else the millions of workers whose jobs depend on the auto industry can be readily reemployed, and regional catastrophe averted, if the industry continues its "hard landing."

Aside from adopting a trade policy which recognizes the need to prevent wholesale destruction of domestic employment, the government could also do a great deal to ease the industry's current plight by reversing the monetary policies which played so significant and unfortunate a role in creating it. Auto workers have been front-line victims of the Federal Reserve Board's so-called anti-inflation fight.

Even if preservation of auto employment is elevated to a much higher rung on the government's policy ladder, there will still be the potential for substantial dislocation and job loss in the auto industry in the months and years ahead. It would be highly desirable for government to plan now to predict and mitigate those dislocations, by targeted stimulation of job-creating non-automotive investment and a comprehensive labor market policy including income maintenance, retraining, job-search assistance, and the like. Instead, we face cutbacks in the already inadequate programs in these and other areas. To beleaguered auto workers, the government's response to date resembles that of a fire fighter who refuses to extinguish the flames in a burning building, and who then—when the people inside are forced to jump—blames the victims for the fire and abruptly removes the net.

In the long run, in order to be effective, industrial policy requires a coherence which only comprehensive economic planning can provide. Unfortunately, this insight will give scant comfort to the thousands of auto workers who are still unemployed more than two years after the onset of the current disastrous slump.

NOTES

1. U.S. Congress, Senate, Committee on Banking, Housing and Urban Affairs, Subcommittee on Economic Stabilization, *The Effect of Expanding Japanese Automobile Imports on the Domestic Economy*, Hearing, 96th Cong., 2nd sess., April 3, 1980, Statement of William J. Abernathy, Harvard University Business School, pp. 96-97.
2. Gerald Bloomfield, *The World Automotive Industry* (North Pomfret, VT: David & Charles Inc., 1978), pp. 18-20.
3. Motor Vehicle Manufacturers Association, *MVMA Motor Vehicle Facts and Figures, '81* (Detroit, MVMA, 1981), p. 65.

4. VW, Toyota, Nissan, Fiat, Renault, British Leyland, Citroen, and Peugeot.
5. Ward's Communications, Inc., *Ward's Automotive Yearbook*, 42nd ed., 1980 (Detroit: Ward's, 1980), p. 97.
6. *Wall Street Journal*, March 20, 1981, p. 24.
7. *Harvard Business Review*, January/February 1981, p. 77.
8. *Forbes*, March 16, 1981, p. 50.
9. The other top producers in descending order were USA, Japan, W. Germany, France, USSR, Italy, Canada, UK, and Spain. (Brazil ranked barely above Spain.)
10. Comptroller General of the United States, *United States-Japan Trade: Issues and Problems*, September 21, 1979, Chapter 3, Automotive Trade, pp. 38-58; U.S. Congress, House, Committee on Ways and Means, Subcommittee on Trade, *Auto Situation: 1980*, Report, 96th Cong., 2nd sess., June 6, 1980, Appendix C, pp. 78-80.
11. Bloomfield, p. 228.
12. U.S. International Trade Commission, *Certain Motor Vehicles and Certain Chassis and Bodies Therefor: Investigation No. TA-201-44*; Prehearing Report to the Commission and Parties, September 10, 1980, p. A-27.

Part II:

Government Intervention on Behalf of Troubled Industry

4

Lessons from the Maritime Aid Program

Gerald R. Jantscher*

The United States merchant marine and shipbuilding industry have received federal aid longer than any other U.S. industries. And they have received aid in more diverse forms than all but a few other industries. In a review of government assistance to troubled industries, there ought to be lessons that can be drawn or observations that can be made from the extensive history of federal aid to U.S. ship operators and shipbuilders. Has assistance helped make them more efficient? If so, which forms of assistance have been most effective? If assistance has not been effective, why hasn't it? What mistakes in the program ought to be avoided in similar programs of assistance to other industries?

In the first section of this chapter, the various aids that are given to the maritime industries are described. Estimates of the recent cost of these aids are also presented. In the second section, we consider how effective these aids have been in creating modern, competitive industries and whether there is any prospect that assistance will one day be unnecessary. In the last section, we consider some of the reasons why the assistance program has not been more effective, what lessons may be learned from its history that will help us design better assistance programs for other troubled industries, and what changes to the program might improve its effectiveness.

FORMS OF FEDERAL AID TO THE MARITIME INDUSTRIES AND THEIR COST

Government assistance to the U.S. merchant marine and shipbuilding industry began early in the very first Congress, with the passage of an act that set

* Principal Tax Policy Analyst, U.S. General Accounting Office, Washington, D.C. None of the opinions expressed in this chapter should be attributed to the U.S. General Accounting Office or to its officers or other staff members.

preferential duties on imports arriving to this country in the ships of U.S. citizens. During the next several years, other acts placed higher tonnage duties on foreign vessels entering U.S. ports than on U.S. vessels and excluded foreign vessels from the U.S. coasting trades. The principal form of aid to the shipbuilding industry during these years was the establishment by law of a protected market for its product—the U.S. merchant marine. U.S. registry and the privileges it conferred were restricted to vessels built in this country.

Some of these earliest aids have lasted to the present day. Other important aids were added in the 1930s. All of them can be gathered into three classes: (1) direct subsidies to selected shipbuilders and ship operators, including subsidies that are administered through the federal tax system; (2) indirect subsidies to shipbuilders or ship operators through the provision of goods or services at below-market prices, either directly to the shipbuilders or ship operators or to the suppliers of goods or services to the industries; and (3) the reservation by law of certain markets to U.S. shipbuilders and ship operators. Other federal government activities that assist the shipping industry also assist its foreign competitors—for example, keeping channels free from obstruction and maintaining navigational aids—and are better regarded as aids to U.S. commerce generally than to the U.S. shipping industry in particular.

Direct Subsidies

The direct subsidies to the maritime industries are among the most valuable aids that these industries receive. Two subsidies bulk largest in this group: operating-differential subsidies to ship operators and construction-differential subsidies to shipbuilders. Both were established by the Merchant Marine Act of 1936, and except for a period during the Second World War when they were suspended, both have been in effect for four and a half decades.

Operating-Differential Subsidy. The largest single class of federal expenditures for the maritime industries is the operating-differential subsidies—operating subsidies, for short—that are paid to selected U.S. steamship lines and bulk operators in service in U.S. foreign commerce. The subsidies are intended to maintain in operation a fleet of privately owned U.S.–built and U.S.–registered vessels, manned exclusively by U.S. citizens.

The introduction of subsidies that are paid directly to ship operators and shipbuilders was the principal innovation in the Merchant Marine Act of 1936. The act itself was the outcome of the experience of a decade and a half, during which the federal government attempted without success to foster the growth and prosperity of a competitive U.S. merchant marine to serve the nation's foreign commerce. The Merchant Marine Act of 1928 had provided public subsidies to private shipping lines through the award of lucrative mail contracts. But the program failed, apparently because contracts were awarded without regard to the needs of U.S. shippers or the postal service, and also because it was tainted by scandal. The failure of the program precipitated a debate over whether the government should support a privately owned fleet or acquire and operate its own. In the end, Congress opted for private ownership, supported by a program of public subsidies openly provided and protected by safeguards against waste and misappropriation.

The most important features of the operating-differential subsidy as established by the 1936 act have not changed. The word "differential" in its name refers to the principle of setting the size of the subsidy equal to the difference between the subsidized U.S. operator's costs and the lower costs of a foreign competitor. In light of the unsavory experience with the 1928 program, it no doubt seemed attractive to Congress to set the subsidy in this manner. A subsidy set equal to the difference in costs must have seemed safe against extravagance. Operators with subsidy contracts would receive only enough aid to bring their costs down to those of their competitors. Commercial success would depend thereafter on their own efforts.

The operating-differential subsidy program is administered by the Maritime Administration in the Department of Transportation. This agency is responsible for calculating the subsidy to be paid to the operator. It does so by choosing a representative foreign flag operator in the same trade as the subsidized operator and estimating its costs. The statute specifies which costs may be considered; currently they are the costs of shipboard wages (including all fringe benefits), insurance, maintenance and repairs not compensated by insurance, and the meals served to officers and crews on certain vessels. From its estimates of the costs of the foreign operator and its data on the costs of the U.S. operator, the Maritime Administration is able to calculate the subsidy that is payable to the U.S. operator.[1]

Of the subsidizable costs, payrolls are by far the largest, and nearly all of the operating subsidy that is paid to U.S. operators is due to their higher wage costs. Nearly 90 percent of current operating subsidies are paid in respect of higher payroll costs on U.S. vessels. U.S. seamen earn much higher wages than their foreign counterparts—an average of four times as much in the subsidized liner trades—and the wage subsidy has recently paid three-quarters of their earnings.

The 1936 legislation restricted the payment of operating subsidies to selected U.S. liner operators providing service on "essential" trade routes in U.S. foreign commerce.[2] The definition and identification of "essential" trade routes was left to the Maritime Administration. In practice every route on which a substantial volume of foreign commerce moves to or from this country has been designated an essential trade route. The Maritime Administration has entered into long-term contracts with a number of U.S. liner firms (currently eight) to provide regular service on many, but not all, of these essential trade routes, in return for which the operators are provided with operating subsidies.

The Merchant Marine Act of 1970 amended the 1936 act to permit operating subsidies to be awarded to bulk operators (operators of vessels carrying commodities in bulk), which are typically engaged by the voyage to carry cargo wherever the shipper directs. During the 1970s a large number of U.S. shipowners received operating subsidies to carry grain to the Soviet Union. Nevertheless, the great majority of operating subsidies have been and continue to be paid to liner operators for service in the liner trades.

Operating subsidies have cost the federal government a great deal of money, especially since the early 1960s. Between 1936 and the end of fiscal year 1980, $5,824 million was expended in operating subsidy payments. The bulk of this sum—all but about $985 million—has been spent since 1960; half the total has been spent in just the last ten years. For the past several years, operating subsidy payments have totaled, in round numbers, $300 million a year. By 1982 they are due to exceed $400 million a year.

Construction-Differential Subsidy. The second subsidy established by the 1936 act is the construction-differential subsidy to U.S. shipbuilders. Construction subsidies are paid to shipbuilders for the construction of new ships or reconstruction or reconditioning of old ones.[3] The subsidy is intended to lower the cost of U.S.-built ships to parity with the cost of foreign-built ships. As in the name of the operating subsidy, the word "differential" refers to the principle of setting the subsidy equal to the difference between U.S. and foreign costs. In the case of the construction subsidy, however, it is not the difference between the U.S. shipbuilder's costs and the costs of a foreign shipbuilder, as estimated by the Maritime Administration, that is covered by the subsidy. Instead, the subsidy is set equal to the difference between the *price* of a new vessel from a U.S. shipyard and the estimated price of a similar new vessel from a foreign yard. This marks a slight but by no means unimportant difference from the operating subsidy program. In the operating subsidy program, the Maritime Administration is subsidizing the cost of factor inputs; in the construction subsidy program, it is subsidizing the sale of outputs.

U.S. shipyards are high-cost producers of ships, and have not been competitive with foreign shipyards, except perhaps in the construction of certain specialized vessels, since the days of wooden ships. For much of the post–World War II period, U.S. shipyards have been unable to build oceangoing cargo ships for less than twice the cost of similar ships from foreign yards. During most of the 1960s, for example, construction subsidy payments equalled or exceeded 50 percent of the cost of construction. Innovations introduced in the Merchant Marine Act of 1970 promised to reduce the subsidy in time to 35 percent, and in fact, during the early 1970s, subsidy rates gradually declined. By the middle of the decade, however, it was clear that whatever advantage U.S. shipbuilders had gained on foreign yards could not be maintained, and for the last several years construction subsidy rates have returned to about 50 percent.

Construction subsidies are available for ships that will be operated under the U.S. flag in the nation's essential foreign commerce. Ships built with subsidy may not be used in the protected domestic trades, such as the oil trade between Alaska and the west coast. Until 1970 the Maritime Administration used its limited construction subsidy funds to assist the lines receiving operating subsidies to replace their vessels periodically as they were obliged to do by their operating subsidy contracts. Following the passage of the Merchant Marine Act of 1970, the Maritime Administration began to allocate much of its construction subsidy funds to the building of bulk carriers and tankers. Recently a variety of vessels has been built with subsidies, including vessels for the liner trades, others for the dry bulk trades, and some tankers and liquefied natural gas carriers.

Between 1936 and the end of fiscal year 1980, construction subsidy expenditures amounted to $3,338 million. Like operating subsidy expenditures, the larger part of this amount has been spent only recently—all but $454 million since 1960 and more than $1 billion since 1975. Construction subsidies have recently totaled about $200 million per year.

In summary, operating subsidy and construction subsidy payments have totaled more than $9 billion since the first payments were authorized by the Merchant Marine Act of 1936. Lately the two programs have been funded at a level of about a half billion dollars annually.

Tax Expenditures for the Merchant Marine. The U.S. merchant marine is also the beneficiary of a unique tax expenditure. Shipowners may establish so-called capital construction funds and deposit earnings from their shipping operations in them. Later they may withdraw sums to buy new ships. Deposits of earnings are deductible from shipowners' income for income tax purposes. Earnings on deposits already in the funds are also nontaxable. Ultimately, income tax may have to be paid on both, however, through a reduction in the depreciation deductions that shipowners may claim on the vessels they buy with moneys from these funds. Meanwhile they have enjoyed the substantial benefit of postponing the payment of income tax for a period of years. The most recent estimate of the cost of this assistance to the federal treasury placed the amount at around $75 million a year.

Indirect Subsidies

Several smaller government programs provide indirect subsidies to the maritime industries. The Maritime Administration sponsors research and development programs that are intended to enhance the competitiveness of the two industries. It engages in market development for U.S. ship operators by approaching shippers on the operators' behalf and urging them to patronize U.S. carriers. The federal government operates the U.S. Merchant Marine Academy at Kings Point, N.Y., for the purpose of training officers for the U.S. commercial fleet and helps support six similar state maritime schools. Construction loans and mortgages on U.S.–built ships for the U.S. merchant marine may be guaranteed against default by the Maritime Administration. The Maritime Administration also offers U.S. shipowners insurance against war loss or damage when commercial insurance is not available. In addition, until 1982 the U.S. Public Health Service operated hospitals and clinics that provided health care services to certain qualifying groups of beneficiaries, the largest of which was American merchant seamen.

Cabotage and Cargo Preference

Another important aid that the federal government gives the U.S. maritime industries is access to protected markets, that is, markets from which foreign competitors are by law excluded. This was one of the earliest forms of federal assistance to these industries, and even after the direct subsidies were initiated, it continued to be among the most important. The cabotage laws of the United States reserve the oceanborne commerce between U.S. ports to U.S. flag, U.S.–built vessels. At one time the U.S. domestic trades supported a sizable volume of commerce, giving employment to large numbers of ships and seamen, many more than were engaged in the nation's foreign commerce. The domestic trades have declined, however, and for much of the post–World War II period have not supported as large a U.S. merchant fleet as the nation's foreign trades. Today most of the domestic oceangoing fleet is employed carrying oil from the Gulf coast to Middle Atlantic ports and from Alaska to the west coast. In view of the minuscule fraction of oil imports that are brought to this country in U.S. flag vessels, it is plausible to suppose that the U.S. tanker fleet is able to operate in these trades only because foreign tankers are barred from them.

The cargo preference laws reserve a portion of the nation's foreign commerce to U.S. flag, U.S.–built vessels. The principal cargo preference law is the Cargo Preference Act of 1954, which reserves 50 percent of so-called government-impelled cargoes to the U.S. merchant marine. These cargoes include goods bought by the government for its own account, goods donated to agencies or nations overseas, and goods that are touched in some other way by the federal government's participation in their financing or sale. Examples include foreign aid cargoes, Food-for-Peace shipments of U.S. commodities, U.S. exports financed by the U.S. Export-Import Bank, and military goods on their way to foreign buyers. Military cargoes for U.S. forces overseas have been reserved in their entirety to U.S. flag vessels since 1904 by act of Congress. The majority of preference cargoes are exports; shipments of oil for the U.S. Strategic Petroleum Reserve are the most notable example of preference imports.

Only a small fraction of the cargoes that move in U.S. foreign trade are subject to the cargo preference laws. In the past, however, the fraction was larger and its reservation to U.S. carriers was a valuable aid to the U.S. maritime industries. Estimates of its value are not routinely prepared, but several years ago I prepared one for much of the post–World War II period.[4] Assistance to the shipowning industry was measured as the difference between the cost of shipping preference cargoes aboard high-cost U.S. flag vessels and the cost of shipping them aboard low-cost foreign ships. Between 1952 and 1972, the movement of military cargoes aboard privately owned U.S. flag vessels added around $3.8 billion to Department of Defense shipping costs, much of it, of course, during the conflict in Vietnam. The cost of shipping Food-for-Peace cargoes during the same period was increased by around $1 billion through the required use of U.S. flag ships. Foreign aid shipments under the programs of the Agency for International Development and its predecessor agencies cost about $600 million more between 1948 and 1970 by reason of the cargo preference laws. Thus, by the early 1970s the assistance received by the U.S. merchant fleet through the cargo preference laws during the postwar period had exceeded $5 billion, more than the sums provided during the same period as operating subsidies. Since then the amount of assistance that the fleet receives from cargo preference has declined, and today the operating subsidy program presumably is delivering more aid.

The full costs of cabotage are more difficult to determine than the costs of cargo preference. The additional cost of shipping cargoes in U.S. flag, U.S.-built vessels instead of in cheaper foreign carriers has no doubt diverted many shipments to truck or rail or even air. Or no shipment may take place and entire markets may be lost to certain products. Lumber producers in the Pacific Northwest maintain that because they must use U.S. flag vessels to transport their products to the U.S. east coast, Canadian producers in British Columbia, who use foreign ships, have displaced them from east coast markets. As a result, no U.S. lumber moves between the coasts.[5] These extra costs to shippers and consumers—the indirect costs of the cabotage laws—are practically impossible to measure, but should not on that account be overlooked or neglected. They are probably sizable.

Even the direct costs of cabotage cannot be measured precisely, but some idea of their magnitude can be gained. In 1975, I attempted to estimate them for much of the postwar period.[6] One of the direct costs of cabotage is the cost of the requirement that vessels serving the domestic trades must be built in U.S. shipyards. Between 1950 and 1970 this restriction added between $900 million and $1 billion to the cost of new vessels and conversion of old ones for the U.S. domestic fleet. No figures are available for the period since 1970, but in view of the many vessels that have been built to carry Alaskan oil to the U.S. west coast, it would be reasonable to add many hundreds of millions of dollars to these numbers.

The other direct cost of cabotage is the extra cost of operating vessels in the domestic trades under the U.S. flag. I calculated that between 1950 and 1970, this cost probably exceeded $2 billion. No estimates are available for the period since 1970.

ACCOMPLISHMENTS OF THE AID PROGRAM

By one test, the federal aid program to the maritime industries has been a success. It has helped keep in being a sizable merchant fleet manned by U.S. citizens that carries a modest fraction of the goods that move in U.S. ocean-borne foreign commerce. I have argued elsewhere that the proper justification for public assistance to the shipping and shipbuilding industries is the contribution they make to the nation's security.[7] It is important to keep this objective in mind when appraising the program and its accomplishments, because the goal dictates the measuring stick. If shipping and shipbuilding really are essential to national security, we should be willing to tolerate more waste—in the strict economic sense—in a program of assistance to preserve these industries than if the purpose of the program was to assist a troubled industry to renew itself and become competitive in world markets. A program that failed to create a viable, self-sufficient industry might still be deemed successful if it added appreciably to national security.

Nevertheless, in this discussion I shall focus on the purely commercial accomplishments of the assistance program. In a conference dealing with the revitalization of American industries and having as one purpose the identification of effective policies for accomplishing this goal, success must be measured by the degree to which the program has created efficient, competitive industries. Not even as rich a nation as ours can be undiscriminating in its support of money-losing industries on national security grounds. In each case, the argument for doing so must be judged on its own merits.

It is a regrettable fact that despite the provision of well over $10 billion of public assistance to the U.S. shipping and shipbuilding industries since the Second World War, they have not been transformed into vigorous, efficient competitors in world markets. Consider the shipbuilding industry first. During the 1960s, construction-differential subsidies regularly amounted to half or more of the cost of new vessels from U.S. shipyards, meaning that the cost of building the ships here was at least double the cost of building them abroad. The Merchant Marine Act of 1970 inaugurated a multibillion-dollar ship-construction program that was intended to add 300 vessels to the U.S. merchant marine over the next ten years. Anticipating criticism of the cost of the program, officials of the Maritime Administration stressed that innovations in the construction subsidy program that were included in the same legislation would increase the efficiency of U.S. yards and enable construction subsidies to be reduced as the prices of U.S.-built vessels fell. Officials emphasized especially the savings to be realized from the serial construction of large numbers of similar vessels over a period of years. As a result, although the legal limits on the size of construction subsidies were not lowered, the 1970 act did establish a series of increasing productivity goals, corresponding to reduced subsidy rates, to take effect over the next five years. It was expected that by 1976 construction subsidies would not exceed 35 percent of the cost of a new vessel.

Shipbuilders were able to meet these goals for the first several years of the program, aided no doubt by a weakening U.S. dollar that made foreign ships more costly for Americans. Gradually, however, it became clear that the optimistic goals that had been set in 1970 could not be realized. By 1976 it was apparent both that the 300-ship program was dead and that U.S. shipbuilders could not maintain their improved position vis-à-vis foreign shipyards. Construction subsidy rates increased, and in fiscal year 1979 they ranged between 48.5 and 49.5 percent, about where they had been a decade before.

In addition to the size of construction subsidies, other indicators are available that show how noncompetitive U.S. shipbuilders continue to be after so many years of receiving public assistance. Not one oceangoing merchant vessel has been built in this country for foreign registry in nearly two decades. Delivery times from U.S. yards are much longer than they are from foreign yards. For reasons that have never been well explained, Americans are simply not competitive with foreigners in shipbuilding, and decades of public assistance to the industry have not altered this fact. Or is it possible that the assistance itself has helped make the industry noncompetitive? It may be germane to note that in another field of enterprise closely related to shipbuilding, the construction of deep-sea drilling rigs, American builders are intensely competitive with foreign producers, despite the fact that they receive no federal aid for their efforts.

The story is similar with the merchant marine—but also different in a few important respects. The chief difference is that the U.S. merchant marine contains one outstanding success story, a liner company that pioneered the development of containerized shipping and capitalized upon its early successes to become a strong and secure operator. Sea-Land Service is one of the leading liner companies in the world, have attained this position in less than a quarter of a century. Its ships are registered under the United States flag and are crewed by U.S. citizens, the same high-cost labor that other U.S. operators use. Yet the remarkable fact is that Sea-Land has achieved its preeminence without the benefit of any operating subsidies. It did receive public assistance of another kind early in its life. Sea-Land began its operations in the 1950s when it introduced containerized shipping between the U.S. mainland and Puerto Rico. In this trade it benefited from the absence of low-cost foreign competition, excluded by the cabotage laws. When it later expanded its operations into the foreign trades, it benefited from the reservation of preference cargoes to U.S. flag vessels. It is questionable, however, whether the preference trade was crucial to the line's success. By the early 1970s Sea-Land had added new foreign-built vessels to its fleet. Foreign-built vessels are disqualified from carrying preference cargoes until three years after their registration under the U.S. flag. Nevertheless, Sea-Land has continued to prosper as a result of its high productivity.

The record of the rest of the U.S. oceangoing merchant marine is much less distinguished. Despite receiving operating subsidies, two U.S. steamship lines recently failed and a third, in weakened condition, was absorbed by another. Other companies are stronger, and some might even be able to carry on if their subsidies were terminated; but the condition of the operators as a whole is no testimony to the invigorating effects of public assistance. If the program were ended, the U.S. merchant marine would surely shrink and U.S. flag participation in the carriage of our commerce would doubtless decline.

Table 4.1 shows U.S. flag participation in the nation's foreign trade for selected years since the Second World War. The figures express the fraction of commercial cargoes, both by weight and by value, that move each year in U.S. bottoms. Whichever series one favors—weight or value—the evidence is plain that the subsidy program has not prevented the share of commerce that moves in U.S. ships from falling. Leaving aside the separate question of whether the decline has had unwelcome consequences, at least it is clear that the

Table 4.1. Percent Share of U.S. Flag Cargo Vessels in U.S. Oceanborne Foreign Trade, by Weight and Value, Selected Years, 1947-79

Measure	1947	1951	1956	1960	1964	1968	1972	1976	1979
By value	n.a.	n.a.	33.8	26.4	25.8	20.7	18.4	17.8	14.7
By weight	57.6	39.8	20.7	11.1	9.2	6.0	4.6	4.8	4.2

SOURCE: *Annual Report of the Maritime Administration for Fiscal Year 1970*, pp. 27-28; *Annual Report of the Maritime Administration for Fiscal Year 1980*, p. 19.
n.a. = not available.

operating subsidy program has not succeeded in arresting the decline, which it was intended to do.[8]

Other indices of prosperity could be examined, such as the number of jobs in the merchant marine, the health of the domestic fleet, which the cabotage laws protect from foreign competition, or the number of ships in the subsidized merchant marine. All would show the same trends. The commercial accomplishments of the federal aid program are so meager that they afford only a pretense for its continuation. The real justification for assistance to these industries must be based on their contribution to national security; otherwise, it would be folly to persist in such waste.

LESSONS TO BE LEARNED FROM THE FEDERAL AID PROGRAM

What instruction do we gain from a review of the federal aid program to the maritime industries? Are there lessons to be learned that may guide policy-making in far-off fields? The disappointing conclusion in the preceding section was that the U.S. maritime industries have few or no commercial achievements to their credit that are attributable to the aid program; that two centuries of assistance in one form or another, including four decades during which sizable amounts of aid have been given in a diversity of forms, have failed to create an efficient, competitive merchant marine or shipbuilding industry. Might one be pardoned for abbreviating this section and deciding that the only certain lesson from this experience is that the assistance that was given doesn't work? Even if one is dissatisfied with so narrow a conclusion, the nearly total commercial failure of the program makes it very difficult to extract positive lessons from its history instead of purely negative ones: to decide, that is, what instruments work best rather than what doesn't work. In particular, there is scarcely any basis for judging the different forms of federal aid and concluding, for instance, that regulatory assistance is more or less effective than direct subsidies. All apparently are equally ineffective.

In my opinion, the history of the aid program does teach a few useful lessons, even if it fails to answer other questions. I begin my discussion of these with the most particular lesson and continue to more general ones.

Subsidizing Labor Costs

Disinterested observers who have examined the operating subsidy program have criticized it for discouraging operators from striving after production economies. It may even be argued that the subsidy actually promotes *in*efficiency. This tendency arises from the manner in which the subsidy is calculated.

The operating subsidy lowers the cost of shipboard labor on the vessels of subsidized operators to the cost of labor aboard the vessels of their foreign competitors. As a result, while the operators have every incentive to use whatever labor they hire as productively as possible, they have no incentive to economize on the amount of that labor, since any dollar saved in payroll costs ultimately means a dollar less received in subsidy, not a dollar added to profits. In other words, the marginal cost of additional labor—or marginal saving from employing less labor—is zero. Elsewhere in the U.S. economy, high labor costs have spurred capital investment and promoted capital-intensive methods of production, with consequent improvements in productivity. Subsidized operators are immune against the incentives that these costs create, which may explain why their economic performance has been so disappointing.

In addition to discouraging operators from economizing on labor, the design of the operating subsidy has helped boost unit labor costs by encouraging shipboard labor unions to vigorously press the operators for high wages and generous fringe benefits. For the reasons already explained, management has little incentive to resist labor's pressure, since the subsidy it receives is equal to the difference between U.S. shipboard labor costs and foreign labor costs. The latter are fixed, no matter what terms labor and management in this country agree on; therefore, the additional payroll costs resulting from a generous settlement are borne in toto by the federal government. The same pressure has also helped keep manning levels higher aboard U.S. vessels than aboard competing foreign ships, despite high unit costs of U.S. labor.

The Maritime Administration has attempted to oppose these effects by administrative measures. The 1936 act contains language empowering the agency to disregard operators' costs that are excessive or unreasonable, and once, late in the 1960s, it attempted to do so after the shipboard unions had won particularly lucrative contracts from the operators. Although it had little success, other pressures were brought to bear upon both parties to moderate the growth of wages. The 1970 act included a provision to limit the rate of increase of subsidizable wage costs; and although the limit was generous, it is a fact that during the 1970s labor costs increased less rapidly than they had before. This improvement—as the federal government must regard it—surely had something to do as well with the decline in the number of shipboard jobs in the U.S. merchant marine as the fleet shrank. It has been a buyer's market for labor services in the U.S. merchant marine during the 1970s, as surely as it was a seller's market during the second half of the 1960s when extra shipping was needed during the Vietnam War.

Efforts by the Maritime Administration to obtain reductions in crew sizes have had some effect. Manning levels have declined since the 1960s, but remain higher than those aboard foreign flag vessels or the levels that U.S.

Coast Guard safety regulations require. Crews of thirty-three or thirty-four men are carried by some new U.S. vessels that would sail with only twenty-eight men if registered abroad.

The lesson to be drawn from this part of the maritime aid program is that industries should not be aided by subsidizing one factor input.[9] The design of the operating subsidy has encouraged a waste of labor in the U.S. merchant fleet and weakened incentives for operators to increase productivity by substituting capital for labor. Legislative admonitions to the Maritime Administration to prod subsidy recipients to be more efficient have not been very effective. A new method of subsidizing shipping operations is needed that contains no direct link between the size of the subsidy and an operator's costs.

Several alternatives to the present system merit consideration. In the most radical departure from current practice, subsidies might be awarded by competitive bidding. The government could entertain offers from many operators to provide a specified frequency of service on certain routes in return for a federal payment. The subsidy contract would be awarded to the operator who agreed to provide the service most cheaply. A less radical alternative would make the subsidy a variable payment that depended on some measure of the operator's output; for example, ton-miles of cargo carried. These and other methods of subsidizing shipping operations must be explored if we desire to supplant the present system, not simply discard it.

Forcing One Weak Industry to Help Another

A second observation that is prompted by a review of the maritime aid program is that the burden of supporting one weak industry should never be thrust upon another weak one. If it is, efforts to help the second industry may be nullified, and in the end both industries may suffer. Assistance to the U.S. shipbuilding industry has been funneled through the U.S. merchant marine by a combination of legislative and contractual requirements that force shipowners to patronize domestic yards. For nearly a century and a quarter after 1789, only U.S.–built ships were eligible for the privilege of U.S. registry. In 1912 this restriction was removed for ships serving the nation's foreign commerce, but retained for the then much larger fleet serving the domestic trades. To this day, the cabotage laws continue to exclude foreign-built ships from the domestic trades. Foreign-built ships may engage in the nation's foreign trade, but may not be employed by contractors receiving operating subsidies. Subsidized operations may only be conducted with U.S.–built vessels. Even the preference cargo system favors domestic yards, with its ban upon the carriage of many preference cargoes in foreign-built vessels until they have been documented for three years under U.S. registry.

A captive market has thus been created for the product of the U.S. ship-building industry. Observation suggests that the ills of the U.S. merchant marine are traceable in part—perhaps in large part—to the shipowners' inability to buy their capital inputs in a wider market, as their competitors may do. The decline of the domestic fleet in particular must have been greatly aggravated by the ban upon purchases from foreign builders. The high-priced products of U.S. yards made domestic shipping services much dearer than they would otherwise have been and helped make ocean carriage an unattractive alternative to rail or highway transport. In the case of service to Alaska and Hawaii, much or all of the additional cost of transportation presumably could be passed on to the residents of those states, since no practical alternative to ocean transport exists for the carriage of many goods. But ultimately substitutes for costly U.S. goods—made costly in part by the high price of U.S. ships—can be found even in these markets in the form of goods from foreign producers, often carried to market in foreign ships. It would be helpful to know, for example, how much of the success of Japanese automobile manufacturers in the Hawaiian market has been due to the high cost of building ships in U.S. yards. As foreign goods displace U.S. goods, the domestic fleet carries a dwindling share of the goods that move to these offshore markets.

In principle, the availability of construction-differential subsidies to ship-owners with operating subsidy contracts should exactly offset their disad-vantage from having to patronize U.S. yards. The construction subsidy is supposed to equal the excess of the actual U.S. price of a ship over the estimated foreign price of the same vessel. American operators complain, however, that the subsidies are too small and that the price they pay net of subsidy remains higher than what they would pay for a similar vessel built abroad. Perhaps they exaggerate: it is clearly in their interest to do all they can to obtain as large a construction subsidy as possible. On the other hand, the Maritime Administration is also under pressure to be thrifty with its funds. And it has the upper hand over the operators, who must replace their ships with new U.S.-built vessels or default on their operating subsidy con-tracts.

On balance, and judging from evidence that has been submitted to Con-gress, one must conclude that construction subsidies are currently inade-quate: that the difference between the U.S. and foreign prices of new vessels exceeds the maximum subsidy—half the U.S. price—that may now be awarded. Thus, in consequence of the operating and construction subsidy programs, subsidized operators face *lower* labor prices and *higher* capital prices than they would otherwise face—a bizarre distortion of factor prices that practi-cally guarantees depressed productivity. It is scarcely necessary to seek further for an explanation of this industry's ills.

But price is not all. Even if the construction subsidy were perfectly administered and it exactly offset the extra cost of the U.S.-built vessel, the patronage requirement would still be burdensome. The U.S. commercial shipbuilding industry is rather smaller than those of other nations, and domestic suppliers to the industry are few. The buyer who must patronize a U.S. yard often finds that none can offer early delivery. His competitor overseas can order a ship from a foreign yard and specify machinery and equipment from different sources. The stringent "buy American" provisions in U.S. law require American buyers to choose from the offerings of U.S. producers. These tend to be limited in number and variety owing to the small size of the U.S. market. The lack of competition among suppliers also helps keep prices high.

The merchant marine has been burdened by its obligation to support the domestic shipbuilding industry. Assistance to the two industries should be divided by permitting U.S. operators to buy their capital equipment wherever commercial considerations dictate. If U.S. shipbuilders have to be aided, they should be aided directly, not through the creation of a captive market.

Demoralizing Effects of Assistance

The third lesson that I suggest may be learned from a review of this program is less scientific than the others—or at least less capable of being verified; but if valid, it may contain the most important implications of the three for other aid programs. No one, I believe, can study the assistance that the federal government gives to the nation's maritime industries without being struck by the demoralizing effects of the program on its recipients. Perhaps these are the inevitable product of an aid program that asks so little of its beneficiaries and that promises everlasting assistance. If so, certain features to be discussed below should be included in similar programs to suppress those effects before they arise.

The acute sense of dependence on government assistance that the aid program has fostered has caused the maritime industries to spend too much of their energies on socially unproductive activities. A small industry has been established in Washington whose sole purpose seems to be to ensure that the flow of aid continues unabated. Since the mid-1960s, representatives of maritime interests have vigorously pressed the federal government for a series of actions that at a minimum would maintain assistance to the industries at its customary level or, in several cases, dramatically augment it. The success or failure of the industries' pleadings is beside the point here. What is censurable is the waste of effort and attention that has been lavished on this activity, as well as the mistaken priorities that it indicates. It has also entangled the two industries in the process of political decision making, prompted numerous allegations of impropriety, led to several indictments, trials, and convictions of public officials and industry personnel, and threatened to discredit the entire aid program.

The maritime industries have become highly defensive about the public aid they receive. This has had the unfortunate consequence of stimulating them to present exaggerated or frankly spurious claims in support of the aid program. The authentic justification for the program—its contribution to national security—has often been neglected in favor of commercial or economic arguments on its behalf. I have discussed these elsewhere and explained why they lack substance.[10] Nevertheless, the supporters of the program persist in presenting them, perhaps in the conviction that a continuing aid program of this magnitude is better safeguarded the more numerous and diverse are the arguments they offer. It is clear that many of these arguments are solemnly believed by their exponents, some of whom now take federal assistance for granted, having abandoned hope that their industries can ever be self-supporting. This is a deeply unhealthy attitude that can only impede progress toward the goal of creating an efficient, competitive industry, the fault for which I locate in nearly two centuries of public assistance.

Perhaps national security considerations require us to indefinitely subsidize the U.S. merchant marine; but if we undertake to subsidize other industries for economic or commercial reasons, the history of the maritime program suggests that the provision of aid should be contingent upon the industry's making demonstrable progress toward self-sufficiency. The government should establish performance goals that the industry must meet if assistance is to continue. For example, goals might be established to be reached by the third, fifth, and seventh years of the program, each more ambitious than the last and marking a further improvement in the performance of the industry. If any goal is not met, the aid program should be terminated, either at once or within a year or two.

Whatever interim performance goals may be established, it should be made clear at the outset of the program that assistance will be given for a limited time only, say five years or ten. If this promise is kept, the industry will have little time to become accustomed to constant assistance from the federal government and the danger of its becoming dependent on federal aid will be lessened.

These recommendations presuppose the necessary resolution among policymakers to withdraw assistance from a vulnerable industry if the aid program fails. If the will to do so is lacking, we risk creating crippled industries, increasingly dependent on growing subsidies, less and less efficient, requiring more protection from competitors, and placing an increasing burden on the rest of the economy.

NOTES

1. For a more detailed explanation of how the operating subsidy is calculated, see Allen R. Ferguson and others, *The Economic Value of the United States Merchant Marine* (Evanston, Ill.: Northwestern University, Transportation Center, 1961), pp. 45-55.
2. Liners serve as common carriers, sailing along fixed routes on regular schedules and accepting cargoes from many different shippers for delivery at ports along their routes.
3. The bulk of construction subsidies—well over 90 percent of the total—has been paid in respect of new construction.
4. See Gerald R. Jantscher, *Bread upon the Waters: Federal Aids to the Maritime Industries* (Washington, D.C.: Brookings Institution, 1975), pp. 80-98.
5. Concerning this case, see "Jones Act Waiver to Allow Foreign-Flag Vessels to Carry West Coast Forest Products," a hearing held on June 23, 1981, in *Merchant Marine Miscellaneous—Part 2*, Hearings before the Subcommittee on Merchant Marine of the House Committee on Merchant Marine and Fisheries, 97 Cong., 1st sess. (1982).
6. Jantscher, *Bread upon the Waters*, pp. 49-52.
7. See, e.g., ibid., p. 142.
8. A finer classification than appears in table 4.1 would show that U.S. flag participation has declined in all classes of foreign trade: the liner trade, dry bulk trade, and tanker trade. Most operating subsidies are paid to liner operators, but even U.S. liner operators are now carrying a smaller share of the nation's commerce that moves in liners than they did five, ten, or twenty years ago.
9. Readers may note that this recommendation is at variance with the current tendency among federal policymakers to establish new capital subsidies and enlarge old ones, not merely for one industry, but for many. Such subsidies could create economic distortions as damaging to efficiency as those created by subsidies of the operating-differential form. To date, however, existing and proposed capital subsidies have offset a much smaller fraction of capital costs than the operating subsidy has of labor costs, and none has come close to reducing the marginal cost of capital to zero.
10. Jantscher, *Bread upon the Waters*, chap. 8.

Part III:

Government and Healthy Industries

5

The Case of Semiconductors

Thomas P. Egan

The U.S. semiconductor industry has enjoyed meteoric growth and has provided the technology for revolutionary changes in dozens of fields. It is usually considered to be an example of American industrial know-how at its internationally competitive best. This chapter summarizes the role that government policy has played in the past success of this industry and the implications of government policies for the semiconductor industry and American industry in general.

Much of the material in this chapter (particularly the second section) is drawn from a recent study done by Charles River Associates for the Experimental Technology Incentives Program of the U.S. Department of Commerce.* This study has been published as a book on the semiconductor industry written by this author and colleagues Robert Wilson and Peter Ashton (Wilson, Ashton, & Egan, 1980). The book contains an expanded treatment of the topics covered in this chapter and other topics related to the semiconductor industry.

This chapter is organized into three sections. The first section provides a background description of the semiconductor industry and its technology. Such a description is necessary to differentiate the characteristics of this industry from other industries along dimensions likely to be influenced by government policies. For example, an industry with a very short product life-cycle may react differently to a set of patent policies than one characterized by a longer product life-cycle.

The second section of the chapter reviews the historical interaction of government policies and the semiconductor industry. This interaction has occurred in three distinct phases (supportive, laissez-faire, and inhibiting), and section two discusses the set of policies most relevant in each phase.

The third section focuses on what past and proposed government policies imply for the future of the semiconductor industry and American industry generally. In this third section we point out that even within a healthy industry, current government policies can have important negative impacts

---

* The views expressed in this chapter are the author's and do not necessarily represent the views of Charles River Associates.

on American firms, and should be reconsidered in light of the increasingly vigorous challenge offered by foreign firms.

THE SEMICONDUCTOR INDUSTRY

A semiconductor is a material which can conduct electric current only in some situations—unlike copper wire, which can always conduct current. The electrical properties of semiconductor material, usually silicon crystal, depend on the types, amounts, and spatial configurations of impurities added to the host silicon crystal material. Semiconductor products are marketed as "discrete" circuit elements such as a single transistor or as a complete or "integrated" electronic circuit (for example, a desk calculator circuit). In an integrated circuit, thousands of individual circuit elements (transistors, resistors, and diodes) are implanted, via selective impurity additions, in a single quarter-inch-square silicon crystal "chip."

The manufacturing of semiconductor products is done in a batch-type process. The production cost per unit of a specific semiconductor product— say, integrated circuit catalogue number 8086—depends directly on the number of good units per batch (or yield) that a manufacturer can obtain.

Over the market lifetime of a particular semiconductor product, process yields will improve and costs per unit will fall with expanding quantity shipments. This "experience-curve"- or "learning-curve"-induced fall in costs is the key stimulus for rapidly falling prices and, therefore, for increasing quantities demanded. If a manufacturer with superior engineering talent increases a product's yield faster than rival firms do, the former's market share can be increased by cutting prices. At the same time, profit per unit targets can be maintained because costs have been lowered through yield improvement. Total firm profits are increased because more units are sold, until the next round of price cuts not matched by yield improvements.

In the last analysis, the customer of the semiconductor industry cares mainly about the price per circuit function (for example, price per unit of computing power or unit of computer memory storage). A semiconductor firm with poor yields for a specific product currently favored in the marketplace can get back in the race by inventing a new integrated circuit product containing more computer functions built into the single silicon crystal chip. If yields on the new product allow sales at a price per computer function lower than the price per function offered by the current market favorite, customers will switch to the newer product, and the learning-curve cycle begins again.

This pattern of successive yield improvement and innovation shows up clearly in the case of semiconductor computer memories. In 1973, a state-of-the-art memory product contained about 1,000 storage cells (or bits) and sold for 0.4¢ per bit. By 1977, the learning curve had brought the price of the 1,000-bit product below 0.2¢ per bit, but customers were switching to the newer 4,000-bit unit selling for slightly above 0.1¢ per bit. This pattern has repeated itself continuously in the semiconductor industry over the last thirty years. New products regularly replace old ones in two- to five-year product life-cycles, and costs and prices per electronic function decrease rapidly. This rapid decrease has led, in turn, to the rapid penetration of semiconductors into all forms of equipment such as ICBM missiles, large computers, desk calculators, watches, machine tools, and auto ignition controls.

Given the rapid pace of innovation and the cost cutting necessary to stay competitive, success for the semiconductor firm depends centrally on having an engineering team which is almost continuously inventing products that the market wants and which can maintain or exceed industry average yields on the products being produced and shipped.

Several other semiconductor industry characteristics should be noted before we turn to a discussion of government policies.

- The industry's products have a very high value-added-to-weight ratio.
- Until recently the capital requirements for starting a new firm were relatively modest.
- The employee working environment in terms of physical safety and comfort is relatively benign.
- A semiconductor factory poses no serious environmental threats to its host community.

The first two of these characteristics influence the structure of the industry, while the latter two influence the regulatory environment of the industry. A very high value-added-to-weight ratio implies that freight cost considerations will not influence plant location decisions or the spatial distribution of markets and market shares. Furthermore, the high value-added-to-weight ratio nullifies any foreign competitors' labor cost advantages. U.S. firms can rapidly respond to higher costs at home and competition from countries having low labor costs, by moving the labor-intensive stages of production to other low-labor-cost areas (such as Korea).

Modest start-up capital requirements have historically been a spur to innovation and competition in the semiconductor industry. For thirty years the industry has seen numerous start-up and spin-off firm entrants. Some new market entrants have prospered, while many others have not. Given the short product life-cycle typical of this industry, even firms dominant in one period can fall precipitously in the next period if key engineers leave to join a competing firm or form a new firm. Such new firm formation was encouraged historically by the modest amounts of capital needed for a start-up and its adequate availability from the venture-capital market.

Within the past few years, the semiconductor industry has been undergoing important changes. As computer function density per chip has increased, semiconductor production technology has become more complex. Reflecting this increased complexity, the cost of an efficient chip-production facility has tripled in the last five years and is expected to double again by 1985. Presently a state-of-the-art manufacturing facility's start-up capital requirement exceeds $10 million. As the entry of new firms and expansion of established firms have become more expensive, semiconductor manufacturers have outgrown the lending capability of the venture-capital market and have turned to other sources of capital. These new sources of capital are frequently either domestic or foreign end-users of semiconductor devices.

At the same time that foreign firms are investing in the U.S. semiconductor industry, import competition is becoming significant, especially in some of the more advanced semiconductor products. In addition, the semiconductor industries of Japan, Germany, France, and the United Kingdom, with the financial support of their respective governments, have undertaken major research and development (R&D) efforts to produce advanced semiconductor technology and capture a larger share of worldwide sales from U.S. firms. This threat from foreign competition in an industry historically dominated by U.S. firms, combined with a concern over whether U.S. semiconductor firms and executives continue to have the entrepreneurial incentives and access to capital that drove the industry in its first three decades, is leading both industry executives and federal policymakers to reassess current policies toward the industry.

GOVERNMENT POLICY AND THE SEMICONDUCTOR INDUSTRY

The federal government has played a significant role in the development and growth of the semiconductor industry. Federal policies affecting the semiconductor industry have had a changing role and importance in different stages of the industry's development over time.

The effect of government policies over time can be seen by dividing the semiconductor industry into three distinct periods. During the early years of the industry (the 1950s and early 1960s), extensive interaction existed between government agencies (particularly the military and NASA) and firms in the industry. The interaction arose from the government's great interest in the military and space applications of semiconductor technology and its willingness to fund company R&D directed toward more complex and more reliable semiconductor products. In addition to this push to semiconductor technology, the government also exerted a demand-pull influence. The federal government was the industry's principal customer, and the profits offered by procurement contracts attracted many new firms to the industry.

The second distinct period, throughout the 1960s, may be described as one of laissez-faire. During this time, government demand, while still important, decreased rapidly relative to total semiconductor product demand. Although the military and NASA remained interested in the development of new semiconductor products, new commercial applications were found that were more attractive to many of the firms in the industry. At the same time, no new policies were adopted or implemented that had negative influences on firms' incentives to innovate.

The third distinct period, which started in the late 1960s, can be characterized as one of increased frustration by industry executives with government policy. Government tax and trade policies have played an increasingly important role in the semiconductor industry of late. As the industry grew worldwide in scope, foreign competition heightened, spurred in part by the support that foreign governments have given to their semiconductor industries. Various changes in policy (or lack of policy responsiveness in some instances) have led U.S. semiconductor executives to view the role of government policy with a critical eye, and the once cordial relationship between government and the semiconductor industry has now taken on a more adversarial tone.

Six major government policies or groups of policies have had a substantial impact on the semiconductor industry, and three (patent policies, labor laws, and environmental regulations) have not. The six sets of influential policies are: procurement; R&D funding; antitrust; trade—export and import policies; tax; and manpower.

All six influential policies affect industries throughout the economy, although three—procurement, government funding of R&D, and antitrust— had special significance in the early years of the semiconductor industry. Trade, tax, and manpower policies are current semiconductor industry concerns. Health, safety, and environmental regulations have not played an important role in this industry because semiconductor technology is not destructive to the environment. The impact of the six relevant policies and the role of patent policies are summarized in the following paragraphs.

Procurement

The Department of Defense (DOD) and NASA were major purchasers of semiconductors during the 1950s and early 1960s. These agencies made a strong commitment to the use of semiconductor devices because they were more cost-effective and performed better in military and space equipment than could alternative technologies (Braun & MacDonald, 1978, pp. 80-82). In addition to accounting for a large portion of total demand, the government was willing to pay substantially higher prices, only part of which reflected the higher cost of military-specification quality-assurance testing. Government demand was also relatively stable and secure (Golding, 1971, p. 336). As a result, procurement policy had a direct impact on the risks firms faced, particularly market risk.

Although it is difficult to document specific links, procurement contracts apparently accelerated the development of new products, particularly the integrated circuit. In other words, while procurement policy may not have resulted in semiconductor innovations that otherwise would not have occurred, it did advance the timing of some innovations. This timing was important especially in the 1950s and 1960s, since it enabled U.S. firms to gain the innovative and competitive edge in the world market.

The combination of the rapid development of new products and the assured demand provided by the government induced many firms to pursue innovative strategies and new-market opportunities. As military production proceeded, learning-curve economies were realized, costs fell, and firms were able to price products more cheaply, enabling them to penetrate consumer and industrial markets.

The environment in which firms competed was indirectly affected by procurement policy in the early years of the industry. Procurement contracts tended to encourage new firms to enter the market, thereby contributing to a highly competitive market environment (Tilton, 1971, p. 91). New firms often targeted their strategies toward the military, at least initially, since they knew that the demand was strong and that premium prices would be paid for their devices (Schnell, 1978). Also, these younger firms, eager to capture a foothold in the market, actively sought military business and were flexible in tailoring their designs to government needs.

Procurement contracts also had impacts on firms' organization and their training of engineers to deal with contracting officers. Since government demands are often highly specialized, personnel specifically designated to handle government work had to be trained. Production people within the industry often disliked government business due to the problems of producing high-reliability military products. However, marketing people liked military business because of its lucrative potential. Thus, often a firm had to face internal management division concerning its strategy with respect to the military demand.

Spillover from government work into the commercial sector occurred in several ways. For example, the production experience that a firm gained in manufacturing integrated circuits for a military program benefited its commercial-production process (Golding, 1971, p. 342). Also, because of the tough performance standards imposed by the government, only a small proportion of the products manufactured would meet these criteria. The remaining products could often be sold at a lower but still profitable price in less exacting civilian applications because of the high prices received on sales to the government.

As the industry moved into the 1960s, military demand declined in importance relative to total semiconductor demand (Braun & MacDonald, 1978, p. 4). Nevertheless, the invention of the integrated circuit in the 1960s and its rapid diffusion were greatly aided by the government, especially the NASA Apollo program and the Air Force Minuteman II project. Again, integrated-circuit technology and its use were rapidly diffused and readily accepted in commercial markets in part because of the government's acceptance of this new technology.

In the late 1960s and 1970s, military demand continued to decline relative to total demand, and procurement contracting officers became more cost-conscious. NASA's Apollo project was operational and no longer needed large quantities of new semiconductors. Also, NASA and Department of Defense (DOD) agencies became more cost-conscious in their procurement contracts.

During the late 1960s and early 1970s, a shake-out of several firms that had historically been military suppliers occurred. These firms were not able to cope with the new environment of the more cost-conscious military purchasers and the intense price competition in sales to civilian users (OECD, 1968, p. 74).

Recently, government purchasers have relied primarily on established firms as suppliers, decreasing the government market opportunities for new entry firms or successful spin-offs. In 1978 government sales of integrated circuits comprised only 10 percent of total sales (*Status*, 1979, p. 43). Not only had government policy changed, but also the industry had matured. The industry's performance and growth are no longer dependent upon the level of government procurement.

Government Funding of R&D

Government funding of R&D for semiconductors originated in DOD and NASA as a means of developing new technology to meet the nation's military and space needs. At an early stage, these government agencies became convinced of the importance of semiconductor electronics to the military and space programs, and therefore pushed for the development of more reliable, faster, and smaller circuits. This "technology-push" factor led firms to conduct extensive research activities (Kleiman, 1966, p. 68).

R&D funding by the public sector proceeds in a manner similar to procurement. Basically, the government is buying a product as it does in procurement, but the product in this case is the research (and/or the development) of a new product or process. During the 1950s the majority of R&D funds went to the established firms that had good reputations for research. However, by the early 1960s many of the newer, highly innovative companies were being given lucrative research contracts.

The effect of R&D funding on firms' strategies impacted their innovative behavior in two ways. R&D funding by the government emphasized the urgency of the situation, thereby inducing greater R&D investments by private firms (Kleiman, 1966, p. 68). This "urgency effect" cut development lead times when firms saw the lucrative benefits of these devices. Throughout the middle and late 1950s government funding covered engineering design and development and private firms funded production facilities, adding to total industry capacity (Tilton, 1971, p. 92).

A second important impact of government R&D funding on innovative behavior was the reduction in the technical risk in developing new products, since firms needed to invest less in R&D. Also, firms' perceptions of risk may have been altered, especially in the 1950s and 1960s, since this large-scale government action may have increased their confidence that technical breakthroughs were possible.

Entry conditions were also affected in the early years of the industry by the pattern of government R&D funding. The majority of R&D funds went to established firms (Tilton, 1971, p. 95). Established firms may have been favored because they were more interested in doing broad, general research and had a strong record of past performance and success in conducting research efforts.

The generation of basic knowledge and skills gained from government-funded R&D created important spillover effects in the semiconductor industry. "The firm benefited through the transfer of production experience gained during the course of the R&D program to the manufacture of commercial devices" (Golding, 1971, p. 342). Also, the cooperation among industry firms, universities, and the government surrounding early R&D efforts increased the impetus for technological change in the 1950s and early 1960s (Tanaka, 1979, p. 8).

During the 1960s the government role as R&D funder began to diminish. Research programs became more goal-oriented, with flexibility in research becoming more restricted. Also research focused less on basic than on applied areas, and funding of related university research dropped considerably. In addition, federal R&D programs were not as well structured, and research efforts tended to be scattered too widely to be effective. According to an industry executive, much of the money went to "second-echelon" firms—that is, firms with little primary interest in semiconductors (CRA interviews, 1980).

During the 1970s, government support of R&D subsided significantly with important effects on the industry. Basic research in electronics is not being performed now as extensively as in the 1950s. Universities, with a few exceptions (such as Cornell, Arizona, Stanford, MIT, and Berkeley), are not doing the leading-edge work they once were, and are receiving less funding from the government. Internal funding generated by universities is not sufficient to keep them on the technological forefront (Hogan, 1979, p. 8). Companies now have to fund the bulk of their R&D, and with the rising costs of R&D, it has become more difficult.

A problem with government-funded R&D has been the government's insistence on claiming title to patents generated from government-funded R&D. NASA began this trend, and now additional government agencies (for example, the Department of Energy) claim title to such patents and license them freely, with no royalty payments. This practice may discourage firms from undertaking government-funded research efforts because they cannot derive any significant advantage from the technical know-how generated by such a project. Firms also are reluctant to consult with government engineers because they fear competitors may gain access to important proprietary information through the Freedom of Information Act (CRA interviews, 1980).

Current policy issues with respect to government R&D funding involve foreign government subsidies to their electronics firms. This support allegedly gives foreign firms unfair advantages in competing and developing new technologies. The Japanese government, for example, is backing a major research effort (*Business Week*, December 3, 1979). In Europe, government support also has risen. The French government is spending $140 million on five companies and joint ventures in research. Great Britain and West Germany are also spending sizable sums to develop capabilities.

Nevertheless, these massive spending efforts must be viewed in the context of the research efforts of U.S. firms. In 1978, U.S. semiconductor firms spent over $400 million in R&D; also, the DOD will commit more than $150 million over a period of several years to develop very-high-speed integrated-circuit technology. Thus, U.S. firms are currently able to spend sums large enough to develop new products and new technology. Whether this adequacy can continue is problematic, as we will examine in later sections of the chapter.

Antitrust Policy

Although U.S. antitrust policy has had only a limited direct effect upon the innovative record of the semiconductor industry, some evidence indicates that it has had an impact upon the industry's environment and structure as well as upon the strategies of individual firms. In 1956 AT&T settled a seven-year antitrust suit with the Justice Department concerning a patent-pooling agreement among General Electric, RCA, Westinghouse, and AT&T. Western Electric was allowed to remain part of AT&T, but was enjoined from selling any output, including semiconductors, to commercial customers. In addition, the company was forced to license all its existing patents royalty-free to any domestic firm and guarantee licensing at reasonable royalty charges on all future patents (Tilton, 1971, p. 76; Kraus, 1973, p. 28). Since AT&T's major activities were centered in telecommunications and it was dependent on innovations in many areas of electronics, including semiconductor components, for its success, it was willing to exchange information about new technologies. Other firms followed suit, entering into cross-licensing agreements as a means of staying abreast of new developments in the various areas of electronic components (Tilton, 1971, p. 74).

During the antitrust suit, AT&T refrained from any measure that might indicate an attempt to dominate the fledgling semiconductor market (Tilton, 1971, p. 76). Technological advances were openly publicized, and Bell Laboratories held several conferences and seminars to inform industrial representatives about their innovative progress (Kraus, 1973, p. 26; Tilton, 1971, p. 75; Braun & MacDonald, 1978, p. 54). A liberal patent-licensing policy was pursued.

Fear of similar antitrust problems may have encouraged other large receiving-tube firms to follow AT&T's liberal licensing policy. This easy access to important patents in the early and mid-1950s allowed many new firms to enter the emerging semiconductor market (Tilton, 1971, p. 77). The industry became more competitive with new entry, and the liberal licensing practices rapidly diffused the stock of basic knowledge.

Trade Policies

As the volume of world trade in semiconductors and digital integrated circuits has increased in recent years, the trade policies of the United States and other nations have taken on added importance. The primary trade issues in the United States today concern access by U.S. firms to the Japanese market and subsidies by foreign governments to their semiconductor industries.

Prior to 1965, U.S. international trade in semiconductor devices was relatively minor. Export sales in no year exceeded 5 percent of total factory sales (Finan, 1975, p. 90). Consumption of semiconductors abroad was minimal and imports into the United States were quite low. The motivating factor behind foreign imports of U.S.-produced semiconductors in the 1960s was access to new technology. U.S. trade policy imposed virtually no restrictions on exports to other free-world countries. The policy impacted the environment directly by diffusing information regarding new product developments to foreign competitors. Foreign firms were able to study and copy these new innovations, thereby allowing them to develop new products more rapidly than if export restriction had prevented them.

After 1965, a shift in the pattern of trade occurred and the total volume of trade increased significantly. U.S. firms began to set up offshore assembly plants and invest abroad in complete production facilities. In part, this setup was due to domestic competitive pressure to reduce costs, especially in the labor-intensive assembly phase of production (U.S. DOC *Report*, 1979, p. 69). Note that this move offshore also forced the Japanese firms to go offshore (Chang, 1972). Foreign consumption of semiconductors rose steadily throughout the late 1960s and 1970s. Prices for semiconductors abroad began to drop significantly, making foreign tariffs a problem for U.S. firms exporting into foreign countries while trying to remain price-competitive (Finan, 1975, p. 94).

Currently, semiconductor industry executives are concerned about the relatively passive posture of the U.S. government with regard to foreign competiton, particularly from Japan. The semiconductor industry vigorously maintains that it welcomes competition. However, the U.S. industry also maintains that foreign government subsidies and protectionist policies preclude fair competition. The main threat is perceived to be from Japan. Some of the alleged Japanese unfairness arises from inherent structural differences between the U.S. and Japanese systems.

The Japanese quasi-nationalized bank credit system allows Japanese firms to be highly leveraged, and therefore they can earn high returns on equity with the relatively low prices needed to penetrate foreign markets. Also, the financial backing of the Japanese banks allows these firms to pursue aggressive capacity-expansion plans without the large earnings base required of U.S. firms (Noyce, 1979). Potential Japanese customers for U.S.-made semiconductors have a strong "buy Japanese" attitude (Noyce, 1979). Many of them are also vertically integrated with their own semiconductor manufacturing divisions (Tanaka, 1980).

However, going beyond these structural differences the Japanese government's policies with regard to its semiconductor industry is more actively supportive than the relatively laissez-faire U.S. government trade policies. Specifically, the Japanese government targets certain industries (including its semiconductor industry) for export market penetration. Such target industries may receive R&D subsidies and tariff protection (Noyce, 1979). (The Japanese have recently agreed to some lowering of existing tariff barriers to U.S. semiconductors.) Tariff protection in turn permits Japanese firms to practice price discrimination. The tariffs permit higher prices and profits in the protected home market, and such home market profits permit vigorous price-cutting strategies in the target U.S. export market (Noyce, 1979).

The combined effect of these structural differences and active government-support policies is perceived by the semiconductor industry to be particularly threatening now that Japanese semiconductor technology is on a par with U.S. technology. The thrust of the threat stems from forecasts that Japanese price cutting and the potential excess supply overhanging the target U.S. market will prevent U.S. firms from generating the profits necessary to finance the large R&D and plant expansion budgets vital for maintaining a viably competitive position in the growing and technically evolving semiconductor marketplace (*Fortune*, March 23, 1981; Noyce, 1979). However, if, as some analysts believe, the demand for state-of-the-art semiconductors will continue to grow rapidly, excess supply situations are not likely to develop.

The Japanese also have been accused by industry executives of unfairly enforcing their patent holdings (by aggressively applying their own patents and infringing on those of U.S. firms) in the United States to gain market power.

It is also important to note that the most intense competiton between U.S. and Japanese firms currently centers around one market—state-of-the-art computer memories. However, this market is potentially the largest in the history of the semiconductor industry (*Fortune*, March 23, 1981). In the three years since the current state-of-the-art product (a 16,000-bit memory) was introduced, the Japanese have made rapid progress, capturing over 40 percent of worldwide sales in 1979 (*Business Week*, December 3, 1979). The fear expressed by U.S. executives is that the Japanese will parlay this success into several others, particularly the new 64,000-bit memory, and eventually dominate all semiconductor sales (*Forbes*, November 26, 1979; *Fortune*, March 23, 1981).

While the available information about the relative weakness of U.S. trade policies and the competitive unfairness of the Japanese comes largely from U.S. semiconductor industry spokesmen, the industry charges have to be regarded as credible. The Japanese Electronics Industries Association concedes that the Japanese capital market operates differently than the U.S. market; that the Japanese government has encouraged its industry to pursue world computer and semiconductor markets; and that the Japanese government has provided a $100 million very large scale integration program semiconductor R&D subsidy to Japanese firms (Tanaka, 1980).

The more difficult question for the policy analyst is the determination of the importance of the remaining nontariff protectionist barriers that the U.S. industry alleges are in place. Two questions must be considered: Do such barriers exist? Do they merit U.S. government policy intervention?

With respect to the existence of such barriers, it seems that, as the industry alleges, many informal barriers exist (Noyce, 1979). To the extent that they exist, they probably represent a degree of unfairness. However, U.S. government intervention to establish trade barrier equality seems warranted only when a barrier is a formal tariff or subsidy established by the Japanese government. In contrast, Japanese private sector policies established at the firm or industry level do not seem to merit direct U.S. government intervention unless they severely handicap the U.S. industry's domestic and worldwide operations. To the extent that U.S. semiconductor products are superior, the Japanese computer and other equipment manufacturers technically penalize themselves with "buy Japanese" policies directed at their potential U.S. semiconductor industry suppliers.

Furthermore, if the forecasted rate of growth of the U.S. market for state-of-the-art semiconductors materializes, U.S. firms will have their hands full just keeping pace with domestic U.S. demand. They may have little surplus to sell in Japan over the next few years. If forecasts are accurate, the real threat from Japan stems from Japanese imports in the growing U.S. market. This threat can be countered only through adequate U.S. production capacity, innovation, and yield improvements.

The appropriate U.S. government policy to meet this threat would seem to be better directed, at least in the near term, to encouraging capital formation for plant expansion rather than to a preoccupation with Japanese trade barriers. However, if substantial barriers exist, they should be equalized in the longer run through U.S. government intervention.

Tax Policies

In addition to trade policies, another set of government policies affecting the semiconductor industry has drawn attention in recent years. These are tax policies and various tax measures, which allegedly have diminished the incentives of firms to innovate.

Tax policies affecting innovation have become important to the semiconductor industry only in recent years. In the early years of the industry, tax policies had little direct impact on firms. This trend continued throughout the 1960s until 1969, when the tax rate on capital gains was increased from 25 percent to 48 percent (over a period of three years). A series of other changes followed. Many of the semiconductor executives that the Charles River Associates study team interviewed asserted that changes in tax policies in the last twelve years have made capital more difficult to obtain and have restricted the ability of firms to expand capacity, enter new product areas, and grow at historical rates.

Several tax policies (investment tax credits, capital gains tax, taxation of stock options, and other stock credits) are discussed in the following subsection to point out the various effects they have had on capital formation, entry of new firms, and incentives to invest in R&D. Each of these tax policies is general in nature—that is, it affects firms in all industries. None was tailored specifically to the semiconductor industry, although all of them have had important effects in this industry as well as in other high-technology industries.

Investment Tax Credits. The investment tax credit is available for investments in machinery and equipment, but not for buildings or R&D, and is currently set at a rate of 10 percent (AEI, 1978, p. 11). Until 1978, when it was made permanent, the credit was a temporary measure that adjusted (or abolished) as policymakers believed economic conditions warranted. Studies have indicated that it may be a useful and effective incentive for business investment and that it promotes faster, long-term growth in the capital stock (American Enterprise Institute, 1978).

The investment tax credit may affect the firm's asset structure by providing an incentive to invest in assets that qualify for the credit (such as equipment and machinery). This incentive in turn may influence a firm's strategies; expansion of capacity may allow a firm to move into new product areas, since the credit can be applied to the equipment needed to expand capacity.

Innovative behavior may be indirectly affected, since the investment tax credit may leave firms with more funds to invest in R&D. Also, current proposals are under discussion (such as those by the Semiconductor Industry Association) to make the investment tax credit applicable to R&D expenditures. This application could directly affect innovation since firms would have a greater incentive to invest in R&D (Nesheim, 1979, p. 16). Application of the investment tax credit to R&D expenditures is currently an important issue with semiconductor executives and is viewed as one way of staying even with foreign government incentives to their high-technology firms (Nesheim, 1979, p. 17).

Capital Gains Tax.   The capital gains tax created a great deal of controversy among semiconductor executives during the 1970s. Between 1969 and 1976, Congress increased the effective tax rate of capital gains. The net effect was to increase the maximum rate from 25 percent in 1969 to over 49 percent in 1978. The Tax Reform Act of 1978 then reduced this maximum rate to 28 percent.

Prior to the 1978 act, many economists, business executives, and members of Congress expressed concern that these changes would stifle capital formation, would slow growth and productivity, and would prevent new, small firms from raising investment (venture) capital. This latter issue, the ability of firms to raise capital, had the greatest impact on the semiconductor industry. Because of the increased capital gains tax rate in 1969, individual investors in new companies faced a reduced incentive to invest in a new venture. Venture capitalists view the investment decision in terms of a risk-return trade-off and are interested in high-risk, high-return situations.

Venture-capital availability in every industry will fluctuate over time depending on economic conditions and business cycles. Nevertheless, venture capital will be more readily available to firms in a rapidly growing industry such as semiconductors, as opposed to more mature, slower-growing industries. In the former, the risk-return trade-off often appears more attractive, especially during boom economic conditions (CRA, 1976, p. S-7). In a strong economic environment, the venture-capital market is usually very active. However, during downturns, capital "dries up," and obtaining money for a new venture becomes more difficult. Thus innovation decreases.

The lack of venture capital has only manifested itself in the semiconductor industry during the last decade. Prior to that time, venture-capital costs of entry were relatively low, since only a modest investment (about $1 million) was required to set up an efficient manufacturing operation. Thus, there was less demand for large sums of venture capital. Second, the rapid pace of technological change and growth in the industry during the 1950s and 1960s made the profit opportunities for venture capitalists good.

In the late 1960s and early 1970s, venture capital became more difficult to raise for new semiconductor ventures. This difficulty was due in part to the change in the capital gains tax. Also, the capital costs of entry had risen considerably, thereby requiring larger initial outlays. Estimates of capital costs of entry range from $100,000 to $1 million in the 1950s, to $10 million in 1970, to $30–40 million today for a state-of-the-art manufacturing facility (*Forbes*, 1979, p. 56; Tilton, 1971, p. 88). These increases (and the resulting decrease in entry) stem from the increasingly complex and costly technology required to make each new device. As a result, through 1978, venture capital did not flow into the industry, in part because entry costs are too high to make a venture-capital offering feasible. Finally, the return on venture-capital investments dropped and several financings turned sour.

The important consequence of the lack of venture capital may be a decrease in innovation. Innovation can decrease both from the lack of entry by new innovative firms and from reduced pressures on existing firms. Many of the major integrated-circuit innovations came from firms spinning off from existing firms. On the other hand, foreign competition may provide the incentive that established firms need to maintain the innovative pace. Furthermore, today's higher plant costs may serve to discourage new entrants regardless of the capital gains tax rate, since such costs are beyond the amount usually advanced by venture-capital firms. Thus it is difficult to draw a firm conclusion about the role that capital gains rates will play in the future. However, a recent *Wall Street Journal* article (March 18, 1981, p. 37) notes that consequent to the 1978 rate reduction, venture capital is rushing back into emerging semiconductor and other high-technology firms.

Treatment of Stock Options.   The tax treatment of stock options and the elimination of the qualified stock option in 1976 have influenced the ability of semiconductor firms to attract top personnel from other firms. Since skilled-labor resources have historically been in short supply in this industry, firms have used the stock option as a means of luring top-notch personnel to new firms. Employee-ownership plans, the profits of which were taxed at a relatively low rate, were viewed as an attractive incentive to engineers to move to new firms seeking qualified personnel. These plans made possible large incomes contingent upon the success of the new firm and allowed taxation at the capital gains rate, which was lower than the personal income tax rate.

Changes in the tax laws now make these options less attractive to employees and new firms. Previously, qualified options were given to key personnel, and no tax was assessed either at the time of the grant or at the time of exercise. At the time of resale, the shares were taxed at the capital gains rate. These special options were phased out beginning in 1976, and stock options no longer receive special tax exempt treatment (U.S. Senate, 1978, p. 43).

Firms now prefer to use other employee-incentive plans such as bonuses and profit sharing; however, none is as potentially lucrative as was the qualified stock option. Semiconductor executives believe a return to the qualified stock option would benefit the industry. These options had an important impact in attracting people to new firms, making it easier to start a new firm. This effect on entry is particularly significant, given that new, small firms have been an important source of innovation in the industry. However, since the importance of new small-firm entrants may be diminishing, qualified stock option tax breaks may not be needed as a spur to future innovation in the semiconductor industry.

Other Tax Policies.   Recent changes in the U.S. income tax policy have eliminated the favorable treatment for Americans working in foreign countries for U.S. firms. Overseas personnel no longer earn their first $25,000 tax-free. As a result, companies find that convincing top-quality management to live outside the country is difficult. Companies are finding it more difficult to penetrate export markets because of the scarcity of the requisite management expertise within the native labor force. Concern has been expressed over the effect of this problem on the growth of the U.S. semiconductor industry.

Manpower Policies

The semiconductor industry is best characterized by its people rather than its companies since company success directly depends upon individual expertise (Braun & MacDonald, 1978, p. 128). Therefore, government policies that affect the quality and availability of manpower in the industry have an important impact on industry growth and structure.

Government funding, particularly from the DOD and NASA programs, greatly aided the electronics industry in the 1950s. During that period, DOD allocated $1 million to $2 million annually to more than 100 doctoral candidates for basic research in solid-state electronics (Utterback & Murray, 1977, p. 17). Universities received funding for the necessary facilities and equipment to attract top-quality research personnel for government projects. The promotion of university research and training provided the highly technical labor force needed for the development of the commercial industry. Expertise gained on government projects could be applied to the growing demand for consumer applications. This was particularly important in facilitating the growth of small firms and encouraging new entrants.

Since the 1950s and mid-1960s, government support for R&D and man-power training to universities and firms has markedly declined. Several major firms claim that support is currently nonexistent. Many executives have agreed that the universities provide an important training ground for the technical manpower required by the industry. Generally, however, executives believe that university facilities and equipment are too obsolete and hinder up-to-date training of future engineers, and that the government should increase its funding to universities to help update their engineering facilities and programs (CRA interviews, 1980). Nevertheless, industry executives also believe that the quality of personnel attracted to the industry has not diminished to date.

Federal tax credits for grants by U.S. corporations to colleges and universities for fundamental research might aid the semiconductor industry and other industries. The proposal might positively affect technical innovation by encouraging the expansion of the base of fundamental knowledge and may increase the supply of talented, highly skilled engineering students who will be the future innovative leaders in U.S. business.

In sum, the supply and mobility of manpower were initially promoted by government policies, especially with university funding for research training. Government actions have faltered, however, and several major firms believe that the cut in university funding and the new tax policies concerning stock options and overseas income have limited the availability of highly skilled technical manpower.

Patents

The consensus among industry executives is that patents provide little incentive for innovation in the semiconductor industry. There are two main reasons for the failure of patents to provide an incentive. First, semiconductor patents are so numerous that firms have to cross-license each other, because several individual firms usually hold patents on separate stages of the manufacturing processes. Without cross-licensing, any of several firms could block others from producing, and wasteful legal confrontations would result. Second, the time required to obtain a patent is slow in relation to the speed with which semiconductor technology changes. As one executive put it to a colleague, "The payoff comes from charging ahead with the innovation. Patents may provide some protection later" (CRA interviews, 1980). On a related point, one executive noted that disclosure was not a disincentive to patenting. Patents are disclosed only when issued, not while pending. Since the technology changes rapidly and information spreads so fast in the semiconductor industry, it is usually possible to tie up an application long enough in the Patent Office to avoid any disclosure problem.

Several other factors also contribute to the low patent incentive. For example, process and production equipment innovations are frequently more valuable as trade secrets. Finally, one firm cited Justice Department opposition to the use of patents to obtain a dominant market position. As a result, royalties have been relatively low. Firms have felt that they risk antitrust litigation if they charge high royalties or otherwise use patents to build a market position (CRA interviews, 1980).

Despite the failure of patents to provide an incentive for innovation, most firms obtain patents for defensive purposes. Patents are viewed as a bargaining chip in cross-licensing negotiations and as a means to minimize royalty payments. The larger firms generally patent most inventions, but some cite the cost of patenting as a deterrent.

According to industry executives, in the 1950s and 1960s, most patent negotiations were entirely among U.S. firms. As other countries caught up, however, U.S. companies found it necessary to build strong patent positions abroad. This factor has greatly increased the cost of patent filing because filings are necessary in about ten countries. Thus, U.S. firms tend to pick and choose what they patent.

In the 1980s, Japanese patent aggressiveness and U.S. reluctance to patent could be a problem. A reverse flow of royalties to Japan could well develop in the 1980s.

Some of the firms that obtained strong patent positions early in the semiconductor industry history earned large royalty income and other benefits such as access to foreign markets and technology. Although difficult to prove conclusively, these benefits may have facilitated subsequent innovation.

CONCLUSIONS AND POLICY ISSUES

In our characterization of the semiconductor industry and our review of government policies pertaining to that industry, several points have emerged which we can draw upon to recommend appropriate policies for the semiconductor industry and U.S. industry generally.

U.S. semiconductor firms face a very short product life-cycle, sell in a very competitive marketplace, and face escalating R&D and plant-expansion capital requirements.

The industry's technology makes it relatively immune to the risks and costs associated with environmental and worker health and safety regulations.

Antitrust policy, short product life-cycle, and industry practices have rendered patent policies, as currently practiced, unimportant for this industry.

Early in its history, government procurement contracts, R&D funding, and support to universities were very beneficial for this industry. The success of the semiconductor industry has, in turn, been extremely beneficial for U.S. trade balances, employment, productivity, and technology leadership.

In other words, the private and social return on the government's investment has been very high.

Government tax policies such as capital gains taxes, the elimination of the qualified stock option, the exclusion of R&D expenditures from investment tax credit incentives, and the elimination of tax incentives for overseas employment currently are detrimental to the semiconductor industry. They inhibit what has always been the innovative spur to and the lifeblood of the semiconductor industry—namely, rapid innovation encouraged by a climate of vigorous entrepreneurial spirit. This climate thrived in the 1950s and 1960s under tax policies encouraging human and financial capital formation and mobility, and withered somewhat under the more restrictive tax policies of the 1970s. Because of the rapid increases in new plant costs, government tax policies may no longer be as influential as they have been in the recent past.

A vigorous challenge to the U.S. semiconductor industry is being offered by Japanese firms encouraged and subsidized by the Japanese government and Japanese financial institutions. Given the typically short product life-cycles and the consequent speed and ease with which firms can be forced from positions of industry leadership to obscurity, this challenge is a potentially serious threat to the U.S. semiconductor industry and all the U.S. industries which will rely on semiconductor products to increase their own productivity and remain competitive in their own markets.

The points just listed can be examined from the perspective of what the U.S. policy should be toward U.S. industry generally and the semiconductor industry in particular. We now discuss this issue.

Policy Proposals

Currently the semiconductor industry shares with much of the rest of U.S. industry the acute need for capital to finance R&D, plant expansion, and plant modernization. Therefore, policies designed to encourage capital investment in the United States are likely to have a positive effect on this industry and most others. In light of the vigorous challenge being mounted by inflation and foreign competition, such policies deserve the high priority they are currently receiving. In addition, the semiconductor industry has moved into an era where the capital needed to start a new firm is larger than a typical venture-capital firm or syndicate can underwrite. Therefore, the key innovations necessary for the industry to remain competitive may not occur as frequently as in the past through small start-up firms funded by venture capitalists and managed by entrepreneurial defectors from large, established firms. Changes in capital market regulations and institutions which encourage the funding of more capital-intensive but risky innovative start-up industries and firms may be a productive policy step.

In addition, the semiconductor industry's history shows that direct R&D assistance has been very beneficial for the semiconductor industry, and therefore for the country indirectly. In the future, government assistance such as basic R&D subsidies might be beneficially applied to very carefully selected specific industries faced with severe foreign competition and current earnings inadequate to attract R&D capital. However, such subsidies should be granted only after careful study demonstrates the industry's strategic value to the economy, that the industry is a special target for foreign imports, and that the industry cannot obtain adequate R&D support in the private sector. Furthermore, as in the semiconductor industry case, the R&D results obtained should be made available to all present and potential U.S.–firm market entrants. Such government basic research grants might best be made to universities rather than leading firms in the target industry, to minimize the danger that the R&D subsidies would go to the less innovatively inclined firms in the industry. Basic R&D grants to universities yield the added benefit of subsidizing the training of highly skilled personnel necessary for continued innovative leadership.

The semiconductor industry experience offers a third lesson generally applicable to U.S. industries that rely on frequent innovation to remain competitors in domestic and world markets. The mobility and rewards available to the most innovative and entrepreneurial individuals must not be constrained by taxes. If U.S. high-technology industries are to offset the subsidies and tariff support given their foreign competitors, it must be possible for innovators to "strike it rich." Since it is impossible to determine, a priori, who such innovative individuals are, qualified stock options and other tax incentives must be made available to all substantive risk takers. If such incentives are not available, many of our high-technology industries may fall one by one as they come up on a foreign government's target list. The individual or small-firm innovator and entrepreneur may be our only truly effective weapon against our larger, well-protected and well-financed foreign adversaries. The history of the semiconductor industry demonstrates this theme repeatedly. Large, well-financed vacuum tube manufacturers fell prey to the first silicon transistors made by small, new start-up firms in the 1950s. In the 1960s many established transistor makers fell to large and small firm innovators of integrated circuits. In the early 1970s, large core-memory manufacturers lost the random-access–memory field in five years to tiny Intel Corporation's part number 1103, a 1,000-bit random-access memory. The semiconductor industry's history is replete with many similar examples.

In an innovation-encouraging tax environment, foreign competitors who are highly leveraged with debt may be quite vulnerable—especially when product life-cycles are short. If a small or large innovator succeeds in capturing a market from a large, highly debt-leveraged competitor, the large debt must still be serviced. If the debt is guaranteed by foreign governments, foreign taxpayers may have to service the debt or let the wounded giant topple.

Innovators and entrepreneurs in the semiconductor industry and other industries will have to be encouraged by lucrative financial and other inducements to make risky intra- and inter-firm mobility moves. For example, a large firm may financially encourage innovative individuals to start up and run wholly owned but autonomously managed subsidiary firms. If this general pattern is appropriate, each industry will have to identify the individuals and organizational patterns best suited to its own survival and growth. The appropriate role of government in this setting is to ensure that it creates no income tax or other capital-formation impediments to the necessary adaptations.

One final characteristic that the semiconductor industry has in common with other U.S. industries is that it enjoys little tariff protection in domestic markets and faces tariff and other barriers in some foreign markets. While it is not a position that one trained in economics moves to easily, this author believes that, under current international market conditions, the U.S. government should raise tariff barriers where our industries face substantial barriers abroad. The objective of such policies should not be to protect inherently uncompetitive U.S. industries, but rather to create leverage to enable the government to negotiate a mutual reduction in tariffs and other protectionist policies. Foreign semiconductor firms as well as foreign firms in many other industries need access to the large U.S. market for growth and survival. However, the semiconductor industry experience demonstrates that foreign governments will not lower protectionist barriers unless it is in their self-interest to do so. For example, in 1967 Texas Instruments (TI) forced the Japanese to grant them the right to construct the only foreign-owned semiconductor facility in Japan because TI caught Japanese firms infringing on key TI patents and threatened judicial action to exclude all infringing Japanese products from the U.S. market (Noyce, 1979, p. 75).

Policy Cost-Effectiveness

To correctly forecast the cost-effectiveness of the policies just proposed, it is ideally necessary to specify the national objectives sought and their relevant time horizon. Specifically, some politically determined social target framework comprising short- and long-run productivity, employment, balance of trade, national security, energy, environmental, and sectoral improvement goals would have to be specified as a "yardstick" to produce such a cost-effectiveness forecast. Since such a "macro objective function" is very unlikely to evolve politically in time to meet the industry vitalization challenge, some more local, or "micro," cost-effectiveness criteria will be needed. Some of these criteria are now discussed.

With respect to capital-formation policies, a well-designed policy will be cost-effective if it is institutionally well thought out and consistent. The policy designer should attempt to ascertain how the proposed policy will affect capital-market institutions and the incentives of the various classes of investors. In addition, it will be necessary to forecast the impact that the proposed policy will have on the major classes of demanders of capital. Such analyses are difficult, but necessary if cost-effective capital-formation policies are to be implemented.

With respect to basic R&D subsidies, the cost-effectiveness of a proposed policy is very difficult to ascertain, since the payoff for the social investment will often occur in an unknown time horizon and specific technology. Despite this difficulty, the semiconductor experience teaches that such policies can ultimately be very cost-effective when directed at promising new broad-technology areas. The semiconductor industry experience also demonstrates that it is nearly impossible to forecast specific technology and firm "winners" and "losers." Despite the overall growth of the semiconductor industry, many semiconductor innovations that were highly regarded, a priori, have failed. Therefore, cost-effective basic R&D subsidies to target industries will have to span a broad enough range of technology options to ensure the inclusion of the ultimate long-run "winners." Such a broad range may well imply the necessity for a taxpayer tolerance of a lack of short-run payoffs and cost-effectiveness.

Similarly, with regard to entrepreneurial encouragement policies, it is impossible to forecast long-run winners. Incentives to potential risk takers must be abundant and technologically broad to ensure long-run policy success. Again, this may imply a lack of short-run policy cost-effectiveness. The long-run employment and productivity growth payoff comes only when successful entrepreneurs start to build the mid-sized and large-sized plants that are warranted by their early successes. Given the historical role that American entrepreneurs have played in our nation's long-run employment and productivity growth, a taxpayer tolerance of a lack of short-run cost-effectiveness is likely to be very productive.

Whatever the ultimate cost-effectiveness of R&D and entrepreneurial encouragement policies, the taxpayer will have to expect that a substantial time lag may exist between policy implementation and payoff.

CONCLUSION

In closing, we would note that the semiconductor industry experience has little of relevance to say about the environmental and other government regulatory problems facing other industries. However, it does share a broad range of concerns with other U.S. industries, particularly high-technology industries. In the main, what is good for U.S. industry generally is good for the semiconductor industry, and vice versa. Most important are inducing innovation and capital formation and the achieving of equitable international trade barrier agreements. In addition, the semiconductor industry shares with a subset of U.S. industry an appreciation of the vital role played by R&D.

Given the high social returns to such policies in the semiconductor industry experience, the government's aggressive adoption of these types of policies may be a highly desirable taxpayer investment to make, especially in light of the vigorous efforts our foreign competitors are making in these directions.

REFERENCES

American Enterprise Institute (AEI) for Public Policy Research. "The Administration's 1978 Tax Package." Legislative Analyses No. 28, 95th Congress, May 15, 1978.

Braun, Ernest and MacDonald, Stuart. *Revolution in Miniature: The History and Impact of Semiconductor Electronics*. New York, N.Y., and Cambridge, England: Cambridge University Press, 1978.

Business Week, "Japan Is Here to Stay." December 3, 1979, pp. 81, 85-86.

Chang, Y. S. *The Analysis of the Offshore Activities of the Japanese Electronics Industry*. International Bank for Reconstruction and Development, November, 1972.

Charles River Associates (CRA). *Analysis of Venture Capital Market Imperfections*. Prepared for NBS. Cambridge, Mass.: CRA, 1976.

Charles River Associates (CRA). Interviews with Industry Executives, 1980.

Finan, William F. *The International Transfer of Semiconductor Technology Through U.S.-Based Firms*. Working Paper No. 118. Washington, D.C.: National Bureau of Economic Research, December, 1975.

Forbes. "The Micro War Heats Up." November 26, 1979, pp. 49-58.

Fortune. "The Japanese Chip Challenge." March 23, 1981, pp. 115-122.

Golding, Anthony M. "Semiconductor Industry in Britain and the United States: A Case Study in Innovation, Growth and the Diffusion of Technology." Ph.D. dissertation, University of Sussex, England, 1971.

Hogan, C. Lester. Statement at the Technology Workshop on Semiconductor Electronics. Palo Alto, California, June 14, 1979.

Kleiman, Herbert S. "A Case Study of Innovation," *Business Horizons* (Winter 1966), pp. 63-70.

Kleiman, Herbert S. *The U.S. Government Role in the Integrated Circuit Innovation*. Final Report. Prepared by Battelle-Columbus Labs for OECD, February 25, 1977.

Kraus, Jerome. "An Economic Study of the U.S. Semiconductor Industry." Ph.D. dissertation, New School for Social Research, 1973.

Nesheim, John L. Statement before the U.S. Senate Subcommittee on Taxation and Debt Management on Behalf of the Semiconductor Industry Association. June 18, 1979.

Noyce, Robert. Testimony on Behalf of the Semiconductor Industry Association before the Subcommittee on Trade of the Committee on Ways and Means of the House of Representatives. November 30, 1979, p. 74.

Organization for Economic Cooperation and Development (OECD). *Gaps in Technology: Electronic Components*. Paris: OECD, 1968.

Schnell, Jerome. "Government Programs and the Growth of High Technology Industries." *Research Policy* 7 (1978): 2-24.

Status. Publication of Integrated Circuit Engineering Corporation, Scottsdale, Arizona, 1979.

Tanaka, William H. Statement before the U.S. International Trade Commission on Behalf of the Electronics Industries Association of Japan. Investigation No. 332-102, May 30, 1979.

Tanaka, William H. Testimony on Behalf of the Electronics Industries Association of Japan before the Subcommittee on International Finance of the Committee on Banking, Housing, and Urban Affairs of the United States Senate, January 15, 1980.

Tilton, J. *International Diffusion of Technology: The Case of Semiconductors.* Washington, D.C.: The Brookings Institution, 1971.

U.S. Department of Commerce (DOC). *Report on the Semiconductor Industry.* Washington D.C.: U.S. Government Printing Office, September, 1979, p. 33.

U.S. Senate. "Industrial Technology, Hearings Before the Committee on Commerce, Science, and Transportation," 95th Congress, 2nd Session, October 30, 1978. Serial No. 95-138.

Utterback, J., and Murray, A. *Influence on Defense Procurement and Sponsorship of Research and Development of the Civilian Electronics Industry.* Cambridge, Mass.: Massachusetts Institute of Technology, Center for Policy Alternatives, June 1977.

Wilson, Robert W., Ashton, Peter K., and Egan, Thomas P. *Innovation, Competition, and Government Policy in the Semiconductor Industry.* Lexington, Mass.: Lexington Books, D. C. Heath and Company, 1980

6

Healthy Industries
and Public Policy

W. Bruce Erickson and Ian Maitland*

This chapter presents the findings of case studies of six healthy industries: commercial jet aircraft, computers, forest products, frozen foods, metal cans, and pharmaceuticals. The case studies were undertaken to try to ascertain the major reasons for the success of healthy industries, and to establish what role, if any, existing public policies played in their development.

In selecting these industries, we used three sampling criteria: an above-average growth in industry revenues, a favorable U.S. trade balance in the commodities produced by the industry, and an above-average return on equity investment. A positive rating on two out of three of these indicators was taken to signify that the industry was a relatively healthy one. As may be seen from figure 6.1, one or two of the industries studied could be considered as borderline cases. (For further data on the industries, see Appendix A at the end of the chapter.) What is more, in three out of the five industries where foreign trade was significant, the relative trade balance deteriorated between 1974 and 1979 (forest products, pharmaceuticals, and aircraft), while in a fourth (computers), exports and imports had grown at the same percentage rate.

We have deliberately chosen to examine a heterogeneous sample of industries to avoid predetermining our results. One consequence of this choice, inevitably, is that some of our findings may apply to only one or another subset of the sample. The sample is limited to so-called mature healthy industries in order to allow us to distinguish the factors contributing to vitality at different stages in the life cycles of healthy industries.

The study is based on case studies prepared by Ph.D. and M.B.A. students at the University of Minnesota. The materials for the case studies were collected by them principally from secondary sources, namely, industry studies, articles, security analysts' reports, and trade publications, as well as from interviews with securities analysts specializing in the industries and from discussions with industry executives.

* The authors would like to acknowledge the invaluable help they received on this project from Murali Mantrala, Dean Schroeder, Jim Ward, Becky Yanisch, Dick Schwab, and John Hegvik.

Industry	Frozen Foods	Forest Products	Pharma- ceuticals	Metal Cans	Computers	Aircraft
SIC #(s)	2037,8	2421,2436	2831,3,4	3411	3573	3721

(1) Growth of Revenues

(2) Trade Balance

(3) Return on Equity

NA

● = Above average, favorable
◐ = Average
○ = Below average, unfavorable

NA = not applicable
Base period for (1) and (2) = 1974 to 1979; for (3) = 1980.

Fig. 6.1 Relative Performance of Six Healthy Industries, 1974-79

Our approach carries with it certain obvious limitations. In order to gain sufficient breadth of experience to permit preliminary generalizations about the causes of industrial vitality, we must forgo intensive examination of a particular industry. Certain other limitations should also be noted. Our sample does not claim to be representative of all healthy U.S. industries. Our report is based, so to speak, on "tertiary" sources (that is, case studies that were themselve largely prepared from secondary sources). In the process of condensation, information was undoubtedly lost and distortions may have crept in. And our findings about "mature" healthy industries may not be applicable in the changed technological, trade, and political environment of today.

THE DEVELOPMENT OF HEALTHY INDUSTRIES: A PARADIGM

This section of the chapter presents our findings regarding the evolution of a normal healthy industry—first, in its early stages and, second, in its maturity. The implications of our findings for the formulation and implementation of policies designed to promote healthy industries are discussed in the second section.

Healthy Industries: The Early Stages

In their modern forms (with the possible exception of forest products), the industries studied here were largely pioneered in the United States. It is therefore worth considering what factors contributed to making the United States an especially nurturing environment for the germination of new industries, paying particular attention to the role of government.

Technological versus commercial leadership. The origins of the six healthy industries can be traced in large part to the commercial application or embodiment in new products or processes of existing technical or scientific knowledge. For example:

- In *computers*, the development of card punchers, card sorters, tabulators, and improved vacuum tubes and switches made the computer realizable once the basic idea was considered seriously.
- In *forest products*, the power-driven saw and saw mill, as well as the commercial use of products like sawdust, changed forest products from a cottage activity into an industry.
- In *frozen foods*, quick-freezing techniques, refrigerated railroad cars, and improvement in refrigeration for groceries and consumers made possible the transportation and storage of frozen foods without impairment of quality.

In several cases, as can be seen, a number of often unrelated technological developments had to occur before the new industry became viable. Nevertheless, the experience of some of the six industries suggests that it may not be unusual for the requisite basic technical knowledge to have been available for a considerable time before its commercial exploitation. This is merely to restate the truism that there is nothing automatic about the transition from a technical advance or invention to a commercially viable product. This distinction is important because, from our case studies, it is apparent that the distinctive advantage of the United States lay not so much in its technological leadership (although it was generally at the forefront of technological developments) as in its commercial leadership. For example, it is well known that the United States lagged behind the U.K. and Germany in jet engines, and the first commercial jet-liner, the British "Comet," was in service in 1952, a full six years before the Boeing 707 entered Pan American service (Phillips, 1971, pp. 123-124). On the other hand, Clarence Birdseye, an American, developed the earliest methods for the quick-freezing of food.

Although Soma (1976, p. 20) attributes the failure of the British to stay abreast of the United States in early computer development to the lack of sustained government support, the importance of the United States' *commercial* edge is evident in the case of computers. As Nicholas Jéquier (1974, p. 198) has pointed out,

> What IBM did in the 1950s and early 1960s was to take the computer out of the ghetto of the scientific world and propose it to its customers as a substitute for the punched card equipment they had been using for their commercial data

processing services. As things turned out, this was a revolutionary innovation in marketing which took everyone by surprise, including many people at IBM.

Jéquier describes the impact on the European market, and especially the UK market, of IBM's 1401 machine:

> These [computer sales] figures are all the more revealing if one considers the important contributions made by English research groups to the development of computing technology. They testify furthermore to what may appear as an unexpected paradox, namely, that the primary causes for the decline of the European computer industry were not technological but commercial . . . what happened in fact is that the commercial superiority established by IBM in the early 1960s laid the basis for the technological superiority which was to follow. (p. 199)

Although starting after Remington Rand (later Sperry Rand), IBM soon caught up in the commercial computer industry. One of the key factors in its breakthrough and in its continued dominance is its constant emphasis on service and support. As Soma (1976) puts it, "A survey of customers conducted by *Datamation* to determine the factors they considered important in comparing computer manufacturing firms found that IBM ranked last in product performance per dollar, but first in after-sales service, product reliability, and support" (p. 43).

In metal cans and to a lesser extent in pharmaceuticals, the United States has accounted for the lion's share of major innovations. However, even here it should be noted that the United States' technological preeminence has not resulted from its basic research effort, but from the applied research conducted in the laboratories of its major corporations. For example, "When we look for the important innovations, the revolutionary technological advances, the discoveries of most far-reaching importance, we find them coming from the laboratories and shops of American Can, Continental Can, and several of the integrated steel producers" (McKie, 1959, p. 247). In the postwar years, the pharmaceutical industry has been the principal source of drug discoveries, although its importance was less pronounced in the 1940s (Schwartzman, 1976, chapter 4).

The role of demand. The basic technologies of computers and jet aircraft were available to several countries, but American firms soon came to dominate these industries. Where did the U.S. advantage lie? The entrepreneurial initiative of men like Thomas J. Watson, Jr. and companies like General Foods (which pioneered the marketing of frozen foods) unquestionably played a part, and it is probable that American management was more entrepreneurial than its European counterparts. It is virtually impossible to assess the independent contribution of this factor, however, because entrepreneurship may be inseparable from the conditions which foster it. Entrepreneurship, that is to say, may not be a function of national culture, but may occur where conditions reward it.

Why was the United States especially hospitable to the early development of the industries studied? Our case studies led us to single out one set of interrelated variables as being of paramount importance: the size, affluence, and sophistication of the American market.

These characteristics of the American market have to some extent offset a built-in bias in the marketplace against new products. In the normal case, a new product can expect to have to compete against a well-established substitute; and in this competition the new product is likely to be inferior both in terms of cost and performance. This inferiority is likely to reflect several or all of the following circumstances:

• Producers using the old technology have fully exploited available "learning-curve" advantages.

• Producers using the old technology have often achieved economies of scale.

• Producers using the old technology have marketing and service operations in place.

• Producers using the old technology have depreciated plants which, in an inflationary era, had often been purchased at low original cost. Because of their size, they are also able to realize financial economies such as lower-cost borrowing and quantity discounts in their purchases of materials.

• Producers using the old technology have achieved customer acceptance for their products.

• Producers using the old technology have the "product infrastructure" in place. (For example, canned-foods manufacturers had warehouses, railroad cars, and consumer storage and stoves in place; frozen-food producers initially had none of their required infrastructure in place.)

The typical situation is depicted in figure 6.2 which shows potential and actual costs, both for the product or service itself and for the associated infrastructure at the time a new technology becomes available. The figure shows that producers using the old technology rarely achieve the maximum reduction in unit costs that are potentially realizable, but invariably come closer to this objective than firms seeking to use a new technology.

How have the size, affluence, and sophistication of the American market helped to remove or lower these barriers to the introduction of new products? This has happened in a number of different ways, chief among which have been the following: The size of the U.S. market has meant that even a specialized market could represent significant dollar volumes of sales. The size and affluence of the U.S. market have meant that there were significant numbers of customers with particular needs who would demand technologically advanced products at premium prices. And high discretionary income

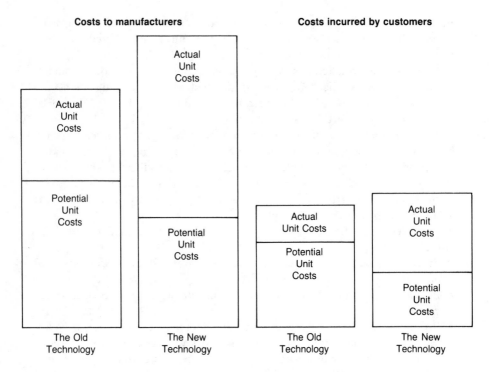

Fig. 6.2 Using Old and New Technologies

in the United States has enabled Americans to develop highly varied life-styles, creating demand for novel goods and services.

Thus, as shown in table 6.1, the U.S. domestic air traffic market has overshadowed the rest of the world. In computers, the development of the large corporation and the growth of corporate international operations, together with rising wages and the resulting substitution of capital for labor, has created enormous demand for computational power. In the early 1970s, for example, the United States had twice the number of computers per billion dollars of GNP and twice the number per million of working population as the nearest other country (Soma, 1976, p. 75). And the affluence of the U.S. market led to a willingness on the part of consumers to pay a premium for the convenience and variety offered by canned and frozen foods.

In other words, the emergence (or transformation) of the industries studied was aided by the existence of specialized markets (strictly speaking, potential specialized markets) of sufficient scale to attract the risk capital necessary for R&D and start-up costs. These markets are what Abernathy (1980) has termed "thin specialty markets," and which in his view have

Table 6.1. Nonfreight Air Transport Market (in millions of passenger kilometers on scheduled routes)

Country of Carrier	1932	1937	1964	1971
Britain	26	79	10,795	19,907
France	22	60	6,697	13,834
United States	236	743	94,134	215,585
World	465	1,500	171,000	494,000

SOURCE: M. S. Hochmuth, "Aerospace," in Raymond Vernon, ed., *Big Business and the State: Changing Relations in Western Europe* (Cambridge, Mass.: Harvard University Press, 1974), p. 155.

played a critical role in the development and commercialization of new technologies.

> Buyers in such markets share common traits: (1) a willingness to pay high premiums for superior performance in a few limited dimensions, and (2) a willingness to accommodate some performance deficiencies in the new technology compared to its existing competitors. Aside from the risks these buyers are willing to assume, they constitute a small affluent market. (Abernathy, 1980, p. 48)

Revolutionary new products need thin specialty markets, because in their initial stages, they are typically inferior—often both in cost and in some important technological dimensions—to their conventional competitors. Abernathy cites the examples of pocket calculators, pocket radios, ballpoint pens, jet engines, and others. The function of thin specialty markets, then, is to nurse these industries through their teething troubles to the point of commercial viability and self-sustained growth. This pattern is illustrated by the evolution of the computer market, as summarized in table 6.2.

The role of government. What contribution did government make to the early development of the healthy industries studied? The role of war and defense spending in the incubation of computer and jet aircraft technology is well known. The computer industry was largely based on data processing equipment developed for the computational needs of the military (for the calculation of ballistic firing tables) and the Census Bureau. All of the earliest electronic computers were built under government contract. IBM's Defense Calculator, announced in 1950, was the first of its 700 series which eventually evolved into a major line of commercial computers (Soma, 1976, p. 18). In the commercial jet aircraft industry, the earliest passenger jets were based on strategic bombers developed for the air force (notably the Boeing 707 or the B-52).

Table 6.2. Computers: Evolution from Specialty to Mass Market

	Market
1950s	Academics and scientists purchase computers for large complicated tasks such as census and research.
1960s	Much broader application of data processing power exploited by large companies as well as government. Purchase made by data processing professionals.
1970s	Use of computers in all aspects of business and some personal applications. Users of system influence and often make final decision.
1980s	"User-friendly" equipment purchased directly by managers and individual private users. Large application purchases form base for network communications.

What is perhaps less well known is the role played by the war and by defense spending in the emergence of the frozen foods industry or the transformation of the pharmaceutical industry. Government policies and actions in World War II created a mass retail market for frozen foods. For example, the government made huge purchases of frozen foods for the armed services. Frozen prepared foods were exempted from rationing. Frozen commodities were rationed until 1944, but not thereafter; and under the rationing "point" system, consumers could buy more of a given commodity by buying it frozen rather than fresh or canned. The Office of Price Administration (OPA) effectively underwrote frozen foods' first mass advertising campaign by requiring widespread publication of the ration points for various foods. The government eventually gave priority in the allotment of steel and other strategic materials to the construction of low-temperature storage plants, retail store frozen foods cabinets, and home freezers. And finally, because of the shortage of standard items, many people were encouraged to experiment with new products, including frozen foods.

As a result of such government actions, by the end of World War II, frozen-food producers were solidly entrenched in the marketplace, both in terms of consumer acceptance and in terms of physical infrastructure (quick-freezing equipment, railroad cars capable of handling frozen foods, frozen-food compartments in supermarkets, and later, home freezers).

In the pharmaceutical industry, it was the development and large-scale production of penicillin to meet wartime needs (in World War II) that began the industry's transition from bulk supplier to finished dosage form manufacturers. In the pre–World War II era, "drug companies were concerned largely with formulating existing drugs and commercial exploitation of findings of original research in universities. However, such an image of the pharmaceutical industry today must be regarded as completely distorted" (Schwartzman, 1976, p. 31). The war meant that, in addition to stepping up the research and development of new antibiotics, the drug companies invested heavily in manufacturing equipment to provide finished goods to meet military needs. As a result, the retail pharmacist's preparation of compounds had become the province of the manufacturer by the war's end. In addition, the development of penicillin was followed by both publicly and privately funded research which led to the discovery of other antibiotics. This signaled the end of the era in which the industry was composed largely of long-established firms producing relatively standardized pharmaceutical preparations.

In our two remaining industries, metal cans and forest products, wartime conditions and military procurement had no comparable impact.

What lessons does wartime experience hold for peacetime industrial vitalization? The answer, we think, is again to be found in Abernathy's concept of thin specialty markets. Directly or indirectly, the government provided an assured market which enabled the fledgling industry to overcome the technological and cost hurdles of initial commercialization; once those hurdles were surmounted, the new technology was in a position to compete on a footing of equality with established technologies. We are suggesting that in computers and jet aircraft, and to a lesser extent in frozen foods and pharmaceuticals, federal procurement and other policies appear to have helped to correct market failures. The high entry costs associated with the commercialization of a new technology might otherwise have impeded or prevented the development of new industries with enormous potential.

Our case studies indicate that government has serendipitously functioned as a thin specialty market; they do not tell us whether government would be effective if it were explicitly to take on the responsibility of fostering healthy industries. After all, foreign experience is littered with the bleached bones of failed government interventions. If resources are not to be squandered on prestige projects, white elephants, bail-outs of declining industries, and so on, it will be necessary to develop criteria to enable policymakers to distinguish between cases where government can and cannot helpfully provide the seed money for new healthy industries.

It would be beyond the scope of this chapter to try to identify those criteria. Nevertheless, certain highly tentative propositions are suggested by our case studies.

Generally, the more capital- and technology-intensive the new industry, the more important has been the role of government procurement in its early stages.

In the shorter term, at least, the healthy industries have depended upon intensive *applied* research rather than on any breakthroughs in pure research.

A crucial factor in the emergence of these industries has been the existence (often underwritten by government) of an *assured market* for products with particular performance characteristics, in spite of probable early deficiencies in other respects. The existence of such a market may be sufficient by itself to call forth the necessary R&D from private sources.

The U.S. market today: A note.   In recent years, spending by both the U.S. government and private American firms on research and development has declined as a percentage of GNP, while the research and development expenditures of other developed Western economies, notably Japan and West Germany, have grown. It is widely believed that the technological gap that may have existed in the past between the United States and its leading commercial rivals is shrinking and in some industries has even disappeared.

Less well known, however, is the probable disappearance of the United States' comparative advantage deriving from its large, affluent, and sophisticated market. Europe (due to the Common Market) and Japan now constitute large and affluent markets. Reductions in international trade barriers have enormously facilitated foreign access to U.S. markets. And customers in highly developed industrialized nations often maintain life-styles as varied as those of U.S. citizens and appear to be at least as receptive to new products as Americans.

Thus, the critical first-mover advantages that were enjoyed by the healthy industries we studied may no longer be as easily available to U.S. companies. As foreign markets come to match the United States in size and affluence, the U.S. advantage in unique "thin specialty markets" for initial commercialization and in larger specialized markets capable of absorbing large-scale commercialization of new products is significantly diminished.

In today's world market, U.S. producers may actually be at a disadvantage. For example, Japan is a major purchaser of American forest products, especially timber from the Pacific Northwest. Japanese specifications and dimensions for wood products are so complex, however, that the United States has remained a supplier of raw timber to the Japanese market rather than a provider of finished goods.

Also, from the viewpoint of, say, a Belgian high-technology firm, the huge U.S. market with largely standardized specifications in most product areas is an attraction. It it well worth modifying its products to meet U.S. specifications and American needs. Equivalent American firms will rarely find it profitable to modify products to meet a jungle of foreign requirements, some of which may be designed deliberately to protect domestic producers. Thus, we suggest that international commerce in new technologies may be affected by a market asymmetry—with the U.S. market highly accessible to foreign entrants, but with foreign markets being less susceptible to penetration by U.S. manufacturers.

Healthy Industries in Maturity

Although they were all in "mature" stages of their life cycles, the industries studied were relatively healthy—not surprisingly, since that is why they were selected for study. In this section we identify some of the more important factors that have affected their continued prosperity, again with particular attention to the impact of public policy.

Before we do so, however, it should be pointed out that a healthy national economy will not necessarily be made up entirely—or even predominantly—of healthy mature industries. Indeed, a more satisfactory index of the health of the economy might be the rate at which mature industries are replaced by newer ones in a Schumpeterian "gale of creative destruction." According to the technological-life-cycle theory of international trade (see Wells, 1972), the comparative advantage of the United States lies in its highly skilled work force. This resource leads the United States to specialize in industries with a high skilled-labor content, that is, new high-technology industries. As industries enter their maturity (that is, as their technology becomes routinized and well known), the skill level that is required declines and the United States' comparative advantage turns into a comparative disadvantage (excessively high labor costs). As a consequence, even healthy mature industries may migrate to lower-skill, lower-wage countries or may become distressed domestic industries.

With this in mind, namely, that the health of particular industries is not to be confused with the health of U.S. industry as a whole, let us turn to the industries we studied in their mature phases. What accounts for their continuing vitality, and how have they been affected by public policy?

As we shall see, although government remained an important factor for our industries in their maturity, it was far less crucial than in their early stages. Another finding is that by and large these industries were self-sustaining, and public policies tended to limit their prosperity rather than promote it.

The heterogeneity of our sample meant that no single set of policies affected all the industries in the same way. As a consequence, the following discussion examines major areas of government intervention sequentially and tries to assess their impact.

Why healthy industries stayed healthy. In several industries—jet aircraft, computers, pharmaceuticals, and, to a lesser extent, metal cans and frozen foods—the United States' early lead was successfully converted into a position of enduring dominance—or, at least, strength. That is to say, these industries benefited from significant first-mover advantages. But the United States has achieved leadership in other industries—such as autos and steel—without securing similar lasting advantages. What was distinctive about the industries under study that enabled them to consolidate early leadership into a position of continuing strength?

The case studies suggest that the United States' first-mover advantages resulted from a number of different (and mutually reinforcing) factors:

• a dynamic technology

- high capital barriers to entry (especially for R&D)
- economies of scale
- customer acceptance
- customer after-sales service support

Three of the industries are highly technology-intensive (jet aircraft, computers, and pharmaceuticals). They are characterized by levels of R&D spending (see Appendix A) far in excess of the national average. What these levels of R&D signify is that the technologies in question are still in a dynamic state; that is, the industries are undergoing continual rapid change, with important innovations quickly overtaken by new advances. In these conditions, the large cash flows from current sales have enabled established U.S. companies to finance the huge R&D outlays necessary to remain at the technological cutting edge of the industry. This is not to argue that these companies have invariably *originated* the major technological breakthroughs. Here the record is mixed: in pharmaceuticals, the large firms have been the industry leaders; in computers, the smaller U.S. firms have been in the forefront (Control Data, Cray Research, Amdahl); and in aircraft, many major innovations have originated outside the industry. It is to argue, rather, that intensive R&D has been vital to assuring that these companies maintain their market share by at least quickly matching innovations developed elsewhere. The classic instance is IBM. According to Soma (1976), the company's strategy is to mount

> a massive research and development effort . . . to ensure that IBM is never more than one to two years behind in all areas of computer technology. Historically, as well as today, IBM has maintained a large research and development expenditure level. IBM R&D effort has not always kept pace with technological developments in the remainder of the computer industry. (p. 151)

In the pharmaceutical industry, larger firms are able to maintain their leadership in part because of the economies of scale in drug research: "Large firms discover and develop proportionately more new drugs than do small firms. This is because they devote proportionately more resources to research and also because, in this field, large laboratories employ resources more productively" (Schwartzman, 1976, p. 9).

These advantages accruing to established firms are reinforced by customer acceptance for their products and by an infrastructure for service support. In the commercial jet aircraft industry, only the dominant American manufacturers have been able to obtain advance purchase commitments from customers in sufficient quantity to cover the costs of designing and developing a new aircraft (Hochmuth, 1974). Foreign passenger aircraft industries would probably not exist without massive government underwriting of their development costs. In the computer industry, once a firm is established with an end user, it is very hard to dislodge (OECD, 1969, p. 113). Soma reports that at least a 10 percent improvement in the price-to-performance ratio is needed before an entrenched customer will even look at a competitor's computer (Soma, 1976, p. 43). Any switch to a competitor's product would entail an arduous process of relearning by the user's employees. When this is coupled with IBM's reputation for after-sales service, product reliability, and support, it constitutes a formidable barrier to the entry of rivals. These facts help to account for IBM's continued dominance overseas as well as at home in mainframe computers (though developments in semiconductor technology are bringing about the structural atomization of the industry and creating new market niches for competitors of IBM, and the trend seriously threatens IBM's dominance).

These factors appear to have been crucial in the cases of the three technology-intensive industries we studied. A variety of other factors—some related, some idiosyncratic—also deserve attention.

Even in the non-technology-intensive industries we investigated, a steady stream of innovations has contributed to their vigor. Notable are the aluminum can, computer-based forest management systems, the development of new applications for wood-based products, the application of freezing technology to new foods, and others.

Government funding of private sector R&D has helped to revolutionize the computer industry by supporting the development of integrated circuits for military applications and the space program. The R&D programs of the civil aircraft industry have largely been financed by military contracts.

The government remains a major customer of the aircraft industry, the computer industry, and even the frozen-foods industry (through purchases for the armed forces and the USDA's child nutrition program). In addition, government has indirectly supported demand for drugs (Medicare and Medicaid) and forest products (whose major customer is the housing market).

Capital availability was not a constraint for the industries studied. Private capital markets were willing and able to supply ample capital, since these industries were properly regarded as good credit risks. In addition, most of the leading firms in these industries retained the bulk of their earnings and used debt finance sparingly.

Both the forest products and frozen-foods industries enjoy a comparative advantage in respect of their raw materials.

Healthy industries in relative decline. Even the stronger of the healthy industries studied exhibited symptoms of flagging vigor. In four cases, the trade balance was deteriorating or stagnant (see Appendix A). And there are other alarming developments: Fujitsu has recently overtaken IBM in the Japanese market; Boeing is meeting its stiffest competition in decades from the Western European Airbus; pharmaceutical R&D has been growing much faster overseas than in the United States; and although the United States is richly endowed with forests, it ran a deficit in forest products of $2.9 billion in 1978.

It is beyond the scope of this chapter to provide any precise estimate of the contribution of government to the loss of vigor of these industries; instead, in what follows we simply highlight some of the principal governmental constraints that have been harmful to their performance. Table 6.3 summarizes the major public policies affecting the industries studied.

First, although in the past the government has contributed to the health of the industries through its direct and indirect support of demand for their products, this sort of help is increasingly viewed as a mixed blessing. The lack of consistency and coherence in government procurement and the onerous paperwork requirements accompanying government contracts have led to the widespread perception of government as a bad customer. Defense procurement has, of course, been particularly subject to abrupt shifts in policy. Budgetary constraints and lack of consensus on a strategic posture for the United States have led, for example, to on-again, off-again plans for the development of the ABM, B-1 bomber, and MX missile. On the one hand, defense contracts (and a federal loan guarantee) have kept McDonnell-Douglas and Lockheed solvent during the teething troubles of their commercial transports, the DC-10 and the L-1011. On the other hand, since the cancellation

Table 6.3. Major Public Policies Affecting the Industries Studied

Industry	Most Important Government Policies
Forest Products	Forest service timber management policies Federal Reserve policies affecting interest rates Environmental regulation
Computers	Government procurement and research support Antitrust actions Export restrictions to communist bloc
Pharmaceuticals	FDA regulation of new drugs Government spending on medical care Wartime military spending Cost-containment measures
Commercial Aircraft	Military procurement Ex-Im Bank financing Antitrust policies
Frozen Foods	USDA mandatory nutritional labeling requirements
Metal Cans	Antitrust actions Restrictions on non-returnable containers and/or mandatory deposits Environmental regulation

of the B-1 bomber, there have been no military contracts for new bombers or large jet transports (traditionally the proving ground for the new technology later incorporated into civilian passenger aircraft). Uncertainties regarding the government's procurement intentions have been exacerbated by the practice of letting contracts on a year-to-year basis. With the lead time for new weapon development having increased to ten or twelve years (from about four years in 1970), the defense industry argues that multiyear contracts are needed to permit more systematic resource planning; this would result in reduced costs and earlier delivery.

But it is not only the defense industry that has been affected by government's failure to maintain consistent long-term policies. Because of its dependence on the housing market, the forest products industry has been particularly sensitive to fluctuations in interest rates. And the innovativeness of the pharmaceutical industry may be hurt by cost-containment measures in medical care (see Schwartzman, 1976, pp. 23-24). These industries, then, have to some extent been the victims of government-imposed boom-and-bust cycles.

Second, the enormous volume of "social" regulations (such as EEOC and OSHA) enacted by Congress and promulgated by government agencies in the late 1960s and the 1970s has undoubtedly had an adverse impact on the industries studied; but, except in a few cases (which we will come to), it is impossible to say with confidence whether these regulations have had a material effect on their long-term health.

In the short term, these industries incurred often substantial extra costs on account of increased government regulation. The metal can industry, for example, has had to install expensive pollution control equipment to control hydrocarbon emissions from solvents used in coating and labeling; it has had to find a replacement for fluorocarbons as propellants in aerosol cans; and it is threatened by the trend in certain states to prohibit nonreturnable beverage containers. The enormous volume of environmental regulations has hurt the forest products industry, primarily through increased restrictions on the supply of timber. The frozen-foods industry has vigorously opposed proposals for mandatory nutritional labeling and has criticized the USDA for other regulations that harm industry growth. It is ironical to note that when the frozen-foods industry was in its infancy and was still regarded with some suspicion, USDA inspection and grading of its products helped to secure consumer acceptance.

The lasting impact of these regulations and others like them is difficult to assess. Individually, the regulations do not appear to have caused any irreversible injury; often the industry has learned to live with the regulation or has innovated its way around it (for example, by inventing a new propellant). What our case studies could not tell us was whether or not the cumulative weight of regulations had weakened the industries.

In two cases, identifiable regulatory policies have had significant impacts. Since the 1962 drug amendments, the FDA has become much more strict in its demands for assurances of efficacy and safety. The costs of R&D have risen accordingly, and it now costs considerably more to develop a new drug than it did before 1962 (Schwartzman, 1976, p. 23). Largely as a result, there has been a precipitous decline in the number of new drugs introduced in the United States. Apart from the obvious social welfare costs of this development, there is the impact on the pharmaceutical industry and its international preeminence. In this regard, certain trends are discernible (Grabowski, 1976):

• U.S. firms have been shifting increasing percentages of their research and development abroad.

• Growth rates in pharmaceutical industry R&D have been much faster overall in foreign countries than in the United States.

• Growth rates on new product sales in foreign countries have far exceeded those in the United States in recent years.

• The majority of drug discoveries by U.S. firms are now first introduced abroad.

• Regulatory differences have also apparently acted to accelerate drug firm investment in manufacturing capacity abroad.

The full potential of the United States' vast stands of trees has not been realized, largely because of restrictive forest management policies pursued by the U.S. Forest Service. The Forest Service owns over half of the nation's softwood saw-timber stocks, and yet the national forests contribute less than a quarter of the softwood saw-timber output. In contrast, the private forest industry, which controls only 16 percent of the softwood saw-timber inventory, accounts for some 38 percent of wood production. Critics of the Forest Service charge that the result of its policies is that an estimated 6 billion board feet of timber in the national forests is wasted every year because mature trees are left to rot and die. They further argue that the nation could have more timber *and* more wilderness if the constraints on efficient production were removed (Lenard, 1981; Smith, 1979).

Third, antitrust policy played a mixed, but on balance probably positive, role in the industries we studied. In the computer industry, antitrust policy has contributed to maintaining a breathing space for smaller firms which have pioneered many significant innovations.

In 1935, as a result of a consent decree, IBM was required to abandon various pricing practices on its cards, and in 1952 IBM was forced to change its leasing practice. Primarily as a result of two private antitrust suits, as well as pressure from the Department of Justice, IBM unbundled its software and service—priced them separately. The fear of vigorous antitrust actions by competitors probably forced IBM to be cautious in its pricing policies among mainframe computers, peripherals, software, and service operations.

In the metal can industry, antitrust decisions or consent decrees in 1916, 1950, and 1956 had the effect of reviving competition.

Nevertheless, the fact that competition is thriving in the industries we studied probably owes more to the operation of market forces and technological change—and, above all, foreign competition—than to the vigorous enforcement of antitrust policies. In computers, as we have noted, the semiconductor has changed the face of the industry and has opened up new market niches for competitors of IBM. In metal cans, fierce competition has been revived by the entry of the aluminum industry into can manufacture and the strong response of the steel industry. Concentration in can manufacture has declined further in recent years with the entry through backward integration into the industry of large beverage producers. In spite of the aircraft industry's high concentration ratio, there is no shortage of competition, thanks largely to its heavily subsidized rivals overseas.

We found evidence that other public policies have had the perverse effects of injuring competition or favoring large producers. For example, the restrictive policies of the U.S Forest Service have favored integrated producers at the expense of smaller ones by increasing the price of standing timber and creating artificial timber shortages. In the pharmaceutical industry, the extensive testing of new drugs required by the FDA has had the effect of entrenching large companies and increasing concentration. Antitrust laws and FCC regulations have combined to delay the entry of AT&T into the computer industry where it might be a formidable competitor for IBM.

In at least one case, our findings raise questions about the continuing relevance of strict antitrust policies regarding joint ventures in an open world economy. Such policies may have harmed the U.S. position in the world passenger aircraft market by precluding joint ventures between American manufacturers. Thus, McDonnell-Douglas and Lockheed developed competing versions of the wide-bodied medium-range jumbo jet (the DC-10 and L-1011) when economic and marketing logic might have favored collaborations between them. No such bar applies to joint ventures with foreign companies, and McDonnell-Douglas is currently looking for a foreign partner for a proposed new 150-passenger airplane. Such collaborations will probably lead to a diffusion of U.S. know-how and intensified foreign competition when the next generation of aircraft is built. In another industry, computers, the current, more relaxed antitrust climate may permit American firms to collaborate on software development.

Fourth, a word needs to be said about U.S. trade policies and the striking contrast they present with the trade policies of other countries. It is interesting to consider the following:

• Foreign governments provide more generous incentives to exporters (for example, return of value added tax and low interest credit to export customers) than does the United States.

• In some cases (notably Japan) nontariff barriers are more systematically used to protect domestic industries.

• No foreign government has made the bribery of political officials in other countries illegal, as the United States has under the Foreign Corrupt Practices Act of 1977.

• U.S. policies regarding the export of military and high-technology goods to communist countries are far more restrictive than those of our allies.

• Until recently at least, the United States has been less generous in the tax treatment of its nationals employed abroad than have its principal trade rivals.

In short, not only has the United States more readily subordinated its commercial interests to its political objectives, but U.S. exporters have not enjoyed the same active collaboration of their government. These differences have unquestionably put American companies, particularly in the aircraft and computer industries, at a competitive disadvantage in export markets.

The computer industry: An illustration.   The growth of the computer industry as depicted in table 6.4 illustrates many of the elements in the initial development and subsequent maturing of representative healthy industry. There are several points to note.

• The initial markets were thin specialty markets—for the U.S. census and the American and British military, and later for specialized scientific applications.

• The United States did not have dominant technological leadership, but was first to commercialize the computer.

• Most of the early technological developments occurred as a result of government research grants or procurement contracts.

• Nonindustry firms made important contributions to the industry (the transistor and the integrated circuit).

• Entrepreneurship played an important role. IBM, not the technological leader, became dominant in the medium-sized range; Digital Computer, in small computers (both largely because of innovative leaders).

• Major technological innovations from the industry came from the smaller firms.

• In the later stages of the industry, the major contribution of government was the development of time-sharing by universities operating under the federal government support.

• As the industry matured, government intervention made less and less difference; increasingly, the innovations came from the private sector.

It should be pointed out that in the early stages, government research support for computers amounted to between $30 million and $50 million; today, according to some estimates, the annual sales of U.S.–made computers and associated equipment manufacturers average between $100 billion and $150 billion.

INDUSTRIAL POLICY AND THE HEALTHY INDUSTRIES

The following public policy recommendations are explicitly based on the assumption that most of any government assistance to industry should be devoted to healthy rather than troubled industries. The recommendations are described at two levels—first, in terms of specific areas of industrial policy, and second in the form of an appropriate strategy for developing and implementing an effective industrial policy for the United States.

Industrial Policy: Some Specific Recommendations

This study of six healthy industries has pointed out that an important market failure (namely, a situation where competitive markets, if left alone, may fail to generate the most desirable outcome in terms of the public interest) may arise in the initial stages of a new technology. For reasons examined in this chapter, new technology may in the normal course of events fail to be developed. Because first-mover advantages appear to be so considerable, a nation that is successful in aiding important new technologies at an early stage can reap substantial economic advantages over many years. The benefit-cost ratio of such government actions can be extraordinary, as evidenced by the $30 million to $50 million research and procurement aid by government to the computer industry during the 1940s and 1950s and the $100 billion or so U.S. computer industry of the 1970s and 1980s. Often, new technologies first appear in specialty markets where highly technical "state of the art" specifications and performance are involved. A major goal of government industrial policy should be to encourage the development of such new technologies and to minimize (consistent with other economic and social priorities) government policies and practices that are harmful to healthy industries in their mature stages. How can these objectives be accomplished?

First, our study suggests that it is important for the United States to maintain a position of technological excellence in basic and applied research, but it is not essential for the United States to be the technological leader in all or most fields. This implies that the United States should maintain adequate supplies of scientists and technologists and provide them with the funds, incentives, and opportunities to conduct research. Specific findings of the study include the following:

• As previously indicated, half of the healthy industries studied spent monies on research and development that greatly exceeded the U.S. average based on percentage of sales data.

• Government research support appears to be most critical at an early stage in the development of a healthy industry.

• Government research support may also be helpful at a mature stage in the development of a healthy industry, but mainly on projects with substantial positive externalities involved (for example, a new computer language).

Table 6.4. Major Computer Developments

Name	Innovation	Government Assistance
	Pre 1940s	
Babbage	Difference Machine	Government research grants
Hollerith	Card tabulating system Computer cards start company that eventually became IBM	Worked for and developed equipment sold to U.S. Census
Power	Card punch, sorter, tabulator Started Powers Accounting Co., now Univac, division of Sperry-Rand	Worked for and developed equipment for U.S. Census
	1940s	
Newman (England) and Evans (U.S.)	Colossus, first computer ENIAC, first widely known computer	Government military grants for codebreaking (Britain) and for ballistics tables (U.S.)
	1950s	
Mauchly and Evans	UNIVAC I, first computer with wide commercial application	Sold to Census Bureau
Shockley, Bardeen, Brattain	Transistor	Discovered at Bell Laboratories, a division of AT&T
Sperry-Rand and IBM	LARC, STRETCH, first computers fully using transistors	Atomic Energy Commission contracts

1960s

Control Data Corporation	CDC 6600, first super-computer	Initial sales largely to government units and universities
Digital Equipment Computers	PDP-1, first minicomputer	No major direct government participation
IBM	7000 Computers line, most commercially successful transistor based computers	First installed in Ballistic Missile Early Warning System
Kilby Noyce	Silicon chips, the basis for the third generation of computers	Largely stimulated by NASA and U.S. Bureau of Standards efforts, to minimize components
IBM	360 line of computers, the most successful commercial line of computers	No major direct government participation
Computer producers and users	FORTRAN and COBOL, standard computer language	FORTRAN developed largely by IBM; COBOL developed as a result of a meeting organized by Department of Defense in May 1959
American Airlines	SABRE, first transaction processing ("on-line") computer system	No direct government participation
Burroughs	First major operating system allowing multi-programming multi-processing and visual storage	No direct government participation
MIT	CTSS, the first time-sharing system	Large-scale government financing

1970s

Gene Amdahl (and others)	Plug compatible peripherals	Largely made possible by antitrust settlements, particularly between TELEX and IBM
Intel and Busicon (Japan)	Microprocessors	Some early financing from government; most financed by industry

SOURCE: Based in part on a Master's Thesis, "A History of Computing" by an MIS specialist, Leslie C. Solheim (University of Minnesota, 1980).

- Government regulatory policy may substantially impede research and development. The pharmaceutical industry has reduced expenditures on research and development and transferred many of its activities abroad in response to FDA regulation of the industry.
- Privately supported research and development innovations in mature healthy industry have come both from large firms (commercial jet aircraft, forest products) and from smaller firms (notably computers).

It also appears to be likely that there are substantial "spillover" effects of being strong in certain key technologies. Thomas Kuhn has argued in *The Structure of Scientific Revolutions* that the emergence of a new scientific paradigm causes a spate of changes over a relatively short period of time in dozens of related scientific subdisciplines. The ramifications of new computer technology in several of the industries studied tends to support this observation. Scientific research in such areas as superconductors, artificial intelligence, materials manipulation, biotechnology, and geological scanning may change the face of the U.S. economy over the coming decades.

Second, our study shows that the commercialization of basic and applied research is more important in the development of healthy industries than is maintaining a position of leadership in the research itself. The critical need is to provide thin specialty markets, and the most frequently used peacetime public policy instrument for this purpose was government procurement.

What are the characteristics that a sound procurement policy should embody, as viewed from the perspective of industrial policy? Several observations are in order:

- Procurement should seek to provide initial demand for state-of-the-art technologies, for new technologies, and for technological interfaces (for example, between computers and communications equipment) not yet economically viable in the private sector.
- Procurement should emphasize setting technologically demanding standards and specifications.
- Procurement programs should be most active during the initial stages of a new technology.
- Procurement programs should emphasize smaller firms with good technological capabilities.
- Procurement contracts should be let on a multiyear basis so as to permit firms to make the required capital investment.

We do not argue here that government should neglect other objectives of government procurement or disregard costs, but there is a strong case for consciously incorporating industrial policy considerations into the procurement process.

Since defense spending is the one major area of federal government activity where expenditures are likely to rise in the immediate future, military procurement is likely to present the most significant opportunities for these recommendations to be implemented. Although we recognize that there are always tensions between the creation of new weapons and forces in being, it is clear that in the past, the rapid development of new technologies—as in computers and electronics—has yielded vast and largely unanticipated benefits to U.S. military capabilities.

Third, the United States has a high stake in international product standardization. Internationalization of the world economy has meant that foreign producers have access to the huge U.S. market, while American manufacturers must confront an often bewildering array of product standards that vary significantly from nation to nation. These factors have probably produced a world market asymmetry; the advantages to American producers of having unique access to this specialty market in the United States have largely disappeared, while mature healthy American industries are placed at a significant competitive disadvantage in international markets. It pays foreign manufacturers to invade the huge U.S. market by meeting American product standards, but it often does not pay American manufacturers to modify their products to meet the standards required in smaller foreign markets.

Fourth, the process of deregulation should benefit healthy industries, but immediate dramatic results should not be expected. As indicated in the first section of this chapter, the types of regulation that have most seriously affected the healthy industries vary greatly from industry to industry—for example, ranging from interest rates and management of U.S. lands in forest products to FDA regulations in pharmaceuticals. The enormous variety of regulations suggests that deregulation is not a panacea capable of revitalizing most healthy industries. Obviously, the process of deregulation, if not carefully carried out, can be exceedingly harmful to other public goals.

Fifth, American antitrust policy needs to be reoriented. In the industries studied, antitrust laws generally had a desirable impact. However, in this very complex field, some changes are in order.

Technological innovations and their subsequent commercialization came from a variety of sources—small firms, large companies, and outsiders to the industry. The "simpleminded" antitrust presumption against well-performing large companies needs to be abandoned. Large companies should not be restricted by antitrust laws and other government policies from invading each other's market (as for example, AT&T and the computer industry).

A vital point is to use antitrust laws to keep entry open. A model of this approach was the use and threatened use of antitrust to enable innovative competitors to build equipment that was compatible with IBM's products and to be reasonably assured that IBM could not use price discrimination to destroy their hard-won positions.

Antitrust attitudes involving domestic joint ventures among nonleading firms in an industry should be relaxed. Various antitrust interpretations involving single-company and joint company marketing of a product in international markets needs to be reexamined.

Relaxing restrictions against horizontal mergers does not seem appropriate. The evidence fails to support the notion that mergers designed to achieve critical size, which were used in foreign countries (for example, in the European aircraft and computer industries), worked at all in reducing American leadership in these industries.

In short, the objectives of antitrust policy insofar as healthy industries are concerned should be to create a "mixed industry structure," with opportunities for both large and small firms in a specific industry, and to maximize the possibility of entry by aggressive entrepreneurs into healthy industries.

Industrial Policy: Developing and Implementing an Overall Strategy

This study of six healthy industries has found that government played an important role, especially in the early developmental stages, in the generation and expansion of healthy industries. The opportunity for government to play this role, it has been argued, is created by significant market failures with respect to the development and early commercialization of new technology. This leads to the conclusion that systematic industrial policy, effectively administered, can contribute to the vitality of a nation's economy.

But difficult questions remain. Is the government capable of helping potentially healthy industries? Won't the political system end up supporting declining industries because of the pressures exerted by powerful constituencies? Once a helping hand is extended by government to an industry can it be withdrawn so that the potentially healthy industry is weaned of its dependence on government? Can government, when necessary, target its help to the genuine innovator, without succumbing to political pressures to distribute largesse to a variety of other interests?

These questions suggest that if a nation is to develop an effective industrial policy, that policy will need to be carefully developed and will have to follow some carefully articulated guidelines if politically opportunistic interference in its development and execution is to be minimized.

In establishing an overall strategy for a nation's industrial policy, three broad approaches, described in some detail in table 6.5 can be identified.

Benign nonintervention. The government allows markets to allocate resources among industries, and carefully weighs business interests against other economic and social goals such as a fair income distribution, income security, protection of the environment, and so on.

Table 6.5. Alternative Strategies in the Formulation of Industrial Policy

Basic Strategy	Major Rationale	Examples of Special Public Policies Given the Strategy
Nonintervention	Government is unlikely to be able to identify much less promote industries of the future.	Traditional government activities—national defense, a system of justice, control of currency, etc.
	Government should seek to promote economic and social values not normally met by the market. Equity and security of income, environmental protection, and equal employment opportunity are examples.	Balanced policies in terms of benefits and costs as measured by contribution to the public interest; e.g., careful consideration of trade-offs between the environmental and economic considerations.
		Reliance on the market except in cases of market failure where active government intervention is desirable.
Selective Intervention	Government can identify and promote the industries of the future.	Traditional government activities (see above).
	Government can either be probusiness, neutral, or a promoter of nonbusiness values depending on the political philosophy of the observer. (Most selective interventionists, however, probably prefer an activist government role.)	Additional government activities to serve nonbusiness economic and social objectives (depending on views of observer).
		Careful identification of favored industries.
		Aid (tax relief, subsidies, export credits, tariff protection, credit allocation, etc.) to designated industries.
Probusiness Activism	Government should encourage business expansion even at short-term costs in other public goals in order to increase the economic base and to counter probusiness actions of other countries.	Traditional government activities (see above).
		Tax relief and subsidies to encourage capital formation, industry research and development, and saving.
	The market should be allowed to decide what industries grow or decline in the probusiness climate except possibly for industries whose foreign competitors are heavily subsidized.	Low or no corporate taxes.
		Expert assistance available to all firms.
		Elimination or reduction of most regulations harmful to business expansion.

Selective intervention.   Industrial policy seeks to identify and promote specific industries, whose success, it is believed, can contribute most heavily to the country's economic and social goals and to the nation's international position.

Probusiness activism.   Industrial policy is neutral with respect to specific industries (except possibly in giving compensating aid to domestic industries that compete with government-favored foreign competitors), allowing the market to determine which domestic industries will prosper. To build and maintain a strong economic base, however, government "tilts" policy toward business interests—for example, by favoring, within reason, business and employment interests over environmental concerns.

It is clear that nations differ in terms of their industrial policies. For example, Japan and, to a lesser extent, West Germany tend to emphasize selective intervention and probusiness activism, while the United States at least rhetorically favors benign nonintervention.

Selective intervention is of particular interest here. It can take two quite different forms.

Aid to healthy industries.   These industries are likely to be "stars" in terms of their ability to help a country meet its goals of price stability (because growth in sales often means lower prices), full employment, improvement in living standards, and international competitiveness.

Aid to declining industries.   In response to political pressures, regional or local concerns, or equity considerations, some observers believe that government should assist so-called "sunset" industries.

The arguments made in this chapter suggest that a carefully conceived and well-administered industrial policy selectively aiding potentially healthy industries in their initial stages by means of government-guaranteed purchases can be effective. The study also supports the view that implementation of many of the public policy recommendations outlined above can help to sustain U.S. strength in mature healthy industries.

The development of a selective interventionist strategy requires that possible healthy industries with high economic potential be identified, that government assistance be directed effectively and economically toward the targeted industries, and that the politics so developed be followed consistently.

After examining some of the available literature on industrial policy, case studies of successful and unsuccessful industries, and our own case studies, we believe that it is possible to identify seven major bases on which our industrial policy designed to aid healthy industries can be founded. These approaches are described in table 6.6. In examining these suggested bases, it

Table 6.6. Alternative Criteria for Selecting Healthy Industries to be Promoted as Part of a Revitalization Program

Type of Industry	Rationale	Possible Illustrative Industries from U.S. Perspective
Rapid growth in sales	Contributes to higher employment and living standards	Electronics Energy
High export growth and content	Improves balance of payments; facilitates growth of domestic economy	Agriculture Forest products Airliners
Comparative advantage	Efficient allocation of resources; likely enduring source of strength	Agriculture Forest products Biomass products
Strong performers	Track record; likely intangible advantages; first-mover advantages	Film (e.g., Kodak) Computers (e.g., IBM) Air-conditioning equipment
Small business	Small businesses often are early in the product life cycle, with rapid growth potential. Small business vigor contributes disproportionately to employment growth and a vigorous, innovative economy. Small businesses are likely to need and benefit most from assistance.	Small business in all industries, perhaps focusing on newly established firms.
High-technology industries	Employs large quantities of high-skill labor; environmentally benign; flexible, can change to new conditions rapidly; provides a high return to capital resources	Jet aircraft Communications equipment
Strategic industries	Likely to be exceptionally high growth industries because they provide vitally needed products; success in strategic industries creates vigor throughout the economy as other industries use innovations from the strategic sector	Integrated circuits Robotics Genetic engineering
Turnabout situation	Possible reversals in product life cycles—as in coal. Underlying potential strength concealed by inept management. If industry can be turned around, existing capital structures and employment (employee, community) relationships need not be destroyed.	Coal Railroad equipment Autos

is prudent to recognize that a specific industry may fall within several categories and that a nation may seek to promote industries in several categories simultaneously. For example, with its vast resources, the U.S. government could elect to promote industries in which it believes it has a comparative advantage, in which it believes it is already a strong performer, and which it believes will be strategic in the future. Japan, for example, appears to have selected a quite different mix of categories—high-growth industries, industries with high export content, and strategic industries.

Based on the six healthy industries examined here, it appears that several conclusions may be drawn.

There is evidence that promotion of strategic industries is desirable. As indicated earlier, it appears that the strong U.S. position in computers significantly helped several other healthy industries. It is widely expected, for example, that a vigorous U.S. genetic engineering industry will significantly help U.S. pharmaceutical manufacturers.

Several of the six healthy industries exploited a U.S. comparative resource advantage over most international competitors. Forest products and frozen foods, for example, displayed exploitation of comparative advantages. Government aid at an early stage in the development of industries of this type appears to be desirable.

The presence of first-mover advantages suggests that government assistance should be directed toward small businesses and innovative small and medium-sized firms in high-technology industries, since mature healthy industries appear to be able to do well on their own.

The major objective of government policy toward mature healthy industries ought, where feasible, to be to avoid regulations that are significantly harmful to the industry—as, for example, the experience of FDA drug industry regulation.

To repeat a familiar theme: in discussions of strategy formulation and implementation, it is often observed that there exist several workable strategies. It is often most important to follow a given strategy consistently and be sure the strategy being followed is reasonable in terms of the environment the organization faces and the organization's own aspirations and aptitudes; so, too, for the development and implementation of sound industrial policy.

Appendix: Selected Statistics for Six Healthy Industries

	Frozen Foods		Forest Products		Pharmaceuticals			Metal Cans	Computers	Aerospace	
SIC#	2037	2038	2421	2436	2831	2833	2834	3411	3573	372/376	3721
Short description	Frozen Fruits & Vegetables	Frozen Specialties	Sawmills & Planing Mills, General	Softwood Veneer & Plywood	Biologicals	Medicinals, Botanicals	Pharmaceutical Preps.	Metal Cans	Electronic Computing Equipment	Aerospace Industry	Aircraft Industry
Value of Shipments[1]											
—1979	$3,888		13,400	4,121	1,114	2,564	14,080	9,950	21,100	55,181	28,000
—1974	$2,468	3,914	7,365	2,124	547	1,094	8,412	6,025	9,122		11,665
Compound annual rate of change	8.1%		10.9	15	13.4	12.7	10.2	9.7	19.2	14.9	
Trade, 1979[1]											
—Exports	165		469	110	252	1,036	344	40	5,250		6,787
—Imports	36		1,005	3	9	822	54	0	4,490 5,960		449
Compound annual rate of change (1974-9)											
—Exports	18.7%		14.5	6	29	10.9	4.1	3.9	19.2	10.6	
—Imports	9.4%		22.8	21	12.5	18.8	22	—	19.0	15.6	
Return on Investment[2]	19.51	10.76	20.81	18.25	22.17	23.06	19.86	24.51	21.38		25.26
Concentration Ratio[3] 4 largest firms											
—1977	22%	40	17	38	32	65	24	59	44	59	
—1963	24%	42 (1972)	11	37 (1972)	36	68	22	74	66(1967)	59	

[1] Source: U.S. Department of Commerce, *1980 Industrial Outlook* (Washington, D.C.: U.S. Department of Commerce, 1980), various pages.

[2] Source: Dun & Bradstreet, *1980 Key Business Ratios* (Dun and Bradstreet), various pages.

[3] Source: U.S. Department of Commerce, *1977 Census of Manufacturers: Concentration in Manufacturing* (MC77-SR-9) (Washington, D.C.: U.S. Department of Commerce, 1981), various pages.

REFERENCES

Abernathy, William J. "Innovation and the Regulatory Paradox: Toward a Theory of Thin Markets." In Douglas H. Ginsburg and William J. Abernathy (eds.), *Government, Technology, and the Automotive Future*, New York: McGraw-Hill, 1980.

Grabowski, Henry G. *Drug Regulation and Innovation*. Washington, D.C.: American Enterprise Institute, 1976.

Hockmuth, M. S. "Aerospace." In Raymond Vernon (ed.), *Big Business and the State: Changing Relations in Western Europe*. Cambridge, Mass.: Harvard University Press, 1974.

Jéquier, Nicolas. "Computers." In R. Vernon (ed.), *Big Business and the State: Changing Relations in Western Europe*. Cambridge, Mass.: Harvard University Press, 1974.

Lenard, Thomas M. "Wasting our National Forests." *Regulation*, July/August, 1981.

McKie, James W. *Tin Cans and Tin Plate: A Study of Competition in Two Related Markets*. Cambridge, Mass.: Harvard University Press, 1959.

OECD. *Gaps in Technology: Electronic Computers*. (Sector report). Paris: Organisation for Economic Cooperation and Development, 1969.

Phillips, Almarin. *Technology and Market Structure*. Lexington, Mass.: D. C. Heath, 1971.

Schwartzman, David. *Innovation in the Pharmaceutical Industry*. Baltimore: Johns Hopkins University Press, 1976.

Smith, Lee. "The Neglected Promise of our Forests." *Fortune*, November 5, 1979.

Soma, John T. *The Computer Industry*. Lexington, Mass.: D. C. Heath, 1976.

Wells, Louis T. *The Product Life Cycle and International Trade*. Boston: Harvard Graduate School of Business, 1972.

Williams. E. W. *Frozen Foods: Biography of an Industry*. Boston: Cahners Publishing Co., 1970.

Part IV:
Industrial Policy in Other Countries

7

Industrial Policy in Japan

Philip H. Trezise

This chapter will express a large measure of skepticism about the reputed efficacy of industrial policy in Japan. I will use the term "industrial policy" in the sense that is now common: that is, that public authorities choose, or participate intimately in choosing, the specific industrial sectors into which capital and labor are to be preferentially directed as well as those sectors that are to be discouraged and discarded. (A *New York Times* editorial put this in the capsule comment, "a national policy—of sunset and sunrise industries.") I will argue the proposition that the Japanese government is not able, any more than other democratic governments are able, to pursue an internally consistent policy of this kind.

The impressive successes in economic growth and social stability in postwar Japan are there to be observed and admired. In my view, they are not owing in any decisive degree to the microeconomic decision making that is often held up as a source of Japanese accomplishments. To say this, however, is not to deny that there has been a pervasive pattern of interventionism in economic life on the part of the permanent civil service and its political masters. The various elements and institutions of that interventionism comprise, or relate to, industrial policy in Japan. I will offer my description of these next.

NATIONAL PLANS

During the allied occupation, reportedly at the suggestion of the supreme commander, General MacArthur, Japan's government established a planning mechanism, the Economic Stabilization Board (ESB). In time, the ESB became the Economic Planning Agency (EPA), sited in the Prime Minister's Office, with a mandate to draw up national economic and social plans as guidelines for the government's economic policy. Since 1955, the EPA has prepared eight or nine medium- or long-term plans, including the famed 1960 plan for doubling national income in ten years.

Planning in Japan engages not only the EPA economists and technicians, but also a broad spectrum of private persons. Indeed, an advisory body made up mainly of businessmen, the prime minister's Economic Council, nominally is charged with preparing the national plan. Its permanent members, supplemented by several hundred distinguished individuals from business, the universities, the press, and organized private groups, are responsible for advising and directing the EPA staff, which itself is supplemented by officials from the several ministries and agencies concerned with economic policy. Once drafted, the plan is submitted to the cabinet, whose approval makes it the nominal guidebook for policy during the prescribed period.

In the national plans can be found estimates or projections of future growth, for the economy as a whole and for major economic sectors. The plans also suggest ways in which public policy should be changed or directed so as to achieve stated national goals. During the period of a plan (the current one runs through 1985), revisions are made and targets or projections are adjusted to take account of unanticipated developments. In a very broad sense, then, the plan may be said to provide a flexible framework for policies toward individual sectors or industries.

MITI "Visions"

Loosely linked to the national plans are periodic statements coming from the Ministry of International Trade & Industry (MITI). In these a preferred pattern for Japan's future industrial structure is envisioned, taking into account judgments about domestic capabilities and assumptions about the external economic forces that will bear upon Japan's fortunes. MITI has had an activist bureaucracy which has not hesitated to lay claim to credit for having determined the character of Japanese postwar growth.[1] Its "vision," after the high-growth decades, 1950–1970, was that the future of Japanese industry lay in becoming predominantly knowledge-intensive. And in fact the computer or data-processing sector was given special emphasis by MITI during the 1970s and did achieve substantial growth.

MITI's overall prescriptions/forecasts, like the EPA plans, are prepared under the aegis of an advisory body, the Industrial Structure Deliberation Council, made up of senior business leaders and other public figures. At the bureau level, MITI officials can turn for consultation to advisory committees, *shingikai*, representatives of individual industries. The "Japan, Incorporated" image, which has business and government acting in closest association and harmony, takes much of its form from this institutionalized structure for exchanges of ideas and information between civil servants and spokesmen for industry.

Regional Planning

Special measures for regions and municipalities can fit within the concept of a national industrial policy. It may be considered desirable, for instance, to provide incentives to encourage investment in areas of labor surplus. These incentives may take the form of tax benefits or low-interest loans to private firms, or they may appear as public investments in highways, port facilities, water supply, and so on.

Like most countries, Japan has sought to locate or relocate business and industry in designated regions and has used the conventional kinds of incentives to that end. This variety of planning has occasionally been complemented by comprehensive reports on the nation's major regions, reports which have gone on to suggest policies that would be helpful in fostering regional development.

Industry-specific Legislation

It is fair to say that Japan is not as legalistic a society as the United States. In practice, government officials have considerable latitude, without specific legal authority, to direct or induce private business to act or refrain from acting, as, for example, to restrict exports of "sensitive" items. Administrative guidance, so-called, while not unique to Japan, is perhaps exercised more commonly and openly than in other democracies.

Nonetheless, the Diet is asked from time to time to enact laws designating one or more industries to which the bureaucracy is expected to give special attention. This kind of legislation may authorize measures to reduce supposed excess capacity, as has frequently been the case for the chronically ailing textile industry. Or it may, as with electronics, give the Diet's general blessing to the promotion of an industry believed to have good prospects for growth. Direct subsidies, if they are to be provided, will be decided through the normal budgetary procedure. But the fact that an industry has been singled out in a law gives weight to a claim for financial aid from public funds or for other benefits available only through official channels.

Budgetary Policy

Plans, visions, or special designation legislation are in themselves mainly hortatory in nature. In a market economy, more material incentives are normally required if resources are to be consciously directed to favored industries. Incentives can take a number of forms, all of them of course partaking of the nature of subsidies. A principal channel for distributing subsidies is the expenditure budget.

Japan's fiscal system has what amounts to four budgets or budget groupings. At the center of the system is the general account. Funds from this budget pay for the usual governmental activities, such as administration, education, welfare services, defense, and payments on the public debt. Also included are grants to local governments, capital spending—that is, public works, and subsidies to specific private sectors.

Overlapping in part with the general account is a set of so-called special accounts and budgets for government-affiliated agencies, such as the national railways. These administrative budgets include a large number of special funds, the most important being the social insurance fund and the Trust Fund Bureau which handles postal savings. Other examples of special accounts are one for road improvement and another for the government's purchase and sale of basic foodstuffs, primarily rice. Most of the varied activities within this group generate revenues, as from the sale of government-owned rice, and make payments, as in purchasing rice from farmers. Many of the special accounts and the government railways incur losses, which are funded by grants appropriated under the general account.

The budgets for the forty-seven prefectures and more than 3,000 municipalities are prepared according to guidelines laid down by the central government. These budgets support a range of local government functions, such as education, water supply, and health services, but also public works They are financed by revenue sharing with the national government, by grants from the general account, and by local taxes and bond issues. Local governments taken together spend more than the central government, although the latter raises much the largest part of total revenue.

Finally, Japan has a form of capital budget known as the Fiscal Loan and Investment Program, FILP, under which lending or investment authority is given to a host of government corporations and institutions. Funds for the FILP come primarily from borrowing from postal savings and other fiduciary deposits accumulated by the Trust Fund Bureau and from government-guaranteed bond issues. A typical FILP agency like the Tokyo Airport Authority will borrow from the Trust Fund Bureau and then lend or invest for purposes considered desirable by the political authorities and the civil service (or perhaps by the agency itself).[2]

This not especially tidy structure of budgets channels a sizable and increasing fraction of Japan's GNP through the government in its various manifestations. The 1980 budget total (before supplemental appropriations) for the general account, for locally financed regional budgets, and the FILP, was 85 trillion yen, or about 34 percent of a GNP of 250 trillion yen. Both the national and the local governments regularly spend some revenues to create fixed assets or inventories of goods, that is, to engage in capital formation. These investments are supplemented by FILP financing for public enterprises and for private industrial sectors. The government's share of gross domestic capital formation has ranged over the years from 20 to 30 percent.

In principle, therefore, the government's investments could be so distributed as to promote "strategic" or "target" private industries as against others. Many observers consider that one of the FILP agencies in particular, the Japan Development Bank (JDB), has had and continues to have a key part in aiding selected industries to expand. The JDB was created in 1951 to advance "economic reconstruction and industrial development," a mission that was redefined in 1972 as one of fostering "industrial development and economic and social progress." Its loans to selected private borrowers, on preferential terms, are thus intended and expected to support investments that are judged to be somehow more in the public interest than others. According to a widely held view, moreover, JDB lending has a multiplier effect on investment in favored sectors, since it is supposed to signal to the commercial banks which companies or industries the government wishes to receive priority treatment.

Taxes and Tariffs

Governments obviously have other means than subsidies, loans, and public investment with which to seek to influence the allocation of a nation's resources. I have mentioned bureaucratic guidance as a means that may be more commonly used in Japan than elsewhere. Of considerably greater potential importance, however, are the instruments of taxation and import protection.

Special tax measures have been prominent in Japan's fiscal system. A 1974 study found more than one hundred separate special provisions, ranging from tax-free treatment of interest income for small savers to various forms of favorable depreciation and depletion allowances, to tax credits for research and development spending. The possibilities of using preferential tax treatment for carrying out industrial policy need not be belabored here.

For import protection to be a fully effective feature of industrial policy, tariffs or other restrictions on imports ought to be applied differentially and skillfully. To treat all imports in the same fashion—say, by means of a uniform *ad valorem* tariff—will not be an effective way of directing capital and labor to selected industrial sectors. Japan's current import regime does in fact operate quite differentially as among the protected sectors. I will come later to an examination of the nature of the differentiation.

Competition Policy

Although Japanese business is certainly rivalrous enough in practice, anti-trust or government enforcement of competition is not a compelling feature of public policy. The Fair Trade Commission, which has a procompetition mandate, has consistently played a role secondary to MITI, a ministry that has usually been preoccupied with evidences of excessive competition rather than the reverse. At all events, resort to anticompetitive arrangements, main-ly cartels, has been frequent, either to mitigate recessionary problems or to promote industrial rationalization. Cartels are approved selectively, of course, depending on which industries MITI or another ministry believes need respites from the rigors of competition. In can be said, therefore, that still another instrument of industrial policy is to be found in the fairly ready availability of competition-restricting measures.

INSTRUMENTS OF JAPAN'S INDUSTRIAL POLICY

The foregoing section has been a catalogue of institutions, instruments, and policies that may be said to make up the elements of a Japanese industrial policy. It is not surprising that some Japan-watchers have concluded that such a policy, operating to select the likely industrial winners and to discourage the losers, has been the prime force in Japan's extraordinary industrial growth. After all, Japanese officials say that they have had an industrial policy designed to foster industries in which Japan has or could have a comparative advantage. Japan's industries on the whole have prospered. The connection appears to be evident.

Still, it seems to me that there are commonsense reasons for having reservations about this easy coupling. Japan is a democracy. A variety of interest groups, each with votes, must be taken into account by government. One knows that politicians and officials cannot simply ignore the weak or unpromising parts of the economy. Politicians must worry about votes. Officials become attached to their constituencies, in Japan as elsewhere. Resources, benefits, and favors have to be distributed to many claimants, not all of whom will be even at average levels of productivity or promise.

One has to be doubtful, too, about the picture of wise bureaucrats sitting down with wise industrialists to plan in some detail the future shape of an economy that now produces, gross, more than a trillion dollars worth of goods and services. It takes nothing from Japanese civil servants, who are chosen through a rigorous examining procedure, to observe that their skills and foresight probably are less than perfect. The same may be said for the figures from private life who participate in or lend their names to official planning and forecasting statements. What officials and advisers say or prescribe obviously can matter. But the allocation of resources in a free market economy—certainly in one as big as Japan's—depends on myriads of decisions taken throughout the country. Over many of these, government and its spokesmen have only indirect or tenuous influence.

These reflections tend to be confirmed by a closer look at the instruments of Japan's industrial policy.

Plans and Planning

The most important thing to be said about Japan's national plans is that none has binding force on anyone. They do not determine budget allocations or government capital formation. They do not impose obligations, legal or otherwise, on either the public or the private sector. Basically they are statements of goals or targets, with suggestions for policy measures which, if adopted and carried out, would help toward achieving the goals. Except, however, as these policies have already been decided by the competent ministries, there is no basis for supposing that specific actions will follow. Often, moreover, the policy prescriptions are so general in nature as to be little more than homilies.[3]

In the national economic and social plans are estimates of GNP growth during the plan period. The average annual rate is then referred to as the government's medium-term growth target—which, in a public relations sense, it is. But the yearly budget, through which the government has its most direct influence on GNP, is compiled, as it must be, with reference to the immediate economic problems facing the country rather than to the five- or seven-year growth target. It is possible, to be sure, that an optimistic forecast of long-term GNP growth by the government will lead the private sector to respond with more investment, helping to make the forecast self-fulfilling. This may well have been the case when Prime Minister Ikeda announced his "double-national-income-in-ten-years" plan in 1960, a target that was reached in eight years. An industrial policy, however, could hardly rest solely on a hoped-for announcement effect from official statements.

Regional planning in Japan, to the extent that it has been something more than a paper exercise, must have had an effect on the movement of resources; for regional development programs often have included material incentives for industrial investment such as tax relief and low-interest loans, along with public investment in roads and other facilities. To my knowledge, no one has attempted to measure or assess the results, perhaps because of the very wide sweep of the plans. For example, as of 1978 no fewer than 1,851 municipalities in the forty-seven prefectures had been subject to "city planning" under the City Planning Law. Or, as former Prime Minister Tanaka reported in his *Building a New Japan*, the Act for the Promotion of the Industrial Development of Underdeveloped Regions, the Act for the Promotion of New Industrial Cities, and the Act for the Development of Special Areas for Industrial Consolidation were supplemented by laws to encourage regional development in Hokkaido, Tohoku (northern Honshu), Hokuriku (western Honshu), Shikoku, Chugoku (southwest Honshu), and Kyushu (that is, except for Okinawa, all the nation's regions other than those centered on Tokyo, Nagoya, and Osaka).[4]

For what it may be worth, however, the prefectures in which Tokyo, Nagoya, and Osaka-Kobe are located, all of which had problems of overdevelopment, grew in population just about as fast as the country as a whole from 1965 to 1979. Hokkaido and the adjacent Tohoku region, which have had a special regional development corporation for many years, lost population relative to the rest of the country, falling from 14.5 percent to 12.9 percent of the total. And Kyushu, except for the already heavily industrialized prefecture of Fukuoka, actually had fewer numbers in 1979 than in 1965.

The "visions" seen by MITI and its Industrial Structure Deliberation Council represent a more pointed form of industrial policymaking. Although these statements are by no means limited in their scope (the vision for the 1980s covers, among other subjects, energy, global interdependence, "internationalization" of the yen, urbanization, development aid, foreign direct investment, national goals, and the quality of Japanese life), they do offer some more or less specific economic and industrial objectives. Thus the current vision identifies a number of technological development tasks for the 1980s in such fields as energy, data processing, telecommunications, and genetics. (None will be unfamiliar to a reader of the London *Economist*'s Science and Technology pages.) It urges more R&D spending, public as well as private. And it sees a role for government in the development of high-cost, high-risk, long-lead-time technologies.

What the vision for the 1980s does not do is provide resources. It does not even propose budgetary priorities. It is certainly not a ten-year "plan" in any operational sense. At most, it presents a description of how some aspects of the Japanese economy and society might appear in the 1990s if MITI and its advisors are sufficiently heeded by the budget makers and private investors— and if, in fact, the technologies listed in the vision prove to be feasible in commercial terms. One must look further for the real world application of industrial policy.

Budgets and Subsidies

As I have said, a bit more than one-third of Japan's current GNP passes through the central and local governments. Both regularly invest in physical assets. Investments financed through the ordinary budget are supplemented by financing provided through the capital budget or FILP to public agencies and enterprises and to private sectors as well. In 1979, the government was responsible for 29 percent of gross domestic capital formation. It would seem, therefore, that public investments could serve to promote private industries specially targeted for expansion, leaving other sectors to fend for themselves in the private capital markets.

The reality is that the bulk of public investment through the regular budgets, national and local, goes where one would expect, to public works: roads, dams, land reclamation, harbors, airports, public housing, water and sewer facilities, and so on. In largest part, this kind of investment is handled through and by the prefectural and local governments, which hardly would be chosen as vehicles for the management of a selective industrial policy. Except for a small "industrial investment" line item (average outlays, 1975-1978 were about $188 million per year) and a much larger and growing sum for energy investments, the fields for public investment through the regular budgets are those that have usually been considered, at least in market economies, as having a straightforwardly public character.

Deficits in a number of government programs are funded through the central government's general account budget. Over the years, the largest of the deficits has been in the foodstuffs control account, which in 1980 was scheduled to get 955 billion yen, or more than $4 billion, mainly to subsidize the price of rice. The national railway system is another major claimant; in 1979 its subsidy exceeded that for rice. Small business gets sizable grants, which have exceeded 200 billion yen in each of the past three fiscal years.

These subsidies, clearly, are for weak sisters. Whatever their other merits or justifications, the big subsidies in the budget do not go to growth industries, past, present, or future.

What about the Fiscal Loan and Investment Program, which seems a more likely instrument for a policy of aids to target industrial sectors? Under the FILP, money borrowed from the Trust Fund Bureau can be invested directly or can be lent to public or private bodies for approved investment purposes. The FILP for fiscal 1980 was set at 18 trillion yen, or upwards of $80 billion. This large amount, made available at better than market terms, offers or appears to offer potential leverage for determining which industries should be enabled to forge ahead in Japan.

Closer examination raises some doubts. The Bank of Japan's annual statistical report[5] identifies the proposed recipients of FILP funds in 1979. In all there were fifty separate entities, plus "local governments," to divide up the FILP pie. Some were allowed small amounts under the program: Japan Airlines, for instance, was entitled to 3.2 billion yen; the Metal Mining Agency, 6.4 billion yen. At the other extreme, four individual borrowers and the category of "local governments" each had available a trillion yen or more: the Housing Loan Corporation, the Peoples' Finance Corporation (one of the small business lending agencies), the Small Business Finance Corporation (another), and the Japan National Railways. Local governments were scheduled to get 2.9 trillion. These five big borrowers, which accounted for more than 60 percent of the FILP, may provide many worthy services to Japanese society, but it is difficult to credit any of them with being closely connected with promising growth sectors, unless housing is so considered.

Other big FILP agencies were the Japan Housing Corporation (public housing), the Export-Import Bank, the Japan Highway Corporation, the Japan Development Bank, and the Agriculture, Forestry, and Fisheries Finance Corporation, each having had borrowing authority in excess of 500 billion yen. These and a few others, such as the Pension Welfare Service Corporation, the Environmental Sanitation Business Finance Corporation, and the Overseas Economic Cooperation Fund, accounted for another 27-plus percent of the FILP. Three dozen smaller government corporations and special accounts were to get the remaining 12 percent of the 1979 FILP.

The fact is that the FILP sweeps in a great hodgepodge of governmental and quasi-governmental activities which have little in common other than having a supportive constituency somewhere in the country. It is plainly not in significant part an industrial-policy program. Most of its financing goes to activities that would be considered of a public character in any society or have become, as in housing finance, a responsibility partially assumed by governments everywhere.

Principal exceptions are the Export-Import Bank (Ex-Im) and the Japan Development Bank (JDB). In the Ex-Im case, a bank able to provide favorable financing for exports must have some influence on industrial development. Ex-Im's export credits have gone in the largest part to finance sales of heavy industry products, led by ships. It is entirely plausible that the expansion of this industrial sector was facilitated by the availability of relatively easy financing for the export business. But subsidized export finance is not unique to Japan. All of Japan's principal competitors offer similar services, using public funds to underwrite credits for selected exports. Each one justifies its policy as necessary to meet competition from the others. It is impossible to know whether Japan's exports would have fared or would now fare as well, less well, or better in a world in which this form of export subsidy was ended by mutual consent.

The Japan Development Bank's role is fairly unambiguous. Its mission, as has been said, is to foster industrial development and economic and social progress. JDB lending to selected private borrowers, on preferential terms, is thus intended and expected to support investments that are judged to be somehow more in the public interest than others. At least so far as the use of public funds is concerned, the JDB's operations do conform to the concept of a selective industrial development policy.[6] As I have said, many foreign observers and Japanese as well believe that the development bank's loans also signal to the private banks those companies or industries that the government wishes to receive special treatment.

During the first twenty years of its life, when all of the JDB's lending came to about $13 billion, the two principal customer industries were merchant shipping (31.5 percent of all loans went to this always troubled industry) and the electric utilities (21.3 percent). Together with regional and urban development (construction projects, ranging from shopping centers to warehouses and truck terminals), these industries accounted for more than three-quarters of all JDB loans. The amounts available for the rest of Japanese industry were simply not great; the "strategic" steel industry, for instance, received less than 1 percent of total JDB lending, or about $110 million in total over two decades.[7]

Since 1972, the emphases in the JDB program have undergone a notable change. Table 7.1 shows that urban-regional-development and quality-of-life (primarily pollution-prevention) investments dominated JDB lending, 1973-1979, with the share represented by energy loans (for nuclear power, oil refining and storage, LNG power generating plants, energy conservation projects, and others) having come back after a long decline. The ocean-shipping category, meanwhile, has fallen to a relatively negligible point. Effectively, the bulk of the post-1972 lending program was for infrastructure and, in a quite literal sense, for improvements in the quality of Japanese life. The impact of this on industrial location, on the efficiency of distribution, on the adjustment to environmental controls, and on productivity in general conceivably was strongly positive. Although Japan was anything but a capital-short country in the 1970s, some of the projects financed by the JDB might have been neglected or delayed if the enterprises concerned had had to borrow on commercial market terms.[8] But it should be observed that the JDB's net lending accounted for just 1 percent of private capital formation, excluding housing, during these years. If all the JDB infrastructure lending had been left to the private capital market, the economy probably would not have developed in a fashion noticeably different from what did happen.

To find a more industry-specific contribution from the JDB, it is necessary (energy projects aside) to go to the technology-development category, which accounted for about 11 percent of all JDB lending during the period, an average of $313 million equivalent per year. The bank says that these loans went to three types of projects: (1) computer leasing, manufacturing, and software; (2) raising the technological level of the electronics and machinery industries; and (3) general technological development. The preoccupation here has been with the computer sector, which has received the largest share of technology-development loans, much of it to help finance a joint leasing company formed under MITI guidance by the major computer producers.[9] Computers have long been considered a strategic or target industry. Other government financial aids, mainly for research and development, have been given to the computer sector; one estimate is that these subsidies came to a not very staggering total of about $340 million for the whole period, 1972-1979.[10]

All this can be summed up in the conclusion that in Japan, public funds have not been directed in any sizable amounts, relative to total investment

Table 7.1. Japan Development Bank—New Loans by Project [millions of U.S. dollars (percent)]

	1973	1974	1975	1976*	1977	1978	1979
Urban Development	328 (19)	354 (17)	451 (18)	469 (18)	469 (17)	611 (20)	840 (18)
Regional Development	263 (18)	324 (16)	364 (15)	380 (15)	447 (16)	612 (20)	717 (15)
Improvement of Quality of Life	317 (18)	578 (28)	765 (31)	794 (31)	920 (34)	689 (30)	851 (18)
Resources & Energy	207 (12)	207 (10)	226 (9)	234 (9)	296 (11)	509 (17)	1306 (27)
Ocean Shipping	314 (18)	256 (12)	245 (10)	254 (10)	181 (7)	90 (3)	158 (3)
Development of Technology	185 (10)	205 (10)	284 (11)	295 (11)	294 (11)	312 (10)	617 (13)
Other	152 (9)	127 (6)	153 (6)	159 (6)	135 (5)	207 (7)	525 (5)
Total	1766	2051	2488	2585	2742	3027	4741

SOURCE: Japan Development Bank, *Annual Reports*, 1975-1979.

* Converted at 296.55 yen = one U.S. dollar. All other dollar figures are from Japan Development Bank.

requirements, to the private industries or economic sectors with high growth potential. Not only appropriated monies, but also the large captive deposits available to the government for investment, have gone and still go in overwhelming part either to ailing but politically important sectors, especially agriculture and small business, or to purposes that in most countries would be considered properly public. It is not accidental or surprising that agriculture receives the largest outright grants or that the government lending agencies for small business command almost four times as much lending power as does the Japan Development Bank (or that the JDB lends mostly to other than the manufacturing industries). In a democracy, it is natural that politicians should worry more about the laggards than about the fast runners. Nor is it easily believable that Japan's horde of public corporations and specialized agencies are all efficient spenders and investors. The very proliferation of these bodies suggests, inescapably, that political as well as economic needs were satisfied by creating new institutions,[11] which then, in the words of the Administrative Management Agency in the Prime Minister's Office, are "apt to survive even after they have completed their tasks."

Tax Incentives

President Reagan's interesting dictum that tax policy should be directed solely to raising revenue has not been the preferred view in postwar Japan. "Special" tax measures, designed to "help attain certain economic policy aims,"[12] have been a continuing feature of the tax system. It should not be supposed, however, that these policy aims were or are exclusively or mainly the promotion of selected industries. To be sure, tax benefits for exporters, almost all discontinued a decade or more ago under pressure from trading partners and the GATT, aided only the export industries (including, ironically, those whose foreign sales were being restricted by the government under "voluntary" arrangements with the United States and other importing countries). But there was always a problem of keeping preferential measures really preferential. The tendency was to spread the benefits to people in related activities until all claimants had been satisfied and none were specially treated.[13]

At all events, the tax system today does not square exactly with the concept of incentives carefully directed to the encouragement of prospective industrial growth sectors.

For example, an extra slice of first-year depreciation is permitted for ten categories of machinery and equipment. The most generous treatment (an additional 27 percent) is given to machinery for the prevention of pollution. Other designated categories are nonpolluting machinery, energy-saving machinery, materials-recycling machinery, certain water supply equipment, oceangoing ships, integrated systems of data-analysis equipment and industrial machinery, commercial aircraft, and buildings which house retail stores. Much of this may well make excellent policy sense, although it is possible to wonder why commercial aircraft or ships or buildings are there. But except for the data-analysis category (which covers industrial robots), the relationship to picking industrial winners is obscure.

Special first-year-depreciation privileges are also offered to investors in "underdeveloped areas, in coal mining regions, in depopulated areas [?], in severely depressed areas, and in industrial development areas." Small and medium-sized enterprises and agricultural cooperatives are similarly indulged. So are craft industries and industry mutual-benefit associations. Up to 27 percent of afforestation expenses may be written off during the first year. Associations "mainly engaged in research work" are entitled to claim special amortization of their equipment.

Accelerated depreciation—extra allowances over several accounting years—is available to commercial and industrial cooperatives (such as in the textile industry), to companies employing handicapped persons, to rental housing enterprises, to owners of crude oil storage tanks, and to investors in fireproof warehouses and grain silos.

Tax-deferrable financial reserves are permitted for overseas market development by small and medium business, for investors in enterprises abroad, and for investors in Okinawa's free trade zone. Other tax-deductible or deferrable arrangements are open to nuclear power facilities, to companies engaged in afforestation, to private railroads, and to firms supplying natural gas to consumers. The computer industry may establish reserves to cover losses from leasing operations and for "repair costs" of defective software programs. Mining companies may deduct exploration costs from income. Japan has experimented with investment tax credits to encourage the purchase of energy-saving and antipollution facilities; the Ministry of Finance has now drawn back, and the tax credits are limited to "permanently depressed" industries and to certain small and medium-sized corporations.

A tax credit for extra research and development expense is probably more pertinent to the notion of an industrial policy. A corporation may deduct 20 percent of R&D spending above a base-period amount, and this credit may be as much as 10 percent of corporate tax. The R&D tax credit is available to all corporations, of course, not merely to prospective winners.

This recital suggests that tax incentives are used in Japan for a variety of purposes, including, quite incidentally, what I have defined as industrial policy.

Trade Policy

We should dispose right away of the proposition that Japan, unlike the United States, has protected the promising growth sectors, but has thrown laggards to the import wolves. It is simply not so.

During the high-growth decades—the 1950s and 1960s—when Japan's industrial structure was undergoing its phenomenal transformation, everything was protected. Until the early 1960s, imports almost without exception were controlled by quotas and exchange restrictions. When some quotas were ended, tariffs were raised. Japan was a reluctant party to the Kennedy round of tariff negotiations. It did not begin really to liberalize its restrictive import regime until the very end of the 1960s, and then only gradually.

When liberalization did come, it was applied most slowly to the weakest, least competitive industries. Agricultural protection stands out, a circumstance far from unique to Japan. Except for agricultural goods which still qualify for quota protection, customs tariffs are the principal means of protection. Present tariff schedules are about at the industrial-country average and are slated to fall to quite low levels. They are skewed, however, to afford greatest protection to the food processing industry, which struggles under the handicap of high material costs because of the restrictions on agricultural imports. The tariff reductions negotiated in the multilateral trade negotiations on computers, film, and a few other products removed or mitigated the principal complaints about duties on other final manufactures.

As to the use of trade policy to expedite the demise of older, inefficient sectors, it is useful to consider the often-cited case of textiles. The weakest textile sector is apparel, which happens also to be a large employer, with almost 5 percent of the manufacturing work force in 1979. It has the lowest value added per worker and so the lowest wages. As might be supposed, it has not been a starring growth industry. Neither has it been disappearing. In contrast to the United States, where apparel employment fell both absolutely and as a share of manufacturing employment, 1973-1979, employment in Japan *rose* absolutely and as a proportion of the manufacturing labor force.

A way to have hastened the decline of the apparel industry would have been to have opened it to full-scale import competition by eliminating tariffs, which range from 11.2 to 17.5 percent. That this has not been done is understandable. A decision deliberately to run down a major industry would be a rare political act anywhere. But if a policy of discouraging the losers does not apply to a sector like apparel, the question can be asked, where might it apply?

The other side of trade policy, of course, is export promotion. As long as it was permitted, Japan used a range of incentives for exports, primarily through the tax system. These eventually attracted opposition from GATT and from Japan's trading partners, and were discontinued. Japan's current export-promotion program consists of Export-Import Bank lending (an "acceptable" export subsidy), a modest tax deferral scheme for small exporters (the United States has a larger one for all exporters), and a set of overseas commercial offices (the Japan Export Trade Recovery Organization). There is not much for industrial policy here.

Competition Policy

It is not wholly clear where policy toward competition should fit within a policy aimed at promoting the most promising industrial sectors. Should it stress competition and survival of the fittest? Or should it aim at combinations and mergers to gain scale economies and other hoped-for benefits?

There is no doubt that MITI at least has been predisposed to the latter notion. Concern about the wastes of "excessive" competition has been a preoccupation of MITI officials, who have regularly sought to foster legal cartels and to bring about mergers. Much of this effort has been directed to industries with numerous small firms, especially textiles and sundries. In the past, too, cartels were frequently formed for the management of the restrictions on exports that Japan's trading partners had insisted upon. A goodly part of competition—or, better, anticompetition—policy was thus directed at the dual economy, in which many tiny firms have coexisted with big industry. It has been and is a kind of industrial policy, but not the kind that is under discussion here.

MITI has sometimes tried to encourage mergers in the more concentrated industries, with indifferent success. In the 1960s an effort to combine the automobile companies into three big firms came to nothing. Japan still has seven of the twenty largest auto-producing firms in the world. A proposed amendment to the antimonopoly law in 1963 would have allowed MITI to exempt industries from the law in order to create large firms that would be better able to compete against foreign rivals. It was opposed by organized industry and the banks, and was not enacted. At present, some MITI officials are floating a revised version, which would permit intervention to control investments in basic industries so as to avoid "overproduction." It is predictable that this effort too will fail.

Where the emphasis on anticompetitive solutions may have been more relevant was in the adjustment to the 1974-1975 recession. The shipbuilding industry, for a major example, was severely distressed by the collapse of the tanker market after the oil crisis. It was guided into a recession cartel which arranged for capacity reductions in a manner that conceivably may have been less costly than a competitive solution. A number of other recession cartels were organized during this period, presumably with the result that the pain of the slump was shared among all or most of the affected firms. It would be interesting to have a careful study of this experience. What it would tell us about the recession-adjustment aspect of industrial policy, I am not certain.

Finally, Gentle Persuasion

This review seems to me to justify a reasonable doubt that industrial policy is a major reason for Japanese industrial accomplishments. Planning, it turns out, is not linked to budgets and resources, except perhaps at the regional or municipal level where no one would look for a coherent policy of selecting industrial winners. A sizable fraction of the nation's GNP goes through the government. In overwhelming part, however, government spending is for normal public purposes, including help to farmers, to the deficit-ridden railways, and to small business. The amounts directed to specific industrial sectors otherwise are quite small, almost trivial. Tax policy aims at a wide range of objectives beyond revenue raising. But most of these objectives are only incidentally related to a recognizable industrial policy. Tariffs are used in Japan, as everywhere, to prop up the weak and vulnerable sectors. Competition policy may have had its uses in easing the adjustment to economic downturns, but its principal application, not very successful, has been to the small-firm portion of Japan's dual economy.

There remains the proposition that governmental guidance does it. The London *Economist* recently carried an essay, "Japan's Gentle Persuaders," which argued that industrial policy is all a matter of persuasion. Policies evolve, it is said, through the interaction of officials with businessmen. As ideas are developed, they become MITI orthodoxy and are propagandized steadily through the ubiquitous Japanese press. In time, Japan's industrialists, motivated by a desire to conform, make MITI's ideas their own.

There probably is something here, although perhaps less than what the *Economist* correspondent saw. It is easily believable that the intensive sectoral discussions organized by MITI do add to the sum of knowledge of the industrialist members. MITI's emphasis in the early 1970s on moving into "knowledge-intensive" industries may well have caused businessmen to look more closely at the possibilities of the computer. (The big business federation, the *Keidanren*, felt it necessary, however, to point out to MITI that computers had their uses in the bad old polluting and raw-material-consuming industries like steel and autos, and that becoming knowledge-intensive did not mean jettisoning Japan's existing industrial structure.) That the government–private-sector consultation and study group process continues obviously suggests that the participants find it helpful.

The more difficult question is how it translates into decision making at the level of the firm. Investment choices must be tied to specific products and production methods. Can one suppose, really, that the management of Hitachi or Toshiba will elect to commit large sums of company funds to specific investments because MITI has had a vision of the technologies of the future? Japan's consumer electronic sector has made a stunning breakthrough with home videotape recorders, which are now the industry's largest export. Is it plausible that MITI's guidance was a primary factor in this? I have not heard it so claimed.

The truth is that the Japanese economy and Japanese society more generally resist pat descriptions and easy explanations. Of course government has had a major role in the nation's economic achievements. Where else would one look to for the monetary and fiscal policies that have underlain the relatively steady course of the economy over thirty years? Of course government and business have had a close relationship in Japan. What would be expected? The Liberal-Democratic party, after all, is the conservative party, while the principal opposition party is committed to a socialist economy. Government and agriculture have had an even closer relationship. And, although agriculture is anything but a high-productivity industry, the government may have been right in deciding to pour large subsidies into it as a contribution to political and social stability in a time of rapid economic change. If so, here was an effective form of industrial policy, but quite different from that usually talked about. Industrial policy in the sense now current, so far as it can be identified, also may have played a part in Japan's success—or, at least, seems not to have noticeably hindered it. But to attribute to industrial policy a crucial role is an expression of faith, not an argument supported by discernible facts.

NOTES

1. A MITI vice-minister (the ranking permanent civil servant) once asserted that "MITI [after the war] decided to establish in Japan industries which require extensive employment of capital and technology, industries that in consideration of comparative cost of production should be the most appropriate for Japan, industries such as steel, oil refining, petrochemicals, automobiles, aircraft, industrial machinery of all sorts, and electronics, including electronic computers. . . . MITI has succeeded in the quarter of a century since the war . . . in building on a cramped land area a giant economy that ranks second in the free world." OECD, *The Industrial Policy of Japan* (Paris: OECD, 1972), pp. 15-17.
2. The Budget Bureau of the Japan Ministry of Finance publishes a small brochure in English, *The Budget in Brief*, which describes the several budgets and the budget process.
3. See Ryutaro Komiya, "Planning in Japan," in Morris Bornstein, ed., *Economic Planning, East and West* (Cambridge, Mass.: Ballinger, 1975).
4. Kakuei Tanaka, *Building a New Japan* (Tokyo: Simul Press, 1972), p. 15.
5. Bank of Japan, *Economic Statistics Annual*, March 1980, p. 214.
6. Many of the smaller government corporations, such as the Hokkaido and Tohoku Development Corporation, and of course the small business financing institutions, also lend to private enterprises. No one has suggested, however, that this lending is expected to fit within a national industrial policy.
7. Hugh Patrick and Henry Rosovsky, eds., *Asia's New Giant* (Washington, D.C.: Brookings Institution, 1978), p. 796.
8. The JDB lending rate, 1974 through 1978, varied from a high of 9.9 percent to a low of 6.05 to 7.1 percent, following closely the best risk rates of the long-term credit banks. JDB, *Annual Reports*, 1974-1978; Bank of Japan, *Economic Statistics Annual*, 1979, p. 78. Since borrowers from the JDB presumably would not as a rule qualify as the best risks, loans to them contained an effective subsidy. Nor does the bank require, as commercial banks often do, that borrowers maintain compensating balances equal to 20 to 40 percent of their borrowings.
9. American Embassy, Tokyo, *Market Information Report, Electronic Computers*, July 1977, p. 7.

10. Comptroller-General of the United States, *U.S.-Japan Trade*, September 21, 1979, chapter 2.

11. Some Japanese are said to believe that the growth of government corporations is ascribable in part to the need to provide post-retirement employment for senior Japanese bureaucrats. See Chalmers Johnson, *Japan's Public Policy Companies* (Washington, D.C.: American Enterprise Institute, 1978), p. 111.

12. Japan Ministry of Finance, *An Outline of Japanese Taxes*, 1980, p. 72.

13. Patrick and Rosovsky, *Asia's New Giant*, p. 353.

8

Industrial Policy in the Federal Republic of Germany

Werner Menden

In recent years, the Federal Republic of Germany's growing role in the world economy has given rise in the United States to an increasing interest in German economic policy, in particular in industrial policies and what is called in Germany *Strukturpolitik*.

In the debate on technological innovation and the revitalization of American industry, which became so pronounced during the last two years of the Carter administration, Americans came to look more and more upon Japan and the Federal Republic of Germany for magic formulas that seemingly enabled these countries to withstand the negative effects of rising oil prices and the general slowdown in the world economy.

Since 1980, unfavorable economic developments in Germany—in particular a high negative balance of payment, a weakened *deutsche mark* (DM) and rising unemployment—caused it to drop out of the exclusive club with Japan and made it excruciatingly clear to everybody that Germany had no magic formula guaranteeing success.

In fact, the key to Germany's previous success was a somewhat fortuitous combination of favorable external and internal conditions—most importantly, a very productive manufacturing sector with strong exports in high-technology goods, a strong currency, liberal trade policies, and the "classical" German attitudes of hard and disciplined work.

After the mid-seventies, a slackening world economy plus rising production costs, problems of structural adaptation, and increasing unemployment introduced sand into the delicate gearing of Germany's export-oriented economic system and resulted in a considerable slowdown of the economy.

Nevertheless, while Germany is increasingly sharing with other industrial nations the negative impacts of global economic developments, it is hoped that with the basic factors contributing to its previous economic growth still in place—the qualification and dedication of its labor force, the innovativeness of its business sector, and the helping hand of the Government's industrial policy—the country will eventually be able to steer its economy to a stable course of gradual but sustained growth.

In this contribution, the main elements of German industrial policy, with special emphasis on the federal government's policies for research and development and innovation, will be outlined. It may be useful to start with some basic facts about the German economy.

ECONOMIC DATA

In 1979 the country produced a GNP of roughly $750 billion, which put it in third place behind the United States ($2,350 billion) and Japan (roughly $1,000 billion). For 1980, it had only a slight increase of about 2 percent real growth in the GNP (expressed in dollars), and for 1981 it can only hope to maintain the level of 1980.

Twenty-nine percent of its GNP, and 45 percent of all manufactured goods, go into exports, a much larger share than the United States or even Japan has (16 percent). This strong export orientation had enabled Germany—at least until 1978—to pay for the increasing cost of its oil-import bill, which in 1978 amounted to roughly 30 billion DM.

With an oil bill of nearly 60 billion DM for 1980 however, the economy ran into its first significant deficit in decades, amounting to a stunning 28 billion DM. We have to expect a deficit of the same order of magnitude for 1981. In this context, it is important to realize that Germany is essentially without domestic mineral resources. It imports not only 95 percent of its oil, but also most of its gas and a large share of its industries' supply of minerals and metals. At the same time, Germany ranks number 1 among the leading industrial countries for the cost of labor, including a high share for social security and fringe benefits.

With ever-increasing costs for the import of commodities and the high cost of labor, its industry has to make the strongest efforts to improve constantly the efficiency of manufacturing processes, by energy conservation as well as by product and process innovations.

ECONOMIC DEVELOPMENT AFTER WORLD WAR II

For someone from this side of the Atlantic trying to analyze the functioning of present German industrial policies, it is helpful to understand the development of Germany after World War II. The war left its economy in a pile of rubble, out of which soon grew the determination to find a new start.

In addition to strong growth-promoting factors (such as the Marshall Plan and the Korean War), the true locomotive of Germany's *Wirtschaftswunder* of the fifties was the currency reform of 1948 and Ludwig Erhard's economic philosophy, firmly rooted in the principle of the market forces guiding the economy. The government's role was restricted to creating favorable conditions for economic growth and to establishing programs for the socially weak and underprivileged sectors and groups.

Erhard's economic policy, in combination with strong social components in the early programs of the postwar Christian Democratic and Social Democratic parties, led to the development of what was to be known as the *Soziale Marktwirtschaft*. This concept sought to combine the advantages of a liberal (in the classic European sense) market-oriented economic policy with a strong commitment in the areas of social security, employment policies, and health insurance.

While purist proponents of economic liberalism may question the strong social commitment in a free-market-oriented economy, the net economic effect of these on the smooth development of the German economy is generally recognized. The maintenance of high political stability even in periods of economic recessions is a related factor of great importance.

Of particular importance in the Federal Republic's political stability is the role played by German labor unions. In striking contrast to the U.S. labor movement, the relation of German unions to business has never been quite as antagonistic. On the contrary, the union movement evolving in Germany after World War II early recognized that the primary goals of "full employment" and a high standard of living could only be achieved and maintained if unions, business, and government combined forces to strive for economic growth. These joint efforts created a strong production system and the reestablishment of the pre–World War II image of quality products "made in Germany."

The comparatively smooth relations that developed between organized labor and business in postwar Germany, in their joint effort to redevelop the economy, was critically influenced by the passing of legislation in 1952 giving labor codetermination rights in certain heavy industries (*Montan-Industrien*).

The fact that the German steel and coal industries were able to survive periods of severe, structural changes in the first decades after the war without significant social unrest can be partially attributed to representatives of labor sharing responsibilities on the companies' boards of directors.

In the late sixties and early seventies, another development helped to foster a continuous dialogue between government, labor unions, and business on issues of economic and industrial policy.

During the years of the "Great Coalition" between the Christian Democrats and the Social Democrats, the government created a new institution called the "concerted action" (*Konzertierte Aktion*), a consultative body in which representatives of the government, unions, business, the federal bank, and scientific institutes met to discuss their mutual assessment of the economic situation as well as policies and strategies to be followed by the various sectors of society.

The objectives on top of the concerted action's agenda were to keep inflation rates low, achieve high employment, maintain a positive balance of trade, and push for economic growth—objectives which appeared difficult to reconcile.

The discussions in the "concerted action" about achievable goals for growth, or productivity, and for employment were instrumental in establishing among the partners a broad common data base and a degree of mutual understanding which would otherwise have been very difficult to achieve.

After a number of years, the "concerted action" ceased to exist when the unions withdrew in the course of a bitter dispute with business over a new codetermination law (1972) extending codetermination to all companies above a certain size (2,000 employees).

Very recently (1980), the federal government has reinitiated a formalized discussion between government, business, unions, and the science community in the framework of what is now called the "technology policy dialogue." Although the thrust of this new dialogue is somewhat different from the old concerted action, inasmuch as it concentrates on the economic and social consequences of new key technologies, the dialogue nonetheless represents a continuation of the government's efforts to establish a basis for mutual understanding between major sectors of society on crucial issues of industrial policy. The group has so far discussed the consequences of microelectronics for future industrial development, with particular emphasis on growth potential and employment.

THE MAIN ELEMENTS OF "STRUKTURPOLITIK"

During the late sixties, the government for the first time enunciated explicit principles for both sectoral and regional structural policies. The chief guideline of these policies—and, as a matter of fact, still a basic guideline of the present industrial policy—is to let market forces control the development of industrial structures, aided by the government providing for a general framework favorable to industrial development.

The implementation of this principle of self-regulation by market forces required, first, that the task of adapting to structural changes should be left essentially to business; second, that the government's role should be restricted to giving assistance on the basis of what was called "help for self-help" (*Hilfe zur Selbsthilfe*), only in specific cases (sectors, regions) where self-regulating mechanisms would fail because of circumstances beyond the control of business.

Although the structural policy principles of 1968 have remained in effect until today, the government clearly has not always strictly adhered to them; deviations, based on political or social considerations, have occurred.

The first major incision in the continuity of postwar German domestic policy was marked by the formation of the coalition between the Social Democrats and the Free Democrats in 1969. It would be wrong, however, to assume that the new political powers decided a radical change in economic policy. While significant reforms were initiated in foreign policy and in education, as well as in other fields of *Gesellschaftspolitik*, the main thrust of industrial policy was still based on the principle of regulation by market forces.

While the mainstream of structural policy was still based on the principle of restricting the government's role to assisting ailing branches of industry in adapting to necessary structural changes, a new element of industrial policy emerged. The new element was more future-oriented and concentrated on industrial sectors with high growth potential. Industrial policy thus became an amalgam of the older liberal guidelines combined with the new emphasis on high-technology industries.

The basic idea of the new policy thrust can be characterized as opportunity-oriented, as opposed to crisis-oriented. Based on the realization that economic growth in a modern industrial society is closely linked to technical progress and innovation, a governmental role is to assist industry, by R&D grants and contracts, in its own innovative efforts, particularly in high-risk and high-technology projects.

Much has been written about the tension between the two major elements of German structural policy. Most of it appears to be exaggerated. The present-day structural policies in Germany represent a constructive mix of the two elements mentioned, with an opportunity-oriented technology policy superimposed on the basic principle of reliance on market forces.

SPECIFIC PROGRAM INITIATIVES IN GERMAN INDUSTRIAL POLICY

The individual programs described below should be understood in the framework of the guidelines outlined above. These programs provide government assistance for self-regulated processes of industrial development; they are not intended to exert government control over the direction of that development. It is the firm belief of the present administration that entrepreneurs and investors are best suited to assess the direction of future developments in individual markets.

However, the government can and should establish—in close communication with major sectors of business, labor, and the scientific community—programs for certain sectors and technical areas where government action is required to support industrial activities if the market forces alone are inadequate. This can result from either high risks, the long-term nature of rewards, or distortions of market mechanisms.

Structural Reporting

Because of the serious difficulties of obtaining accurate information on trends in individual sectors, the federal government recently has started to assemble a body of reliable data on structural changes in the economy. The project involves five economic research institutes, which have been asked to design a system of periodical structural reports for the economy of the Federal Republic. The reports hopefully will be a valuable source of information for government as well as for industry, especially for smaller companies, in their efforts to assess negative impacts as well as opportunities offered by structural trends.

Sectoral Programs in Three Industries

Special sectoral programs, managed by the Federal Ministry of Economics, provide assistance for the shipbuilding, steel, and aerospace industries. In addition, there are programs in the Ministry of Research and Technology providing R&D funds for nuclear, electronic, data processing, and other industries, which will be addressed later.

Shipbuilding. The objective of the Shipyard Assistance Program is to counterbalance the competitive disadvantages suffered by this industrial sector (for example, through subsidies granted to competing industries in other countries). The program provides financial assistance for the sale of German ships, by granting interest subsidies and credits.

Steel. Steel industries have been besieged by structural problems for many years in the European Community and also in the United States. While the German steel industry in general, by virtue of strong investments in modern equipment and a relatively high level of technical capability, was able to remain reasonably competitive compared with steel industries from other countries, it was hit hard by the worldwide growth in production capacity, a high underutilization factor, and the ensuing increase in production costs.

With regard to special hardships incurred by steel industries in the Saar region, the federal and the state governments have come up with a program to provide loan guarantees and conditionally repayable grants. Both programs are meant to alleviate the financial burden of costly investments to modernize the production structure in the Saar.

Aerospace. This sector represents a different situation. Instead of an old, established industrial sector fighting to make the necessary adjustments to structural change, this is the case of a high-technology industry with significant spin-off into other industries and with high growth potential.

In its attempts to gain a significant share of the world market, the small German aerospace industry faces overwhelming competition from abroad, particularly from the dominant U.S. aerospace industry. Strengthening the competitive position of this industry is necessary for its survival. Therefore, the civil segment of the aeronautical industry receives financial help from the government, via repayable development grants and loan guarantees for production. In some respects, this program represents a connecting link between the shipbuilding and steel programs and the R&D programs of the Research Ministry, to be discussed later.

General Programs to Ease Structural Adaptation

A few examples will be mentioned here of programs not directed at specific sectors.

"Investments for the Future."
This medium-term program was introduced in 1977. Some of these funds were used to assist industry in projects for structural development and adaptation. Major areas are construction, transportation, energy, and housing.

Capital-loan Programs
- Loans for setting up new businesses.
- Loans for improving businesses in poorly developed regions or regions with siting disadvantages.
- Loans for restructuring businesses, especially to adapt to new markets and technologies.

Tax Legislation
In the area of tax legislation, a few recent initiatives are relevant to industrial policy:
- A new law to decrease (or even eliminate) the profit tax for small and medium-sized businesses.
- The possibility, for small and medium-sized businesses, to carry back losses incurred (up to 5 million DM), including losses due to retooling of plants and equipment.
- Special tax allowances for R&D investments; The allowance is 20 percent for investments up to 500,000 DM per year and 75 percent for higher amounts (costs for acquisition of patents and know-how as well as for R&D buildings can be included).

Antitrust Legislation
- A new law was passed facilitating cooperation between small or medium-sized companies in technology and innovation, and
- the control of the abuse of monopolistic power was tightened.

Labor
In labor market and employment policies, various measures designed to assist adaptation to structural changes include
- assistance programs to create new jobs, and
- training as well as retraining programs.

Federal Programs for R&D and Innovation in Industry

A large share (about 45 percent) of the government's R&D programs is in direct or indirect support of industrial technology and innovation. These programs with a strong impact on industrial policies will be briefly described.

In 1978, the total national R&D budget for the Federal Republic of Germany was $15 billion, representing approximately 2.1 percent of its GNP. Government outlays amounted to just over $7 billion (federal funds $4.2 billion, state funds $2.8 billion); industry outlays, $7.6 billion; roughly $500 million came from other sources.

In 1980, total federal spending for industrial R&D and innovation was $1.8 billion. A major share of these funds, approximately $1.15 billion, is spent by various departments in "direct funding" programs (grants for specific industrial projects) for civilian R&D, with the lion's share being managed by the Federal Ministry for Research and Technology (BMFT). This department not only controls a dominating share of the total federal R&D funds, but also has the authority to coordinate all federal civilian research programs.

Among the broad range of BMFT R&D programs, the following have strong relevance to industrial policy:
- Energy
- Aerospace and terrestrial transportation
- Communication technologies
- Materials sciences and mineral resources
- Electronics, production technologies, optical R&D, and scientific instruments
- Biotechnology and biomedical engineering.

The objective of these programs, supporting technical fields that might be considered "key technologies" for future economic growth, is to strengthen the scientific and technological capability and competitiveness of German industry.

These programs were initiated (starting with nuclear energy and space programs) in the second half of the fifties. The majority of grants went to a small number of big "high-technology" companies. The reason for this development can be found in the industrial structure itself. In 1975, for instance, small and medium-sized businesses with sales of up to 100 million DM accounted for only 6 percent of the total industrial R&D expenditures, whereas the largest part of the remainder of 94 percent was spent by a very small number of research-intensive large companies. It is perhaps natural that, without specific government action, federal R&D funds have a tendency to flow in a direction where industry already has a strong R&D effort and government funds can be matched by corresponding industrial funds.

In the late seventies, the federal government therefore undertook an effort to counteract the striking imbalance existing between the important role that small business has in innovation and the disadvantage resulting from its small share of government R&D funds. The result of this effort was a special "research and technology policy concept for small and medium size business," a joint program of the BMFT and the Ministry of Economics that was announced in 1978.

This program takes into consideration the special requirements of smaller companies and offers a wide range of measures—such as grants, loans, technical and management consulting—to assist these companies in innovation and adaptation to structural changes. These measures include the following:

- A "first innovation program," through which repayable grants (if the innovation is successful) are given for the costs incurred in the introduction of new products or processes into the market.
- Allowance for the cost of R&D personnel. The government pays for between 25 percent and 40 percent of the cost of such personnel.
- Grants for energy-conserving technologies.
- Support of contract-research. The government pays for up to 30 percent of the cost of research contracted by small companies to research institutes (the maximum contribution to a research project is 120,000 DM per year).
- A cooperative research program, managed by the Federation of Industrial Research Associations of German Industry. In this program, more than seventy industrial research associations, representing the different industrial sectors, assisted by a technical advisory system, define research projects of general interest to the companies in these sectors. The cost of these projects is shared between industry and the government (represented by the Ministry of Economics).
- The establishment of a risk capital organization with major German banks as shareholders. Seventy-five percent of the funds are backed by government guarantees. The organization, called *Wagnis Finanzierungs-Gesellschaft*, provides venture capital and consulting services to new and small, high-technology, innovative companies.

- A special program to strengthen economic growth and competitiveness of industries in Berlin, to compensate for hardships and disadvantages hampering industrial production in this city. Grants are made for technical development projects of small and medium-sized businesses operating in Berlin; some of the grants are repayable.
- Special measures for technology transfer (especially in the areas of information and documentation, patents, and consulting).

The transfer of the vast body of scientific and technological information, generated in academic research institutions and government labs, to small companies presents difficult problems.

Federal and state governments cooperate in a number of complementary programs to ease that transfer. These programs comprise a network of scientific and technical documentation systems; institutions advising small companies on patent problems; "technology transfer agencies" established in a number of universities, which consult businesses on scientific or technological problems; and a growing number of similar agencies assisting businesses on problems incurred with innovation projects. The approach taken by these agencies can be regional, sectoral, or problem-oriented (for example, microelectronics). While some of these latter agencies are associated with chambers of industry and trade, others are associated with productivity-oriented institutions or with unions.

RESULTS OF THE PROGRAMS

Sectoral Programs

Any assessment of the effects of government programs on the viability and competitiveness of specific industrial sectors can easily lead to fallacious conclusions: since the environment in which these industries operate constantly changes both globally and domestically, the effects of government aid or incentives are difficult to single out. Still, a few comments will be made on how some of the efforts have worked so far.

In spite of the fact that the government has granted support for the shipbuilding industry for quite a few years now, it would be exaggerated to claim that the industry in general is now competitive on the world market. However, due to government assistance, including R&D programs, the industry has managed to establish itself in an important and growing niche of the market concerning special cargo vessels, and also in special ships for marine technology.

In the German steel industry, the structural assistance by the government enabled the ailing part of that sector in the Saar region to initiate necessary investments for modernization of plants and equipment, and will hopefully make this industry competitive once the worldwide crisis due to overproduction gives way to normal market conditions.

In the aerospace sector, the appearance of the "Airbus" on the world market for civilian jet aircraft seems to be an indication of an emerging viable industry which, after the recent merger between two major German manufacturers, should be able to compete successfully also for future commercial aircraft projects. Clearly, the development of the "Airbus" as well as other aerospace projects would not have been possible without significant government support.

Federal R&D Programs

There are also some rather striking examples where federal R&D programs helped industries to adapt to technological change. In particular, German manufacturers of nuclear plants and equipment, who are presently competing successfully on the world market, have benefited greatly from a strong research and technology base developed with government funds. In particular, fuel cycle technologies as well as advanced reactor concepts such as the breeder and the high-temperature reactor are being developed mainly with government money.

Another rather striking example is the German clock and watch industry. This sector of small and medium-sized companies with a long tradition of highly skilled workers and high-quality mechanical products was suddenly faced with the appearance of cheap electronic watches, mostly made by U.S. and Japanese manufacturers. Because of the comparatively conservative structure of the industry's management and work force, which lacked both the technological skills and the financial capabilities needed to invest in new manufacturing processes, the necessary structural and technological adaptation was started with a dangerous delay and proceeded only slowly.

In 1977 the government initiated a specific sector-oriented program offering assistance for retraining of workers and engineers, for R&D programs, and for consulting. As a result, the industry has by and large managed to establish itself in the new markets for electronic products.

As a last example, computers should be mentioned. In the sixties, few German manufacturers had evolved. However, due to the overwhelming competition from abroad (at that time, the largest U.S. manufacturer held 75 percent of the German market), their small market share did not enable them to invest vigorously in R&D for new and competitive products; therefore they seemed doomed to suffer continuous losses or to withdraw from the market.

Since computers were considered to be the single most important key technology, the government started a program of R&D assistance, which was mostly oriented to develop advanced hardware. At the same time, government money was made available to academic institutions and research laboratories to buy computers as well as for computer science education. In the second half of the seventies, the direction of the R&D assistance was shifted toward software development and applications.

Today, large mainframes as well as small computers and minicomputers are manufactured in Germany and compete with foreign manufacturers both domestically and abroad.

Finally, as far as the R&D policy concept for small and medium-sized business is concerned, initial results are quite encouraging. In particular, the services of the various technology-transfer agencies are frequently used; government assistance for R&D personnel costs has led to increased research activities in small companies, and requests for funds for contract-research are constantly rising in number. In general, the reaction of the business sector to this concept has been quite favorable.

CONCLUSION

The industrial policies outlined should not be perceived as a framework of static principles and programs, but as a dynamic process of policy development and adaptation to a changing economic and social environment.

In the eighties, Germany, like many industrial countries, will be facing difficult processes of structural adaptation. Since these processes will take place in a period of severe budgetary constraints, the government will no longer be able to react by providing ever-increasing R&D funds. Instead, strong efforts will have to be made to optimize the allocation of limited resources and to further improve the efficiency of existing programs. In big technology projects, the private sector will be asked to contribute a higher share of the cost. Some assistance programs, endeared to their clientele, will have to be cut or even abolished; new programs may have to be started. The evolving industrial policies of the eighties should help to soothe the transition of German industries into the next decades.

REFERENCES

Aktuelle Beiträge zur Wirtschafts- und Finanzpolitik No. 16/81. Presse- und Informationsamt der Bundesregierung, February 1981.

Anderson, Douglas D. "Germany: The Uncertain Stride of a Giant." Harvard Business School, Case Study on German Industrial Policies, Boston, July 1980.

Büchner-Schoepf, Melitta. "Industrial Policy in the Federal Republic of Germany." Paper presented at the International RKW-Roundtable of Industrial Policies, Bonn, October 1979.

Bülow, Andreas V. "Folgen technologischen Wandels für die Arbeitsplätze, Ansätze einer modernen Technologiepolitik." Speech for the List-Society in Düsseldorf, March 1981.

Forschungs- und technologiepolitisches Gesamtkonzept der Bundesregierung fuer kleine und mittlere Unternehmen. Bundesministerium für Forschung und Technologie und Bundesministerium für Wirtschaft (Bonn, 1978).

Jahreswirtschaftsbericht der Bundesregierung für 1981 (Entwurf).

Lambsdorff, Otto Count. "The Federal Republic of Germany at the Beginning of the 80's." Speech delivered at the Council on Foreign Relations, Chicago, March 1981.

Menden, Werner. "Science, Technology and Innovation in the Federal Republic of Germany." Paper presented at a Conference of the Society of Research Administrators, Chicago, October 1980.

Menden, Werner. "Energy Technology in Germany." Speech delivered at a Conference of the American Society of Mechanical Engineers, Washington, D.C., February 1981.

Rembser, Josef. "National Concepts of Innovation Policy." Paper presented at workshop on technological innovation in industry, Berlin, December 1980.

Siebter Subventionsbericht der Bundesregierung. Deutscher Bundestag Drucksache 8/3097 v. 8.8.79.

Sixth Report of the Federal Government on Research, Bonn, 1980.

9

If at First You Don't Succeed, Don't Try Again: Industrial Policy in Britain

Stephen Blank and Paul M. Sacks

The lessons American leaders can draw from Britain's experience with industrial policy are for the most part negative. They spotlight constraints on institutional innovation and policy engineering and suggest further the political menace that can be created by unsuccessful efforts to remedy social and economic ills.

Britain's experience with industrial policy has particular relevance for American leaders because of the similarity of constraints which policymakers face on both shores of the Atlantic. The historical constraints on state intervention in the economy, the inheritance of the laissez-faire tradition, and the relatively limited role of the state bureaucracy are similar in the two countries. Both Britain and the United States are "weak" states when it comes to the role of the state in directing and ordering private sector activities.[1] Leaders in both states are apt to forget this when confronting new problems, and frequently speak as if what is plausible in Japan or France is equally feasible in their own societies. In the 1960s, the British were captured by such a French illusion, and the United States today seems equally smitten with Japan.

Compared to the other countries discussed at the 1981 Humphrey Conference on Industry Vitalization (Japan and Germany), Britain has experimented much more directly with industrial policies and strategies. The essential components of an industrial policy were in existence during Attlee's postwar Labour government. Only in the mid-1960s, when the gravity of their economic dilemma galvanized policymakers into formulating a strategy for reversing Britain's steady decline in international competitiveness, did the government actually seek to formulate an explicit industrial strategy. Since then, however, under successive Labour and Tory governments, strategies for industrial revival have remained high on the policy agenda.

The failure of these efforts is the beginning of this chapter. The more interesting question in the British case is not what governments have tried to do, but why they have failed. Seen from this perspective, the British experience may be more valuable for nations grappling with their own decisions about a strategy of industrial revitalization. British experience illustrates the factors that can inhibit the successful implementation of an industrial policy, and suggests, perhaps, what other nations ought not to do. The most important lesson to be drawn from all of this might well be that doing something badly can be much worse than doing nothing at all.

THE BURDEN OF HISTORY

Although the failure we are discussing is a postwar phenomenon, its roots lie as far back in British history as the first half of the nineteenth century when the structure of government-industry relations was initially established. Indeed, what distinguishes Britain most from Germany and Japan with regard to industrial policy (and, equally, is most similar to the United States) is the pattern of industrialization in British history and the constraints which this legacy imposes on later government efforts at industrial vitalization.

In Britain, in contrast to Germany and Japan, industrialization was not led by the government. Britain's experience is quite the reverse. As the political and economic systems became more modern in the eighteenth and nineteenth centuries, the two systems were progressively disengaged. In what might be termed Britain's first (and most successful) industrial policy, governments sought to sweep away outmoded restrictions and regulations that hindered industrial freedom and to streamline their own administrative machinery. As many scholars have demonstrated, the early nineteenth century did not see the total triumph of laissez-fairism,[2] but during this period the commitment to "complete freedom of trade, backed by a whole philosophy of commercial liberalism and a new popular faith in the virtue of free competitive enterprise" formed the mold for government-industry relations in rapidly industrializing Britain.[3] By mid-century, a truly liberal regime had been firmly implanted. Henceforth, the essential economic function of the British state would be to preserve the freedom of the marketplace, while governments in later industrializing nations, including Germany and Japan, were forced by competitive pressures to protect domestic enterprise and foster national industrial development.[4]

Britain's pattern of industrial development profoundly influenced the economic policy environment well into the present era. One consequence was what Andrew Shonfield called the "instinctive suspicion of positive government" in Britain.[5] There is a deep, continuing reluctance to government involvement in the economic process except, as Charles Kindleberger writes, "in the exercize of the police powers of the state to protect the general safety and welfare."[6] Shonfield continues: "Anything which smacked of a restless or over-energetic state with ideas of guiding the nation on the basis of a long view of its collective economic interest, was instinctively the object of suspicion."[7]

A second, closely related consequence was the deeply ingrained anti-interventionist orientation of Britain's civil service which continued full-blown into the middle of the twentieth century and still exerts a powerful influence in Whitehall today. In a famous critique of the civil service written in the late 1960s, Thomas Balogh, a top advisor to Harold Wilson, emphasized that a large share of Britain's inability to adapt to the demands of the mid–twentieth century "derives ironically perhaps *from the very success of the boldness of the efforts of the Victorian reformers* to give Britain an administrative personnel for a Nightwatchman State presiding over the breathtaking expansion of private industrial capital."[8] Contrast the role of the state bureaucracy in Meiji-era Japan and its continued place at the center of Japan's economic policy machinery today:

> The young *samuri*-bureaucrats of the new Imperial regime embarked on a program of sweeping and autocratic national reforms. The dream of men like Okubo, Kido, Iwakura, and others was first to consolidate the power and authority of the new government against internal opposition; second, to build a strong national state able to defend and assert itself in the arena of world politics. These ambitions set the framework and tempo of national development for the next quarter century. They formed the basis for a close mercantilist alliance between the bureaucrats and the nascent class of financiers and industrialists.[9]

A third consequence of Britain's pattern of industrialization was the development of a particular approach to economic management. Unlike the French or the Japanese, the British developed only a limited inventory of policy instruments. The British policy orientation has consistently favored the global, the minimal, and the indirect approach to economic policy. There is no British equivalent to the *dirigiste* tradition in France or to the system of administrative guidance in Japan. Again and again throughout the postwar period, British officials have searched for automatic forms of economic management that would minimize administrative discretion and preserve the maximum distance between the state and the economy.

The British experience of industrialization also influenced key social patterns. Britain's business community remained highly fragmented, with especially sharp divisions between industry and finance. One result of this fragmentation was that British business never had the capacity to speak to government with even the semblance of a single voice, not at least until the formation of the Confederation of British Industry in 1965. For most of the twentieth century, British industry was more concerned about keeping government away and minimizing its contacts with the public sector than with influencing government policies.[10] The network of contacts and personal connections that provided the social foundation for government policies affecting industry in other countries has never existed in Britain. The institutional linkages that might have provided a voice in government for business leaders or drawn connections between them and government officials remained undeveloped in the absence of any compelling need to create them.

Another equally important consequence of Britain's industrial development was that the interests of finance were not only distinct from those of industry, but even at odds with them. Financial interests came to be identified with the extension and maintenance of Britain's international financial role rather than with the interests of the domestic economy.

> The passivity of the state in economic affairs gave the British bourgeoisie the same luxury of organizational decentralization characteristic of America. Its most formidable opponent arose, in fact, not in Whitehall but in the City. Over time, political power shifted from industry to finance with its international orientation. Unlike German banks, the growth of a powerful financial community was geared not to financing investments at home but to facilitating capital exports. As was true of America after 1945, both business (that is, finance) interests and state ideology converged, preferring liberal imperialism.[11]

British investment bankers developed little stake in domestic industry (as the French investment banking community did); nor was any financial mechanism created for restructuring domestic industry when it was required. Over time, this financial definition of the nation's economic interest was transformed into a national orthodoxy shared by a broad spectrum of political leaders and was increasingly immune from criticism or new ideas.

As long as Britain remained the world's leading economic and financial power, this divergence was not critical. In the post-1945 era, however, when domestic resources were insufficient to support both roles, international financial commitments and interests helped undermine the health of the domestic economy.

The advent of modern mass parties did little to alter this pattern of government-industry relations. A new breed of party leaders came to dominate these new structures and, as a result, the formal institutions of government. The leaders of business remained on the sidelines, for British business did not need a modern party organization to wage a struggle for recognition and influence which it had won decades before. The fact that a modern, merit-based civil service merged into an already well-ensconced liberal regime also had a profound importance. The long history of administrative decentralization and the late emergence of a centralized bureaucracy, together with the deeply ingrained commitment to commercial liberalism and free trade, circumscribed the bureaucratic penetration of the economy and defined government's role as a neutral rule enforcer. What emerged in the second half of the nineteenth century in Britain was a policy in which industrial and financial interests enjoyed a prominent position, but in which neither the private sector nor the state had much inclination nor capacity to intervene in the other's affairs.

Even the rise of the Labour party in the years following World War I did not alter the liberal orientation of Britain's economic policy. Labour's first government in 1924, with only minority support in Parliament, was "in office but not in power, shackled to the Liberals and pursuing a policy of moderation."[12] In 1929, Ramsey MacDonald and the other Labour leaders who formed Labour's second government rejected the ideas of the party's Left. The government's efforts to fight off the effects of the worldwide depression were shaped primarily by civil servants and Chancellor of the Exchequer Philip Snowden's rigidly orthodox view of economic management.

All such schemes to ameliorate rising unemployment failed in the Unemployment Committee where the four ministers were confronted with bleak negatives from the top civil servants . . . if this was not sufficiently discouraging, the Treasury watch-dog was always at hand; and no Chancellor of the Exchequer was more economy-minded and less sympathetic to any proposals of a socialist cast than Philip Snowden.[13]

The historical mold which shaped Britain's experience of industrialization differed vastly from that which formed the German, Japanese, or French experience. The mold produced substantial differences in the relationship of state and society and of government and economy; vital differences in perceptions of the function and role of public power in economic life; significant differences in the attitudes of key public and private sector actors toward government-business relations; and great variations in the tools or policies available to public sector leaders to influence patterns of economic growth and industrial development. These differences, the result of the burden of history, continued to exert a profound influence on the economic policymaking process even after the Second World War and well into the second half of the twentieth century.

Throughout the postwar decades, these historical legacies have constrained British policies toward industry, narrowing and circumscribing the room for maneuver. Despite the new commitments of the managed economy and welfare state, the products of the Great Depression, and World War II, Britain's historical legacy continued to define, limit, and complicate subsequent efforts to revitalize industry. As we shall see, the failure of these efforts stemmed in large measure from the policymakers' inability, in the midst of

industrial crisis, to take full account of a legacy so mighty that it was overlooked.

THE PERSISTENCE OF AD-HOCERY

Britain's liberal orientation was significantly altered by the Great Depression and World War II—by the efforts of governments in the 1930s and
1940s to mobilize the national economy in the face of global political and
economic conflict. Government-industry relations and the pattern of economic policy both changed significantly as the public sector expanded and
assumed vast new responsibilities.

The Great Depression hit Britain hard, but recovery was substantial between 1933 and 1935. Manufacturing output in 1938-1939 was almost one-
third higher than in 1929 and almost 40 percent more than in 1914.[14] Unemployment remained high, particularly in the cities where far too many workers remained on the dole, but total output and industrial productivity increased impressively. The full costs of the war were incalculable; perhaps 10
percent of the nation's wealth was destroyed by enemy action or by overuse,
and 400,000 British citizens died as a result of the war. But there were
positive effects as well. The war brought about a remarkable resurgence of
self-confidence after long years of frustration. Together the British had shared
in the nation's "finest hour," standing alone against the might of Hitler's
forces. The war had been a triumph for traditional British virtues—strength
of character, tenacity, and cooperation. Perhaps most important, the scourge
of unemployment had ended. In 1945, three million more Britons were employed than in 1939.

Despite the bombing, the loss of resources, and the lack of replacement
and new investment, Britain's economy had accomplished miracles of production. Key technological advances had been made and, in many cases (in
electronics, radar, and jet propulsion, for example), there were promises of
important peacetime applications. Thus A. J. P. Taylor concludes his study
of Britain from 1914 to 1945 by stating: "During the Second World War, and
not before, Great Britain took the decisive jump industrially from the nineteenth into the twentieth century."[15]

Not withstanding the damage inflicted by the war, Britain enjoyed a remarkable postwar economic recovery. Impressive achievements were registered in total production, productivity, and in exports. Industrial production
increased by 30 to 40 percent between 1945 and 1950, and annual increases in
industrial output and in productivity were greater between 1949 and 1960
than in the years leading up to World War I or in the 1920s. Britain's
international trade balance improved enormously in these years; for the first
time in its history, Britain consistently ran a surplus in visible trade. All of
this was carried out, it should be remembered, against the background of the

creation of the welfare state, a fairly substantial redistribution of personal income in favor of wage earners, and the maintenance of full employment.

This record may well entitle Britain after 1945 to be considered Europe's first "economic miracle." But we will search in vain in the postwar government's economic policies for much that is miraculous. Insofar as public policies contributed to Britain's postwar economic successes, the Labour government's policies were essentially a continuation of those initiated under the National government and expanded during the war.

In his monumental study of British politics in the collectivist age, Samuel Beer writes that while "the Labour Party . . . talked a great deal more about planning and control of the economy. . . . Historically . . . it was The National Government, nominally a coalition, but in fact amost entirely dominated by its Conservative ministers and their ideas, that laid the foundations of the Managed Economy."[16] Beer traces the origins of many postwar economic policies to the National government—a managed currency, devaluation, bilateral trade agreements, tariffs, import quotas, subsidies, deficiency payments, and control on location of industry. Indeed, in the various plans for "industrial reorganization" that were discussed in this period, one finds the roots of today's industrial policy.[17]

World War II quickened the pace of economic policy change. Relying on a universe of physical controls as well as new Keynesian techniques of financial management, the wartime government was able to mobilize Britain's economy far beyond what the rulers of totalitarian Germany could accomplish. During the war, there was no time for theorizing. Policy and institutional innovation were a response to dire necessity, to the threat to survival itself, and not to theoretical imperatives.

Coming to power in 1945, the Labour government, for the first time with a huge majority in Parliament, might have been capable of rationalizing the experience of the previous decade and of constructing a new framework for economic and industrial policy. Much was in the government's favor. The nation was aware of the severity of the economic crisis it faced. Aside from extensive physical damage, Britain's industrial plant had been run down, its foreign assets liquidated, and gold and silver reserves exhausted. Economic instability and massive unemployment seemed inevitable with the winding down of war production. The very size of Labour's mandate also inhibited opposition to reform. The government's moral authority to lead the country in new directions could not be questioned. Many leaders in industry were convinced that the spectrum of British politics had shifted permanently to the left, toward a planned economy, "and manufacturers and traders seemed ready to accommodate themselves to it with resignation, if not with enthusiasm."[18]

Yet, in the area of economic policy, innovation was limited and instead there was much continuity with the wartime system. The Labour government continued to rely on the wartime control system to implement its economic and industrial policies. Consultation between industry and government went on in the first years of peace just as it had during the war and, as in wartime, the government found that the most effective way to ensure cooperation was to involve industry directly in the policy process. Where changes were made in the control system, they invariably resulted in the loosening rather than the tightening of regulation. Nationalization aside, almost all of the changes in the economic policy made after 1945 served to decentralize decision making and responsibility.

Most importantly, the Labour government created no new policy framework for economic management and industrial revitalization. Efforts at changing the framework, at institutional innovation—other than the minimal program of nationalization—were not taken seriously and, where attempted, quickly dropped. Development councils provide one example of this half-hearted effort at reform, the attempt to create a central planning staff, a second.

In September 1945, Sir Stafford Cripps (then president of the Board of Trade) announced the formation of working parties which would inquire into the problems of a number of industries for which nationalization was not contemplated. Each working party was composed of employers and trade union members from an industry, together with a few independent members and an independent chairman. All save one recommended the establishment of some sort of continuing industrial council. This led in the summer of 1947 to the enactment of the Industrial Development and Organization Act. The act enabled any of eight ministers to establish a development council in an industry or group of related industries by an order, subject to approval by resolution in each House of Parliament. The council could impose levies for research or export promotion and undertake activities to raise productivity.

The development councils might have represented a first, critical step toward a system of national economic planning (in France, Monnet and his associates watched the British experiment carefully[19]) or an industrial revitalization strategy. Industrial leaders at first were violently opposed to the councils. They were unhappy with provisions for trade union representation and feared that a government-controlled majority on a council which had statutory authority over its industry might constitute back-door nationalization. More central to the opposition of many industrialists, however, was a concern that the councils would constitute an alternative structure of industrial organization, a rival with official status to the trade associations.

The Labour government was taken by surprise by the intensity of industrial opposition to the development councils, and never pressed forcefully for their establishment. By the time of the 1951 general election, only seven orders had been made under the act and, of these, only four had actually led to the formation of a council. The government's posture reflected its own uncertainty. If the councils were intended merely to help improve efficiency and performance, it would be pointless to force them on unwilling industries. If, on the other hand, the councils were to have the more fundamental purpose of restructuring key industries, they might then be worth the fight. Not all industrial leaders opposed the development-council concept. Some were especially critical of the older trade associations for failing to provide effective channels of communication with government and with the trade unions. But the Labour government never forced the issue. Pressed for time, reluctant to confront the established industrial structure that had served so well during the war, and diverted by more immediate problems, the government permitted the development council concept to die quietly.

The second case in point concerns efforts to establish a central planning staff. As noted earlier, although the Labour party talked extensively about "planning," it did little to produce a national economic plan.It continued to rely instead on the wartime system of direct physical controls guided by the national income and manpower budgets. Early in 1947, a severe fuel crisis dramatically revealed the government's inability to coordinate economic policy and led to major alterations in the machinery as well as the content of economic policy. Greater emphasis was henceforth to be placed on forward planning, and a new planning body, the Central Economic Planning Staff, was created. A new ministerial position was created to coordinate all economic policy, and early in the fall of 1947, Cripps became the first minister for economic affairs.

The experiment had barely begun, however, when Hugh Dalton was forced to resign from the Exchequer. Cripps succeeded Dalton as chancellor and took with him the function and apparatus of economic planning. With Cripps as chancellor, the role of the Treasury—downgraded since the outbreak of the war—revived. With this revival came a shift in the technique of economic control, away from direct physical controls and toward a greater reliance on indirect economic management. The economic survey of 1947 had approximated a forward plan; after this, efforts to construct some sort of national plan fell away. The attention of the Treasury was increasingly focused on the problem of inflation and on finding a permanent solution to Britain's balance-of-payments problems. The pace of "decontrol" quickened, and with it, the return to more traditional relations between industry and government.

What accounts for this failure to consolidate the economic gains and achievements of the previous ten years in the form of new policies and institutions? Much of the answer is obvious. Britain won the war; its political and economic system which had carried so heavy a burden was still intact; the leaders who had stood so bravely against Hitler were still in place. Victory had been achieved because that system had worked, and because of the loyalty and dedication to that system on the part of Britain's leaders in government and in the private sector. The temptation to continue to do what had worked so well was overwhelming. In the first years after the war, the wartime economic system was patched and mended; its strength lay in the wealth of personal relationships that had developed among politicians, bureaucrats, businessmen, and trade union leaders over the previous decade. When this group wearied, however, and ultimately died, there had been no institutional learning, no new system put in place embodying the lessons learned at so high a cost. The temptation then was unavoidable to return to older habits, to the earlier traditions so deeply ingrained in the system.

Contrast the French situation. France had been defeated, and the French nation widely agreed that defeat was due in large part to the failures of the French economy. France's economy was archaic and hopelessly ineffective; France remained a preindustrial state in an era when national power rested primarily upon industrial potency. As matters stood, the French state could neither protect its citizens from external invasion nor ensure their domestic well-being. Even while the battle of the Rhine was under way, DeGaulle, as leader of the provisional government, called for a national economic renewal, and throughout the political chaos of the next years, the realization of the absolute necessity for economic revival remained. Kindleberger observes that "a basic change seems to have occurred in France after its defeat by Germany in 1940. . . . Essentially this change was agreement—nationally— that economic backwardness was intolerable and that, whatever differences might divide France on other issues, economic progress must be made."[20]

> There was a deep-rooted alteration in the importance attached by society to economic expansion and advance, to effective economic performance. Whether the change was sparked by the Inspection des Finances or was widespread in every echelon of French culture; whether it relied on a small group of planners or was carried out empirically by technocrats at all levels of industry; whether it relied exclusively on increased investment or mainly on changing technology— these are subjects that lie beyond the scope of the present discussion. But war had a great deal to do with the change in attitude.

> And this was a significant difference between the British and the French experience: The British had won the war; the French, though they belonged to the winning side had lost it.[21]

In France, defeat led to a rejection of old men and old machinery; its memory forced an alliance to restore France's economic capacity that cut across other divisions in French society. In Britain, victory exhausted the national leadership and yet created a sense of achievement that made it almost impossible to think of drastic reform. Britain's plucky make-do-and-mend attitude, the stuff of a thousand war legends, enshrined ad hocery as a way of life. "Muddling through" was the national slogan. Kindleberger sums up his views on this subject perhaps too cruelly, but basically correctly: "Unlike the French, who greeted peace with the resolve to restore the national honor and to achieve economic expansion . . . the British emerged from six years of war prepared not to earn, but to enjoy, the fruits of victory."[22]

THE PREDOMINANCE OF POLITICAL GOALS

Ad hocery is not the only reason for Britain's failure after World War II to reform its economic policy mechanism and to focus its attention on industrial reconstruction. The predominance of political goals was perhaps even more important in this regard.[23]

British economic policies after 1945 were dominated and shaped by two overriding objectives. One was to consolidate the welfare state; the second was to restore and protect Britain's position as an international power.

By the end of the war, the British were convinced that the root causes of the conflict were the economic and social conditions of the interwar years. Britain's leaders were determined to avoid the recurrence of these conditions at any cost. Thus the consolidation of the welfare state and the commitment to full employment at home were intimately linked to British efforts to recreate a stable and liberal international commercial and financial order.

British perceptions of their role in the world war after 1945 are easy enough to understand. A victor in the war, a member of the Big Three, the world's third ranking military power, the leader, perhaps, in technology, the head of the Commonwealth—these were all realities. Britain's leaders were aware, of course, of just how weak the country was, and the Labour government struggled to reduce its immediate foreign and military responsibilities. But, as Joseph Frankel observes, it was assumed "that Britain's domestic arrangements, the international system, and Britain's role within it would all return to some approximation of prewar 'normalcy.' "[24]

By the late 1940s, Britain's international role was defined less and less in military terms (where it was clear that Britain would have to play second fiddle to the Americans) and more in terms of commerce and finance. Supported by the Commonwealth, independent of both the United States and Europe, Britain could maintain its position as the world's foremost commercial and financial center. Within this arena, sterling served as the primary mechanism which linked the Commonwealth into a coherent economic entity. Thus the sterling system, resting on fixed exchange rates and London's role as an international banker, provided the key support for Britain's position as a world power.

The stability of the international financial and commercial systems established under Anglo-American leadership at war's end was seen to be essential for the operation of the sterling system and, thus, for ensuring Britain's international role. The restoration of a liberal international financial order ensured, in British eyes, a better world by preventing the disasters of the interwar years and by guaranteeing that Britain would be one of its leaders.

Fact and wish tended to blur at this point. It was not obvious that Britain's international position had been fundamentally altered. Britain's political and economic superiority over Japan and the European nations in the first postwar years was self-evident, and few doubted that the Commonwealth would continue to be Britain's great reservoir of resources. No one was prepared to say that Britain had become a second-class power, nor were British leaders prepared to duck the responsibilities that great-power status, so avidly sought and clung to, conferred. Britain's leaders agreed that it was her duty to maintain peace, law, and stability in the world. Duties were especially clear with regard to the reestablishment of a liberal global economic system, which was perceived as the source of British power. Britain was determined to act like a world power and, if necessary, to hold up herself the very scenery of the set to make it so. Sir Kenneth Younger writes that while Britain's power to discharge its responsibilities might have been limited, "she nonetheless rightly felt herself to be still the same sort of power that she had been before, handicapped indeed by lack of resources, but still cast for a world part, which no one else, for the time being, could play in her stead."[25]

The focus of economic policy immediately after the war was reconstruction and the conversion of the economy to peacetime production. International economic policy was directed primarily toward gathering scarce dollars. By the late 1940s, however, the emphasis was beginning to shift as the initial tasks of restoring the peacetime economy were accomplished. After 1951, the main thrust of British economic policy was directed to the achievement of convertibility, multilateral trade, and "the re-establishment of sterling as a general international currency and of London as an open financial market-place."[26] What evolved thereafter in the 1950s was a complex interlocking policy network, the purpose of which was the preservation of Britain's role as a world power. Included in this network were the restoration of sterling's international transaction and reserve functions, fixed exchange rates, overseas investment directed particularly toward the sterling area, government spending and lending in the Commonwealth and sterling area, and the maintenance of a military and defense presence in these areas.

The role Britain elected to play is entirely understandable; it combined both self-interest and a large measure of international responsibility. But it was a role Britain could no longer afford, and represented the triumph of political aspiration over economic reality.

The problem was that British efforts after 1945 to play the role of global power were excessively expensive and well beyond the nation's resources and capacities. Britain's rearmament program in 1950, the decision to maintain a British army in Europe in 1954, and the rush to restore full convertibility of the pound in 1957, were highly responsible actions from the perspective of the international economic and political order. Yet the reference point for each of these decisions was Britain's role as a world power, not the costs that would actually be borne by the domestic economy. No calculation of Britain's actual ability to bear these costs seems to have been carried out. At times, it appears, Britain was lured or pressured into taking steps (to support the U.S. dollar in the Johnson era, for example) by the manipulation of the "special relationship" with the United States, but this behavior, too, reflected the overwhelming desire of British leaders to walk in the corridors of global power and to play Greece to the American Rome.

The result, especially after 1955, was that British citizens were told again and again that they were living beyond their means and that they would have to accept higher taxes, cutbacks in public services, and slower economic growth if the nation was to remain solvent and to maintain its international competitiveness. The government resorted to more violent attacks on the domestic economy, raising interest rates and restraining investment, in order to support Britain's international aspirations. To an ever-increasing extent, domestic economic policy was determined not by the needs of the national economy, but by the movement of international confidence in the pound, a situation that one of the most acute observers of Britain at the time found "both tragic and absurd."[27]

Severe deflationary packages were imposed on the domestic economy in 1957, 1961, and 1966—although from 1965 until 1970 the economy was in a state of almost continuous retrenchment. Domestic investment was cut or held back by direct government action and indirectly influenced by high interest rates, credit restrictions, and cuts in investment allowances. The indirect effects on the economy were equally serious, and perhaps more dangerous in the long term. Business expectations were depressed by the continuing stop-go cycles, efforts to expand output were limited, and investment was less productive than it should have been.

The contrast with France could not be more vivid. The primary goal of postwar economic policy in France had been to raise the expectations of investors, "to dispell the gloomy fatalism that had marked French business thinking since the depression."[28] Success here undoubtedly enhanced the increases in labor and capital productivity so notable in France in the 1950s and 1960s.

The impact of government economic policy on British business expectations was quite the opposite. After the "stops" in 1961 and 1965, few British entrepreneurs were prepared to take another chance on national economic growth. Expectations shortened drastically, and liquidity was preferred to longer-term growth possibilities. Continued domestic deflation aggravated the structural problems of the British economy. Investment remained low. Frequent deflation (whether or not the economy was actually overheated) and continuous uncertainty reinforced traditional tendencies toward restrictive practices and inhibited more aggressive management.

There had been little disagreement among Britain's leaders after the war about the need to maintain the country's international role. By the early 1960s, however, the policies of the past decade were viewed as increasingly anachronistic by substantial segments of Britain's leadership, and some of these leaders began to urge a reevaluation of national goals and policies, especially as they affected economic growth and performance.

The result was the attempt in 1961 to create a new approach to economic policymaking involving a tripartite commitment to greater coordination in the economy. Although the term "planning" was much used, what was devised bears perhaps more resemblance to a national industrial policy apparatus. The objective was economic and industrial "revitalization"— although no one used that term—to enhance domestic economic performance and create the conditions for more rapid economic growth. The system consisted of three basic elements: the tripartite National Economic Development Council (or "Neddy"), the policy setting body; the National Economic Development Office, composed of economists and technocrats who prepared staff materials for the council and oversaw the work of the organization; and a series of industry-level "Little Neddies"—shades of the long-forgotten development councils—which were to be charged with developing industry-based growth and performance strategies.

The collapse of this effort in 1964 had very serious implications. In the first place, it showed that the priorities of the government had not changed and that the preservation of the existing rate of exchange, a highly political goal, would take precedence over the domestic economy. Second, the opportunity to rally the support of a key segment of British industry (and to mobilize a cadre of Britain's younger and brightest businessmen) was lost. While no Monnet, Wilson might still have played Cripps and established a more effective and productive union between government and industry. Moreover, the disastrous collapse of this effort at planning tainted future approaches to planning and undermined those institutions which had been created in this first start of the planning process. Third, when devaluation did take place (after the government had promised it would never happen), it was too late to achieve any significant benefits. Instead of freeing the economy from external constraints, the 1967 devaluation forced economic policymakers to squeeze the economy even more vigorously and to keep their attention focused even more rigidly on external confidence in the pound.

Economic needs thus remained in Britain subservient to political goals. In France, the desire to regain great-power status was founded on the realization that the first step had to be the renovation of the domestic economy.

Thus, in the 1950s, the French worried less about their international image and, when necessary, bent the rules of good international citizenship to meet the needs of domestic economic growth. The British, however, kept their eyes firmly focused on the international scene and progressively squeezed the domestic economy to support their international aspirations.

THE POLITIZATION OF ECONOMIC POLICY

British economic policy in the 1950s and early 1960s was not a subject of intense political debate. As we have seen in the previous sections of this chapter, there was little disagreement among Britain's leaders on the outlines and objectives of postwar national economic policies. After the middle 1960s, however, the continued failure of successive governments to arrest Britain's all-too-obvious economic decline led to the increasing politization of economic policy. The burden of British history—the deeply ingrained suspicion of positive government, the lack of a dirigiste tradition, the anti-interventionist orientation of the civil service, and the preference for global economic policy vehicles—would have made the development of a new style of economic management more difficult (and possibly quite impossible) in the best of circumstances.[29] But as frustration increased, the very institutions which should have been nourished in the most quiet and protected portion of the garden were placed in the hottest glare of publicity and expectation. The whole process of institutional innovation was thus fatally undermined.

The political parties in the 1950s did not differ substantially in their views of the economy and economic management. In the 1959 general election, for example, party "image" was far more important than issues.[30] The anti-nationalization campaign, launched by conservative business interests in 1958, spotlighted one key ideological difference between the parties, but Labour party leaders emphasized that, aside from the renationalization of the steel industry, they had no plans for further nationalization. (And, in the wake of their third successive electoral defeat, many Labour leaders were determined to drop nationalization as a party objective.) Nationalization aside, few people in the age of "Butskillism" perceived sharp differences between the parties on economic issues. Indeed, the number of people in the summer of 1959 who felt that it mattered little or not at all which party was in power had doubled (to almost 40 percent) over the previous eight years.[31]

In 1959, the two parties asked the British voter to decide who could better administer the mixed-economy welfare state. In 1964, party differences on economic issues were not vastly greater. Labour's task, to be sure, was easier. In 1959, the Tories had campaigned behind Mr. Macmillan who told the country that "you've never had it so good." In 1964 a sharper-tongued Harold Wilson informed the British voters that "you've never been had so good!" As the authors of the Nuffield study of the 1964 election report, "The Labour manifesto pointed to the lack of purposive Conservative planning and the comparatively low rate of economic growth; it attacked 'Stop-Go' policies, high prices, regional stagnation, and the spreading of 'a selfish get-rich-quick' mood."[32] Labour leaders claimed that they could run Britain more efficiently, that they could turn on the "white-hot" technological revolution and revitalize the economy. They promised to establish a ministry of economic affairs to formulate a national plan and a ministry of technology to bring advanced technology into industry. But none of this amounted to a radically different overall policy than what the Conservatives were proposing. The planning experiment, after all, had been initiated by Conservative Chancellor Selwyn Lloyd. Wilson simply argued that he could do it much better. In any case, "the argument on the rate of economic growth never got very far, nor did the modernization themes of any party seem to have great emotive appeal."[33] Labour offered in 1964, not a change in direction, but a newer, more modern, somehow more technological image than did the weary Tories.

Since then, however, economic issues—both the ultimate objectives of economic policy and the policy instruments—have been at the center of political conflict. Consensus has vanished; Butskillism is dead; and the nature and running of the economy have become objects of hot political controversy.

The reason for this is not difficult to understand. Despite the very real achievements of the Labour government in the 1960s, its economic policies were rated by the nation as a glaring and disastrous failure. Britain's economic situation seemed to deteriorate year by year. Staggering between deepening recession and unguided expansion, and suffering the worst of both much of the time, the "British disease" became a global symbol of economic decay and national decline. Inflation and unemployment reached new postwar peaks, and industrial conflict reemerged as a serious social concern for the first time since the war.

For a country that had experienced little institutional change since World War II, the 1960s saw a blitz of new programs, new agencies, and new promises. Government looked like a merry-go-round, a square dance of changing partners, of circling left and circling right, and finally, of coming back home again—to a growing sense of frustration and impotence.

Watching the endless array of makeshift measures, the Conservative party changed, too. To a new generation of Conservative leaders, the final destination of the consensus politics of the 1950s was the gigantic governmental octopus Mr. Wilson had created, which was strangling the British economy. The party's new philosophy, which its leaders labeled "neo-capitalist," included cutting government spending, lowering taxes, reforming the trade unions, making the social welfare services more selective, as well as joining

the EEC. "The aim was to revive British capitalism: to make it more competitive and efficient, to restore its self-confidence. Britain had somehow to be
shaken from its lethargy; this, according to the Conservatives, was the way
to do it."[34]

To the Conservatives, new attitudes were as important as new policies.
Anthony King writes: "Not only did the party acquire new policies, it acquired a new determination, a new willingness to take risks. The politics of
accommodation gave way to the politics of confrontation."[35] The new Tory
leader, Edward Heath, promised a new and radical style of government, a
rejection of the errors of the Labour government, and a return to essentials:
a "quiet revolution."

The Tory diagnosis of Britain's problems boiled down to excessive government intervention. The new government announced that it would create a
more rigorous competitive climate, with less propping up of lame ducks and
ailing industries. Thus, according to John Davies, the new secretary of state
for trade and industry, what the country needed was "to gear its policies to
the great majority of people, who are not lame ducks, who do not need a
hand, who are quite capable of looking after their own interests and only
demand to be allowed to do so."[36]

The first of the Conservative initiatives aimed at disengaging government
from the private sector was the abolition of the Industrial Reorganization
Corporation (IRC), a Labour-designed agency that had functioned during its
brief five-year existence as the government's merchant bank. A second initiative was the repeal of the Industrial Expansion Act. Along with these roll-
backs came the abolition of the Prices and Incomes Board and the Consumer's Council. This was to be just the beginning of the "wholesale massacre of
the various interventionist bodies and devices established by Labour."[37]

Yet, hardly sooner than Mr. Heath had set about removing the debris of
the previous government, he was forced himself to reverse course.[38] From
now on, "U-turns" would characterize British economic and industrial policy. Well before the 1973-1974 winter of confrontation, when the government
and trade unions locked horns in a test of resolve, the new Tory industrial
policy had been tested and abandoned. The tests were the government's
response to the bankruptcies of Rolls-Royce and Upper Clyde Shipbuilders
in 1971. Rolls-Royce's problem had begun in the fall of 1970 when it ran into
trouble meeting the contract terms in its deal to supply engines for the
Lockheed TriStar. The new government had been forced to bail out the
company—to the tune of £42 million. This was not enough, however, to keep
Rolls-Royce from declaring bankruptcy in February 1971. Faced with the
prospect of the demise of a major employer and exporter, the Tory government retreated from its hard-nosed industrial rhetoric and nationalized a
large part of the company, and supplied in addition some £130 million in
additional public funds.[39]

A similar history of U-turns marked the government's behavior in the case of Upper Clyde Shipbuilders. Upon assuming office, the Tories proclaimed that the stream of public money that had been poured into this ailing industry was to be terminated. This decision, too, was reversed in February 1971, but the action proved insufficient to prevent the company from going into liquidation in June. The workers at UCS staged a "work-in" and the government responded by supplying a newly formed company, Govan Shipbuilders, even larger amounts of public backing than its Labour predecessor.[40]

The Tory decision to repeal major sections of the IEA and abolish the IRC did not necessarily mean a full-scale retreat from the principles embodied in these measures. In 1972 the government passed the Industrial Act, which one commentator called "a resurrected IRC with regional off-shoots."[41] The new act created an Industrial Development Executive (IDE) which, unlike the IRC, was located within a government ministry. But its mission was similar to that of its predecessor. The act initially provided some £550 million in public funds to aid industrial development, particularly within the depressed regions, where IDE regional offices were set up. The new act gave virtually unlimited powers to the secretary of state in deciding the forms, quantities, and recipients of this industrial aid. This same legislation was used later by the Labour government as a favored instrument of industrial policy.[42]

In a few areas, what the Conservative government of 1970-1974 did more closely resembled what it had promised. The system of investment grants was abolished, and in their place came increases in investment allowances.[43] Labour's pet tax initiative, the Selective Employment Tax (SET)—which had been aimed at increasing the flow of labor into manufacturing industry—was halved in 1971 and eliminated in 1973. Finally, the Regional Employment Premium (REP), which had provided for an employment subsidy to manufacturing industry in the development area, was phased out by the Tories.

Just as a new Conservative party emerged from the years in opposition in the 1960s, so too, Labour underwent important changes in early 1970s, swinging sharply to the left. "More precisely," King observes, "it adopted a series of programs that had long been advocated by the party's more extreme militants."

In 1973 *Labour's Programme for Britain* reasserted Labour's goal of bringing about 'a fundamental and irreversible shift in the balance of power and wealth in favour of working people and their families.' Its specific proposals included a wealth tax, the nationalization of building land, the municipalization of privately rented housing, the nationalization of the docks and the aircraft and shipbuilding industries, and the creation of a National Enterprise Board which would intervene massively . . . in the workings of the private manufacturing sector.[44]

Vaguely suggesting that the nationalization of "some twenty-five of our largest manufacturers . . . would be required," Labour was clearer on the rest of its program for industry. First, as noted above, a new state holding company would be created to establish a major public stake in manufacturing industry; second would be a new system of planning agreements to be concluded between government and individual companies; and third was a new Industry Act "to provide the next Labour Government with all the industrial powers it will need to meet its economic objectives." Symbolic of these commitments, Anthony Wedgwood Benn, the outspoken leader of the Left, was named secretary of state for industry.

Perhaps still more importantly, just as the Conservatives had pledged in 1970 to root out the last remains of Wilson's programs, so now Labour, too, would wipe the Tory slate clean. "Just as the Conservatives in 1970 had swept away the vestiges of Labour's incomes policy . . . so now the Labour Government swept away the Conservatives' Stage III. . . . Mr. Heath had dispatched Mr. Wilson's Prices and Incomes Board; now Mr. Wilson abolished Mr. Heath's Pay Board."[45] And so on.

The priorities with which its goals would be pursued and the precise way in which they would be implemented both reflected a continuing division within the Labour party between the party's left and the social democratic wing of the party; among those leaders was Denis Healey, the new chancellor of the Exchequer. Labour, however, soon confronted the necessity of its own U-turns. This was all apparent in the discussions which preceded the publication of the white paper *The Regeneration of British Industry* in 1974 and later in the legislative adaptation of these proposals in the Industry Bill, originally published at the start of 1975. As Michael Shanks observes, the Left "wanted to meet the crisis by further *dirigisme*, by extending the state's umbrella further to cover the defective parts of the private sector."[46] By contrast, the Treasury envisaged an NEB which would acquire assets and enter into planning agreements at the consent of firms. Moreover, firms were to be assisted "only if they were likely to achieve a commercial rate of return on the capital."[47] The Treasury's victory was apparent when the bill derived from the white paper was published.

> The National Enterprise Board has more sharply delimited terms of reference, and its boss, Lord Ryder, would report to the Prime Minister and not to Mr. Benn. More important, planning agreements were to be voluntary rather than mandatory, and the participation of the workers' representatives in them was minimized. They were to be seen as an adjunct to sector planning, not a substitute for it. It was clear that the Left was starting to lose ground within the Cabinet.[48]

The pace with which the NEB matured reflected the ambiguity which had surrounded its birth. The Industry Bill did not become law until November

1975. Guidelines governing the NEB's operations were slow in coming, and by the middle of 1976 not a single planning agreement had been reached, nor had a single private sector firm been taken over.[49] What had occurred is that existing government shareholdings in Rolls-Royce, British Leyland, Alfred Herbert, Ferranti, and others had been shifted to the NEB. Thus, the aspiration that the NEB would fill a gap in the capital market, left by the unwillingness of other lenders to risk venture capital on new technologically sophisticated firms, went largely unfulfilled, as the NEB followed its predecessor in becoming primarily a holding company for shares in the least profitable of Britain's industries.

> The NEB's role as venture capital lender of last resort was in fact quite circumscribed. Although much press publicity was given to the NEB role in promoting the founding of companies such as INMOS (a microcircuitry firm based in the USA, with management experienced in the US market), the financial sums involved (perhaps £50 million in 1977), were miniscule compared to the nearly £3 billion per year support given to the old industry.[50]

Whatever its stated intentions, NEB's primary mission turned out to be overseeing the financial operations of companies acquired by government through salvage operations rather than picking and financing winners.

In other areas, the Labour government gravitated away from the ambitions of the party Left, and toward an industrial policy reminiscent of the voluntarism and consensus planning which had characterized the early days of Neddy. The defeat of the party Left in the May 1975 referendum on EEC membership (in which the Left urged rejection of community membership, but lost by a two-to-one margin) marked a turning point in the life of the government. In June of that year, Tony Benn was replaced as secretary of state for industry by Eric Varley, who was more clearly within the social democratic wing of the party. By November the shift in direction had taken a more concrete form with the publication of the white paper on *An Approach to Industrial Strategy*. The new industrial strategy laid out an approach to planning which would work largely within established tripartite structures.

The key to the new approach to industrial strategy lay in a growing realization that the politics of confrontation which had laid waste to so many of the Tory ambitions was likely to result only in further economic paralysis. In July, the Labour government reached accord with the TUC on a voluntary £6 per week pay limitation on all workers earning up to £8500; in September this agreement was ratified, and it was largely adhered to throughout the agreement period. A subsequent voluntary wage restraint was agreed to the following year in what was called stage two, and for much of the late 1970s the Labour party and organized labor were able to negotiate their differences through peak association mechanisms.

Thus the new Labour industrial strategy was based on the official rein-statement of tripartitism. The goals of the new industrial strategy, as laid out in the white paper, would be to correct a series of deficiencies in Britain's manufacturing performance, including low labor productivity, inadequate manpower policies, a low rate of investment, inefficient use of capital, "a capital market which does not give priority to the needs of industry," and "sharp and frequent changes of economic regulators to meet the conflicting needs of economic and social priorities, which make it difficult for compa-nies to plan ahead."[51]

The mechanism to correct these deficiencies once again would be Neddy and forty tripartite special-sector working parties (SWPs) representing some 60 percent of Britain's manufacturing industry. Each sector working party was to identify a set of actions and objectives for that sector and to report these back to the government, which would frame its macroeconomic poli-cies on the basis of this information. Thirty-nine SWPs were established in the first cycle of the process, and were scheduled to report to the NEDC in July 1976.

To some extent, the thirty-nine SWPs which were established were coter-minous with the already established "Little Neddies." But new structures on the government side were created to participate in this process. The Treasury set up an Industrial Policy Department under Alan Lord, and a general steering group under his supervision (but also including representatives of the Department of Industry) was established.

The industrial strategy continued to exist throughout the Labour govern-ment's term of office, although as the industrial editor of the *Financial Times* observed on the strategy's third anniversary. "Few people apart from those directly involved in the Treasury and Industry Department, the NEDO headquarters and 1,000 people who sit on the sector working parties take the exercise very seriously—and some of the representatives from companies resent the cost of the management time involved."[52]

Not surprisingly, the working party reports covered familiar ground. No one claimed that their reports were useless. "The check-list of action re-quired was much more detailed and precise than in previous exercises and most of the reports had a practical, down-to-earth air about them," one observer notes.[53] The best that could be claimed is that they represented a beginning. More cynically, a critic might say that having oversold the indus-try strategy at the beginning, the government grew tired of it when it failed to produce overnight miracles. The same problems remained—suspicion, re-sentment, and lack of experience with this type of intimate interaction be-tween government and industry (not to mention that between industry and the trade unions). Under the best of conditions, it would take many years of steady work to build the infrastructure of experience and understanding that the industrial strategy would require to be successful. But the conditions in the second half of the 1970s were scarcely optimal, and once again, time was the scarcest resource.

Another set of problems illustrates how events forced this government (like others) to abandon its basic commitments. The Labour government had announced its policy (like the previous governments) of backing "winners," not lame ducks. Indeed, the original choice of sectors for the SWPs, according to the white paper, were to be selected and grouped according to the following criteria:

—industries which, judging by past performance and current prospects, are intrinsically likely to be successful;

—industries which, though they fall short of the first category, have the potential for success if appropriate action is taken;

—industries whose performance (as in the case of component suppliers) is most important to the rest of the industry.[54]

In the event, however, the government's actual record proved to be far less hard-nosed.

The weakness of the government's resolve was evident no more than a month after the publication of the white paper, when it was forced to deal with the rapidly deteriorating Chrysler situation. Faced with possible closure and the loss of some 17,000 jobs (6,000 of which were at the Linwood plant in Scotland, where the government was trying to stem growing Scottish demands for devolution), the government announced a £160 million rescue package for Chrysler, even though earlier that same year it had agreed to put £1,500 million into the rival but also aging British Leyland.[55]

The problem with the new industrial policy was not just political pressure, but the nonselectivity inherent in its conception. To be sure, this nonselectivity (for example, the "choice" of some forty sectors as critical under the new strategy) is itself the product of a political system dedicated to full employment, and less than fully confident in its own capacity to "pick winners." The result was a traditional broad-brush approach to industrial assistance. As Lawrence Franko notes,

Firms in 15 sectors received financial subsidies, grants, or credits after 1975 under the 1972 (Industry) Act alone. Aids to firms in these 15 sectors were in addition to R&D grants, export aids, procurement preferences and trade protection extended to yet other sectors. This broad-brush application of sectorial policies was accompanied by a substantial expansion of eligibility of firms for regional policy grants, including grants to enterprises already located in industrialized regions of the country. Definitions of depressed regions were greatly expanded, so that by 1976 all but London and South Eastern England was

considered a development region for purposes of investment incentives, or qualified for the temporary employment subsidy given to firms that agreed to keep
redundant workers on the payroll.[56]

Franko concludes:

British industrial policy during the mid-1970s ended up reinforcing the existing
structural characteristics of U.K. industry instead of helping industry reform
along the lines of national comparative advantage. Britain entered the 1970s
with the least specialized pattern of international trade among the industrial
nations, and the situation changed little over the decade.[57]

Two lessons can be drawn from this unhappy story. The failure of successive
governments in the 1950s to reform Britain's industrial structure created
widespread resentment and frustration with continuing economic decline.
Clear evidence of a loss of economic capacity, rising levels of discomfort that
affected all classes, and renewed social strife led to the breakdown of the
politics of consensus and to the politization of economic policy. One key
effect of this has been to further undermine the process of institutional
development.

The British have been extremely willing to jettison programs, plans, and
institutions long before there has been any opportunity to see what will work
and what will not. Both parties have been impressively ignorant of the
conditions and requirements of institutional innovation. Achievements in
institution building were in fact not negligible in the 1960s. The development
of Neddy and experiments with prices and incomes policies are good examples. But their impact has been limited. Each government, dominated by a
short-term mentality, persisted in seeing each new initiative or institution as
the immediate remedy for the continuing economic crisis. Each new instrument was created in the flare of battle, rushed to the front lines, and thrust
into the thick of the struggle. As each was bloodied in turn, enthusiasm
evaporated. Little thought was given to the needs of longer-term institutional building. Instead of a process of gradual development, there was a parade
of tentative and partially organized vehicles. The result was to degrade the
process, demoralize the participants, and in the end, strengthen those institutions which had traditionally dominated the economic and industrial policy
process.

Still more worrisome is the politization of the entire process of institution building. Lacking an adequate sense of long-term policy, facing declining popular support and the collapse of consensus on economic objectives,
the parties have responded by pledging above all to undo what the other has
done. This is what Michael Stewart has called the Jekyll and Hyde side of
British politics.

In a world of limited resources and virtually unlimited wants, any government must make many hard and unpopular decisions. If the opposition regularly tries to cash in on this unpopularity for electoral reasons, by condemning such decisions however justified and necessary, and promising to reverse them, a different kind of threat is posed to the democratic system. The electorate will be encouraged to believe that this is any easy way out, that hard choices can be avoided, and that all their problems stem from the mistakes of a confused and incompetent government.[58]

As Stewart observes, this phenomenon has been most evident with regard to incomes policy and economic planning in general. The same lack of continuity also affects industrial policy:

Labour replaced investment allowances by investment grants; the Conservatives changed back to investment allowances. Labour introduced SEP; the Conservatives abolished it. Labour introduced REP, to make more use of idle resources in the regions; the Conservatives made no attempt to maintain its effective value. Labour set up the IRC; the Conservatives did away with it.[59]

The second lesson is that, because life does go on and decisions of some sort must be made, the ironic upshot of all of the political clamoring and confrontation over economic and industrial policies is that, time after time, the same old, tried-and-weary answers emerge. Of course Britain has an industrial policy: governments of both political casts grease the loudest wheel, back the lamest ducks, opt for the short-term quick fix, and ignore the longer-term process. The shape of British industrial policy is a "U"; after all of the political huffing and puffing, the determination to start afresh and get down to basics, governments drift back to what has never worked in the past, but at least is familiar.

THATCHER AND BENN: THE POLITICS OF ECONOMIC POLICY POLARIZED

The 1970s saw the end of the consensus on economic policy that had characterized British politics since World War II and of the politization of key economic policy issues. The result was a new pattern in British politics: each government arrived in office determined to wipe out all traces of its predecessor's economic policies, only to be forced, midway through its term, into a violent U-turn. By the end of the 1970s, the mainstream of the two major parties had drifted still further apart. Each now adopted a more and more radical approach to solving Britain's economic problems, and the gap between them widened dangerously.

The extent to which Mr. Heath had tried in 1970 to break with the past had been a surprise to most Whitehall insiders. A moderate, a team player, Heath would have surprised few if he had stepped easily into the comfortable shoes of a postwar Tory prime minister. Nine years later, however, no one expected Mrs. Thatcher to conform to that mold. Her intentions were radical, even revolutionary, from the start. John Nott, then secretary of state for trade, outlined the main purposes of her government about a year after the Conservative victory:

> It is the central purpose of Mrs. Thatcher's government to reverse these trends. To set off in a radical new direction. To undo the controls, the regulations, and the bureaucracy which stifle freedom. To produce a strong state determined to maintain in good repair the frame which surrounds society. But also determined that the frame would not be so heavy or so elaborate as to dominate society.[60]

Nott indicated some of the ways in which this purpose was being implemented, including: the removal of the curb on personal capital movements which had been a feature in Britain since the Second World War; the removal of curbs on wages; the abolition of all controls on prices, including the abolition of the Price Commission; the reduction of the size of the public sector; and efforts to improve the supply side of the economy, particularly in a shift in taxation away from income and toward spending.

Behind these policies rests a well-constructed philosophical edifice, an almost undiluted form of monetarism. Inflation is perceived as the single greatest problem confronting the UK economy, and its solution lies in reducing the growth of the money supply, paralleled by progressive reductions in public sector borrowing.

Spokesmen for the Thatcher team repeatedly stated their opposition to microeconomic policies which intervened in the operations of individual firms, and to government programs that propped up lame ducks. Sir Keith Joseph, Mrs. Thatcher's guru in opposition and then her minister of industry, observed that British industry can only compete when its productivity matches that of its competitors, and urged therefore a monetary squeeze which would force employers to withhold pay increases unrelated to productivity. The result would necessarily be a dramatic shake-out in British industry, allowing the weak to fall by the wayside and permitting the strong to move forward unhindered. In opposition, the Thatcher-Joseph policy for industry included the abolition of the NEB and sale of its shareholdings wherever possible; the repeal of the 1975 Industry Act; a reduction of government aid to industries in financial difficulties; the introduction of private capital into the nationalized industries; and the sale, if possible, of companies in the nationalized aircraft and shipbuilding industries.

Thus, perhaps more than any other British government in the postwar era (and perhaps even in the twentieth century), the Thatcher government came to power with a systematic and coherent economic policy portfolio. Policies of the past, even those adopted by earlier Conservative governments, were to be rejected and evidence of their existence destroyed wherever possible. This time, there would be no turning back, no "pragmatism," no U-turns.

Once in office, the new government put forward a program of incentives to the private sector, reduced income taxes sharply, and trimmed key social services. It took as its most important goal the reduction of public spending and the slowing of the growth of the money supply. Its industrial policy evolved more slowly. Only in March 1980 did a white paper clearly lay down the policy of reducing state aid to industry. The white paper stated that within two or three years the annual amount allocated to such aid would fall by some 50 percent, with the shipbuilding industry, steel, British Leyland, and the NEB (which had not been abolished after all) all receiving substantially less than in the past. In some cases, ministers hoped that they would receive nothing at all, and the white paper categorically stated that "there is no provision for major rescues."

Thus, in March 1980, almost a year after it had come to power, the Thatcher government finally seemed on course. "After Sir Geoffrey Howe's second budget the Conservative government has a coherent economic philosophy with figures attached," wrote a leading British journalist. "It has taken nearly a year to get there. But now we know roughly where we are starting from and broadly where we are going, even if there may be pitfalls along the way."[61]

Pitfalls indeed. In midsummer, the government's "figures" collapsed in the midst of rapidly decreasing confidence both among its supporters in the country and in the House, and even among its ministers, that anyone "knows broadly where we are going." Public spending and the money supply both soared out of control, now in the midst of Britain's worst recession since the 1930s.

Industry felt (or claimed) the most serious brunt of Thatcher's storm. Current rates of interest, said the Confederation of British Industry, were choking off investment, ruining hundreds of businesses, and at the same time pushing the pound so high that British exports were priced out of overseas markets. Key leaders of British industry—even Thatcher supporters such as Sir Michael Edwards of British Leyland, Lord Weinstock of General Electric, and Sir Terrence Beckett, formerly of Ford—made the same point. It was becoming all too clear that the government's determination to launch the reindustrialization of Britain had faded; increasingly the nation feared that Mrs. Thatcher might be presiding over its deindustrialization.

The results of the near (or impending) disaster were twofold, both regrettably predictable. First, despite continued protestations to the contrary, industrial policy eased into more traditional channels—if not a full-fledged U-turn, at least a modified U. Second, the Labour party in opposition shifted still further to the left, as the Bennite forces gathered strength to attempt to seize the party leadership.

In July, in response to the second censure motion she faced, Mrs. Thatcher announced new moves to stimulate industrial development and alleviate unemployment. The government stated that it would give the National Enterprise Board an additional £25 million to establish the first Inmos Microchip production plant in Wales; provide Dunlop with £6.1 million in grants to modernize its tire factories in the Midlands; and establish seven "enterprise zones" in older urban areas. Taken together with the relaxation of cash limits on British steel, announced in June, and on shipbuilding, a "new pragmatism" seemed to have emerged in the government's industrial strategy.

Commentators claimed that the approach to industrial policy now evolving in Downing Street was not vastly different from that preached by Mr. Healy, or even from that practiced by Mr. Callaghan's government. The new phrase, they said, was "constructive intervention."[62] The same experts pointed to a distinct shift of emphasis from the attitudes of Mrs. Thatcher's first year. State intervention in industry was now regarded as good, provided that it is at the right time, in the right place, in the right industry, and can be afforded. Priorities are familiar: Government funds would be directed into places of high unemployment, into industries which were considered to have a future and not just fossilizing old jobs; there were even some whispers that the government might be prepared to reestablish older consultative mechanisms with industry and the trade unions.

In the fall of 1980, highly familiar policies began to take shape. As *The Economist* observed, the government "intends to pump some new money quietly out through the old pipelines."[63] Ministers, it was said, opted with enthusiasm for the "creative use" of the old selective industrial aid schemes, "which have been in place since Mr. Edward Heath suddenly started bailing out lame ducks."[64] By March 1981, it had become clear that the government's efforts to reduce spending on industry and employment had collapsed: "Now these cuts have been abandoned. Major increases are being allowed for in order to prop up ailing industries and cope with unemployment."[65] By the spring, critics and supporters of the government alike were calling on it to launch a Japanese, or German, or French-style "industrial policy."

Meanwhile, policies of the Labour opposition that would affect industry slipped further and further to the left. In the October 1979 annual party conference, the parliamentary party was instructed to declare that any business denationalized by the Tories "will be taken back into public ownership by the next Labour government without compensation." In July 1980, the Left-dominated national executive committee published a document entitled "Draft Labour Manifesto 1980." It was, of course, not the party's manifesto and had not even been circulated officially to the shadow cabinet. But it revealed quite clearly the aims of the increasingly powerful Left. It proposed, among other matters, a significant public stake in each important industrial sector, plus banking and insurance; public ownership of major companies in pharmaceuticals, medical equipment, microelectronics, construction and building materials, the national nuclear corporation, North Sea oil, the power plant industry, commercial ports, cargo handling, and more of road haulage; powers to nationalize individual companies by statutory instrument; much more money for the NEB; a new national investment bank; diversification of existing nationalized industries; and renationalization of denationalized companies without compensation.[66]

A lot of this was simply warmed-over left-wing rhetoric from past party conferences, and no one expected the actual party manifesto to be quite so red when it came to the general election. But the growing strength of the Bennite Left (and the departure of key moderates to form the Social Democratic party) is one (and only one of many) vivid indications of the polarization of the major parties on key issues affecting the economy and industry.

CONCLUSION

Each of the themes of this chapter—the burden of history, the persistence of ad hocery, the predominance of political goals, the politization of economic policy, and the polarization of politics—suggests a reason for the failure of British efforts to develop a successful industrial policy. To a large extent, each represents or corresponds to a different period in modern economic life. There is a clear archaeological relationship among these themes. Each episode in British history set the stage for the next and conferred a legacy on later policymakers of unrecognized or unresolved problems and of policy failures—which was to complicate the task of their successors. Thus the inherited pattern of government-industry relations postponed the initiation of an industrial policy well past the point it might have commenced, and restrained policymakers when the need for an industrial policy began to be compelling. Again, when piecemeal ad hoc policies began to emerge in the postwar years, inherited patterns of government industry relations restrained both the ambition and commitment to such initiatives, and provided the ingredients of the environment which would greet such initiatives with resistance. In the early postwar years, the costs of these early failures were not perceived to be especially high, as other political ambitions pushed industrial issues aside and as economic recovery seemed not to require concerted government action. However, the costs of such priorities—the defense of sterling, full employment, and the welfare state—soon began to be felt, and further complicated later efforts at industrial vitalization. When industrial policies were later articulated in the 1960s, it was against a background of a severely deteriorating international economic position, an unwillingness to let lame duck (high employment) industries fail, and against a private sector still unwilling to let government become an active participant in revitalization. The restraints and difficulties of the past did not vanish; they complicated and politicized newer efforts to attack old problems.

NOTES

1. See Peter Katzenstein's contributions in P. Katzenstein, ed., *Between Power and Plenty; Foreign Economic Policies of Advanced Industrial States* (Madison: The University of Wisconsin Press, 1978).
2. See, for example, Phyllis Deane, *The First Industrial Revolution* (Cambridge: Cambridge University Press, 1965), chapter 13.
3. David Thompson, *England in the Nineteenth Century* (Harmondsworth: Penguin Books, 1950), p. 78.
4. Katzenstein, *Between Power and Plenty*, pp. 895-896.
5. Andrew Shonfield, *Modern Capitalism* (Oxford: Oxford University Press, 1965), p. 94.
6. Charles P. Kindleberger, *Economic Growth in France and Britain*, 1851-1950 (Cambridge: Harvard University Press, 1964), p. 188.
7. Shonfield, *Modern Capitalism*, p. 88.
8. Thomas Balogh, "The Apothesis of the Dilettante," in Hugh Thomas, ed., *Crisis in the Civil Service* (London: Anthony Blond, 1968), p. 35.
9. William W. Lockwood, *The Economic Development of Japan; Growth and Structural Change, 1868-1938* (Princeton, N.J.: Princeton University Press, 1954), reprinted in Barry E. Supple, ed., *The Experience of Economic Growth* (New York: Random House, 1963), p. 380.
10. S. Blank, *Industry and Government in Britain* (Lexington, Mass.: Lexington Books, 1973), p. 5.
11. Katzenstein, *Between Power and Plenty*, p. 910.
12. Charles Lock Mowat, *Britain Between the Wars, 1918-1940* (Chicago: University of Chicago Press, 1955), p. 174.
13. Ibid., p. 359.
14. David S. Landes, *The Unbound Prometheus* (Cambridge: Cambridge University Press, 1969), p. 394.
15. A. J. P. Taylor, *English History 1914-1945* (Oxford: The Clarendon Press, 1965), p. 600.
16. Samuel Beer, *British Politics in the Collectivist Age*, rev. ed. (New York: Vintage Books, 1969), p. 278.
17. See, for example, Harold Macmillan, *Reconstruction: A Plea for a National Policy* (London: Macmillan, 1933).
18. G. C. Allen, *The Structure of Industry in Britain*, 2nd ed., (London: Longmans, 1966), p. 67.
19. "It is ironical to reflect that the first generation of French planners under M. Monnet, groping for a method of inflicting the long-term public interest on private enterprise, turned naturally to Labour Britain for their model. They found what they wanted in the industrial Working Parties. . . . When the French established the *commissions demodernisation* for their key industries and used them as a basis for constructing a nation-wide plan with a clear order of priorities, they believed themselves to be taking over an essentially British device." Shonfield, *Modern Capitalism*, p. 88.
20. Kindleberger, *Economic Growth in France and Britain*, p. 110.

21. Ibid., pp. 318-319.

22. Ibid., p. 320.

23. We have written about this at length elsewhere. See Stephen Blank, "Great Britain: The politics of foreign economic policy, the domestic economy, and the problem of pluralistic stagnation," *International Organization* 31,4 (Autumn 1977).

24. Joseph Frankel, *British Foreign Policy 1945-1973* (London: Oxford University Press, 1975), p. 91.

25. Kenneth Younger, *Changing Perspectives in British Foreign Policy* (London: Oxford University Press 1964), p. 3.

26. Susan Strange, *Sterling and British Policy* (London: Oxford University Press, 1971), p. 64.

27. Andrew Shonfield, *British Economic Policy Since the War* (London: Penguin Books, 1958), p. 218.

28. J. H. MacArthur and Bruce Scott, *Industrial Planning in France* (Cambridge: Graduate School of Business Administration, Harvard University, 1969), p. 483.

29. See Shonfield, *Modern Capitalism*, chapters VI, VIII, and part 4; and Michael Shanks, *The Stagnant Society* (London: Penguin Books, 1961).

30. In the Nuffield study of the 1959 general election, there is no chapter dealing with the main issues of the campaign. See D. E. Butler and Richard Rose, *The British General Election of 1959* (London: Macmillan, 1960).

31. Ibid., p. 19.

32. Ibid., p. 28.

33. D. E. Butler and Anthony King, *The British General Election of 1964* (London: Macmillan, 1965), p. 133.

34. Anthony King, "The Election that Everyone Lost," in Howard R. Penniman, ed., *Britain at the Polls; The Parliamentary Election of February 1974* (Washington, D.C.: American Enterprise Institute, 1974), p. 6.

35. Ibid., p. 6.

36. British Information Services press release.

37. Michael Stewart, *The Jekyll & Hyde Years; Politics and Economic Policy Since 1964* (London: J. M. Dent & Sons, 1977), p. 120.

38. See J. Bruce-Gardyne, *Whatever Happened to the Quiet Revolution?* (London: Charles Knight & Co., 1974).

39. For a fuller account of this episode, see Stewart, *Jekyll & Hyde Years, pp. 134-138.*

40. Ibid., p. 135.

41. Trevor Smith, *Anti-Politics: Consensus, Reform and Protest in Britain* (London: Charles Knight Co., Ltd., 1972), p. 124.

42. Beyond the immediate area of industrial policy, the Heath government wound up aping its Labour predecessors in other areas as well. While it abolished the PIB, it created a separate Pay Board and Prices Commission. Despite their criticism of the National Industrial Relations Court, the Tories resorted to it on more than one occasion. And legislation was introduced which strengthened consumer protection. In mid-1972, a 90-day prices and incomes freeze was resorted to. See ibid., pp. 124-125.

43. The first year allowance on investment in plants and machinery was increased from 60 percent to 80 percent on all expenditures incurred before August 1973.

44. King, "The Election that Everyone Lost," pp. 17-18.

45. Stewart, *Jekyll & Hyde Years*, p. 191.

46. Michael Shanks, *Planning and Politics* (London: George Allen & Unwin, 1977), p. 75.

47. Stewart, *Jekyll & Hyde Years*, p. 216.

48. Shanks, *Planning and Politics*, p. 76.

49. Stewart, *Jekyll & Hyde Years*, p. 217.

50. Lawrence Franko, *European Industrial Policy, Past, Present and Future* (Brussels: The Conference Board, 1980), p. 34.

51. HMSO, *An Approach to Industrial Strategy*, 1975.
52. John Elliot, *Financial Times*, February 5, 1979.
53. Shanks, *Planning and Politics*, p. 83.
54. Cmnd. 6315, *An Approach to Industrial Strategy*, para. 14.
55. For a fuller account of the various considerations in this decision, see Stewart, *Jekyll & Hyde Years*, p. 220.
56. Franko, *European Industrial Policy*, p. 32.
57. Ibid.
58. Stewart, *Jekyll & Hyde Years*, p. 244.
59. Ibid., p. 242.
60. Speech to the National Association of Manufacturers, March 21, 1980.
61. Malcolm Rutherford, *Financial Times*, March 29, 1981.
62. Malcolm Rutherford, *Financial Times*, October 17, 1980.
63. *The Economist*, October 25, 1980.
64. Ibid.
65. *Financial Times*, March 12, 1981.
66. *The Economist*, July 12, 1980.

Index

About the Contributors

Stephen Blank is a partner in Multinational Strategies Inc., a research and consulting organization. He received a Ph.D. in government from Harvard University and taught at the University of Pittsburgh. He has written extensively on multinational corporations and on British politics. His writings on British politics include *Government and Industry in Britain: The Federation of British Industries in Politics* (1973) and "Britain's Economic Problems: Lies and Damned Lies" (1979).

Harlan Cleveland is director of the Hubert H. Humphrey Institute of Public Affairs, and Professor of Public Affairs at the University of Minnesota. Mr. Cleveland was a magazine editor and publisher (*The Reporter*), and graduate school dean (the Maxwell School of Citizenship and Public Affairs at Syracuse University) in the 1950s. During the 1960s he served as assistant secretary of state for International Organization Affairs and as U.S. ambassador to NATO. From 1969 to 1974 he was the president of the University of Hawaii. From 1974 to 1980 he was director of the Program in International Affairs of the Aspen Institute for Humanistic Studies. Among his published writings are *The Overseas Americans* (1960), *The Obligations of Power* (1966), *NATO: The Transatlantic Bargain* (1970), *The Future Executive* (1972), *China Diary* (1976), and *The Third Try at World Order* (1977). He is also the recipient of sixteen honorary degrees, Princeton University's Woodrow Wilson Award, and the U.S. Medal of Freedom.

Margaret Dewar is an assistant professor of planning at the Humphrey Institute of Public Affairs at the University of Minnesota. Her interests are in planning for employment and economic development in the United States. She is the author of *Industry in Trouble: The Federal Government and the New England Fisheries*. She holds an A.B. from Wellesley College, a Masters in City Planning from Harvard University, and a Ph.D. in urban studies and planning from M.I.T.

Thomas P. Egan is a senior research associate at Charles River Associates Inc., in Boston. He received a B.S. degree in physics from Providence College in 1963, an M.B.A. from the University of San Francisco in 1975, and a Ph.D. in economics from the University of California at Davis in 1978. Dr. Egan held various marketing positions in the semiconductor industry before beginning his doctoral training. He has also researched and co-authored several studies in coal market economics and the conversion of American industry to coal.

W. Bruce Erickson is professor of business and government at the University of Minnesota's School of Management. His research has been in industrial organization. He has a special interest in antitrust policy. Before coming to the University of Minnesota, Dr. Erickson taught at Michigan State University and at Bowling Green State University. His publications include *Government and Business*, *Small Business in Minnesota*, *An Introduction to Contemporary Business*, and numerous articles on antitrust issues.

Sheldon Friedman is director of the Research Department of the United Auto Workers. Before joining the UAW in 1975, he served as research associate at the M.I.T. Center for Policy Alternatives, where he did work on protecting workers affected by technological change, as well as the economics of occupational health and safety, equal employment opportunity and seniority. He has written widely on plant closings and economic dislocation. He did undergraduate and graduate work in economics at M.I.T.

Joel S. Hirschhorn is a project director at the Congressional Office of Technology Assessment, where he directed a study on the United States steel industry and now directs an assessment of non-nuclear industrial hazardous wastes. Prior to joining OTA, Dr. Hirschhorn was a professor of engineering at the University of Wisconsin, Madison; a director of research for a manufacturing firm; and a consultant to many firms, both here and abroad, in the areas of research and development planning, acquisitions, patents and innovation activities. He has published over 60 papers in journals, books and newspapers; several books; and articles in encyclopedias. Most recently he has been writing on the steel industry, industrial policy, and the nature of technological innovation and has given testimony to several Senate committees on his work at OTA.

Gerald Jantscher is the Principal Tax Policy Analyst of the U.S. General Accounting Office and directs most of the tax policy studies undertaken by the agency. In his previous position as a research associate at the Brookings Institution, Dr. Jantscher conducted a major analysis of the federal aid program to the U.S. merchant marine and shipbuilding industry. His book on the subject, *Bread upon the Waters*, was published in 1975. Dr. Jantscher received his Ph.D. in economics from Columbia University in 1965 and did postdoctoral work at the University of Manchester (England) under the auspices of a National Science Foundation fellowship.

Ian Maitland is an assistant professor of business, government and society at the University of Minnesota's School of Management. His principal field of interest is comparative political economy. He is the author of *The Causes of Industrial Disorder: A Comparison of a British and a German Factory* (London:

Routledge & Kegan Paul, forthcoming) and articles on industrial relations and incomes policy in Great Britain and on the organization of the Japanese company. Dr. Maitland earned his B.A. in French and German from Oxford University and his Ph.D. in sociology from Columbia University.

Before his return to Germany in June 1981 to rejoin the Federal Ministry for Research and Technology, Werner Menden was the counselor for scientific and technological affairs at the Embassy of the Federal Republic of Germany. Prior to his Washington assignment, Dr. Menden directed the German Office of Advanced Technologies in the Department of Research and Technology, where he established research and development programs in applied physics, electronic components, communications engineering, materials research and transportation technologies. More recently, he was responsible for the offices of Natural Resources and Industrial Production, Physical and Chemical Research and Development, and Environmental Research. Dr. Menden earned an M.S. in physics from the University of Bonn in 1959 and a Ph.D. from the Technical University of Aachen in 1964.

Vera Miller, vice president and director of research of the Amalgamated Clothing and Textile Workers Union, is responsible for the analysis and presentation of data for collective bargaining, arbitration and legislative hearings. She participates in industry-wide negotiations, in various labor-management projects on industrial matters, and in international labor conferences. Dr. Miller is currently active on advisory committees to governmental agencies, including the U.S. Bureau of Labor Statistics. In 1965 she represented the U.S. State Department at an International Women's Conference in Japan and lectured before women's, labor and civic groups in various Japanese cities. Dr. Miller earned a Ph.D. in sociology from the University of Chicago. Her specializations were industrial relations and methods of research.

Paul M. Sacks is a principal at Multinational Strategies Inc., New York City. Prior to joining MNS, Dr. Sacks worked at the Chase Manhattan Bank, where he helped to develop their political risk system, and served as Chase World Information Corporation's Regional Analyst for Western Europe. He is a specialist in West European politics, and has extensive overseas research experience in the United Kingdom and in Ireland, and most recently in France and Nigeria. Sacks holds a Ph.D. in political science from the University of California, Los Angeles, and a B.A. from the University of Rochester.

Philip H. Trezise, a senior fellow at the Brookings Institution for the past ten years, has extensive experience in international affairs. Prior to his move to the Brookings Institution, he served as assistant secretary of state for economic affairs and U.S. ambassador to OECD in Paris. Mr. Trezise is the author of *The Atlantic Connection*, and contributed to *Asia's New Giant: How the Japanese Economy Works*, *Setting National Priorities: Agenda for the 80's*, and *The Politics of Trade*. He served as editor of *The European Monetary System: Its Promise and Prospects*.